John's Creation
A Model for Understanding the Gospel of John

© Copyright 2005 John Pople
All rights reserved. No part of this publication may be reproduced, stored in a retrieval system, or transmitted, in any form or by any means, electronic, mechanical, photocopying, recording, or otherwise, without the written prior permission of the author.

Note for Librarians: A cataloguing record for this book is available from Library and Archives Canada at www.collectionscanada.ca/amicus/index-e.html
ISBN 1-4120-7430-4

Printed in Victoria, BC, Canada. Printed on paper with minimum 30% recycled fibre. Trafford's print shop runs on "green energy" from solar, wind and other environmentally-friendly power sources.

TRAFFORD
PUBLISHING

Offices in Canada, USA, Ireland and UK
This book was published *on-demand* in cooperation with Trafford Publishing. On-demand publishing is a unique process and service of making a book available for retail sale to the public taking advantage of on-demand manufacturing and Internet marketing. On-demand publishing includes promotions, retail sales, manufacturing, order fulfilment, accounting and collecting royalties on behalf of the author.

Book sales for North America and international:
Trafford Publishing, 6E–2333 Government St.,
Victoria, BC v8T 4P4 CANADA
phone 250 383 6864 (toll-free 1 888 232 4444)
fax 250 383 6804; email to orders@trafford.com
Book sales in Europe:
Trafford Publishing (UK) Limited, 9 Park End Street, 2nd Floor
Oxford, UK OX1 1HH UNITED KINGDOM
phone 44 (0)1865 722 113 (local rate 0845 230 9601)
facsimile 44 (0)1865 722 868; info.uk@trafford.com
Order online at:
trafford.com/05-2326

10 9 8 7 6 5 4 3 2

For His glory. Not mine; or yours

PREFACE

It is, after all, a most extraordinary book.

The gospel of John provides one of the deepest insights, if not the deepest insight, into the life of the Lord Jesus Christ. Other scriptures, including Matthew, Mark and Luke, give us a comprehensive account of Jesus' words and actions. But John often stands alone in granting us an intimate glimpse of especially telling moments in Jesus' conversation or action that allows us to perceive our Savior's character and purpose more clearly.

While the other gospels offer detailed chronology of Jesus' life, John especially provides us with the keys to unlock its meaning; using careful descriptions which add extra depth and meaning. Sequences of events present in the other gospels are often absent in his: John is concerned with the layers of meaning and motivation which lie behind these external happenings. Thus it is the particular moments and events that reveal the underlying spiritual drive which he emphasizes. The view he gives is as if a veil had been momentarily parted revealing the meanings underlying the form and action with external shapes and players. In John these external appearances pall and the spiritual world, which resides behind, shines through before.

One such moment occurs in Jesus' midnight conversation with the ruler of the Jewish council, Nicodemus. In this conversation, exclusive to John, God's purpose with man is expressed in terms of love:

For God so loved the world that He gave His only begotten Son, that whoever believes in Him should not perish but have everlasting life (3:16).

Only John articulates this principle of love so profoundly and concisely; no other author matches his depth and clarity in expressing God's love in His purpose with mankind in so few words. John alone shows in one sentence the extent of God's love for His children, and what He was prepared to give so that we might have a chance of life eternal.

John's presentation extends to both a deeper revelation of the character and purpose of the Savior himself and also to the use of broader concepts; he shows how the development of Jesus' ministry reflects that of the Earth on a macroscopic scale. Therefore the same principles underlying the creation of the world underlie Christ's life here in the gospel according to John. The theme of Jesus mirroring – and refining – the creation sequence of the world will be expanded in what follows.

This study gets its impetus from being sensitive to these underlying patterns, by noticing and exploring these unique moments. But before examining these themes in detail; especially those which use the spiritual creation as a pattern for Jesus' ministry; let us consider some examples that typify the uniqueness and intimacy of John's gospel: moments in which John pierces through peripheral layers of meaning to reveal the very heart of Jesus. Consider this bold statement from the tenth chapter:

"I and my Father are one." (10:30)

This is the most profound declaration of unity between the Son and his Father in all of scripture: how better could we understand the Lord Jesus! As far as describing Jesus' role in this world – and the next – it is perfect. We should never feel the need to add vindication, corroboration or qualification to this most beautiful statement: it is simply perfect as it is.

Expanding the theme of love, John's beautiful message breaks through once more in his account of the last supper:

"A new command I give you: Love one another. As I have loved you, so you must love one another. By this all men will know that you are my disciples, if you love one another." (13:34-35)

How clear are Jesus' commands! This simple statement sweeps a sharp, two edged sword through fussy human attempts to define exactly what constitutes a disciple of Jesus. Christ himself has spoken, and no one can gainsay him! Whatever qualities the disciple needs, or however proficient he might be in his understanding, if he omits the love the Lord himself specifies, he cannot be recognized as a disciple of the Lord he professes. All four gospels record events from that same, dreadful evening; but only John lets us steal close enough to share a place on Jesus' breast and clearly perceive the spirit of Jesus' message for us; to learn of the love that he has commanded, invited and, indeed, provoked us to share with each other.

Only John describes discipleship as the enviable status of being a friend of Jesus:

> "My command is this: Love each other as I have loved you. Greater love has no one than this, that he lay down his life for his friends. You are my friends if you do what I command. I no longer call you servants, because a servant does not know his master's business. Instead, I have called you friends, for everything that I learned from my Father I have made known to you. You did not choose me, but I chose you and appointed you to go and bear fruit..." (15:12-16)

What a wonderful elevation of status to learn that following Jesus' commands transforms us from being an unprofitable servant [1] into the friend of Jesus Christ! A friend of Jesus cannot therefore act blindly. He acts in full knowledge of the directives underlying Jesus' purpose: thus there must exist a direct link between the deeds of a disciple and Jesus' own works (15:12). What a privilege this is to be a disciple of Jesus: to share a degree of knowledge, motivation and purpose with the Master himself, although what is more, with this illuminating knowledge comes responsibility: to be chosen also means to be commissioned 'to bear fruit.' Yet notice how this same passage eliminates any prideful thoughts that might result from our elevation to the state

---

[1] As Paul's argument concerning Onesimus (Philemon 11).

of Jesus' friends. We have not had the intelligence of mind nor the godliness of heart to choose Jesus. John educates us rather that Jesus has had the grace, the very grace of God, to choose us.

In addition to these commissions, John also preserves for us amazing statements of comfort. From these same pages Jesus tells us:

> "I will not leave you as orphans; I will come to you. Before long, the world will not see me anymore, but you will see me. Because I live, you also will live." (14:18-20)
> "I have told you these things, so that in me you may have peace. In this world you will have trouble. But take heart! I have overcome the world." (16:33)

Jesus will come to us, he promises, to overcome the world that would otherwise destroy us. When these words are properly absorbed, if they can ever be properly absorbed, what immense comfort is ours who have heard them!

Finally, in the shortest verse of all scripture, John records one of the Bible's most intimate moments:

> Jesus wept. (11:35)

Only John allows us to eavesdrop so closely on the very heart and mind of our Master. Although we certainly find evidence of Jesus' compassion outside of John's gospel, John's witness alone records that Jesus actually wept. The Jews accompanying Jesus supposed he wept because his friend Lazarus had died. This may be true; but it seems unlikely that Lazarus' death in itself made Jesus weep: Jesus already knew Lazarus was dead and, more importantly he, and he alone, knew that Lazarus would walk again before the day was done. Perhaps Jesus wept from the sympathy he felt with the grief of those around him, or perhaps he wept because Lazarus' death brought into sharp relief the fragility of all flesh; that mankind is like a field of flowers: crumpled and blown away by the winds of time and chance. Or he may have wept because these events were causing Jesus to appreciate more and more the gulf that was widening between the things he needed his disciples to understand, and what they (and we?) were able to understand. This may have proven the most powerful pathos of all. We are not told why Jesus wept, and therefore we cannot be sure. But we can be sure that these two simple words give us an insight into the extent of Jesus' empathy and compassion unparalleled by other witnesses.

All these verses are unique to John's gospel, which we have such a great privilege to share and enjoy. Furthermore, this remarkable gospel is not only studded by these singular quotes, but is also underlain by broader concepts, such as light and glory, of which John reveals their complexity and beauty more fully than other accounts. Indeed in all matters of spiritual weight John always troubles to guide our understanding to deeper levels.

Objectives of this Study

It is proper that the reader be aware of the persuasions and qualifications of the author so he is best placed to form his own opinion of the relevance of this work. Primarily I am a Christian, baptized into the saving name of the Lord Jesus, and consequently a member of the Christadelphian (Brethren in Christ) faith. My professional training culminates in a physics doctorate in the fields of laser optics and materials science. I work in scientific research at a synchrotron source (a particle accelerator), being daily called to utilize critical and hypothetical analysis, as well as detection and characterization of statistically significant coherent patterns within source streams yielding both coherent and incoherent data. These skills, as with all blessings from God, find useful employ in humble approach of the scriptures and feature significantly in forming this work. I have not been schooled in languages nor literary critique, thus this work will not attempt to offer a linguistic analysis of John's gospel, (meanings of Greek and Aramaic words or practices, where necessary, are referenced from expert sources), nor advance critique upon the veracity or authorship of the gospel *per se*. My Christian faith (and other considerations not detailed here) convinces me the scriptural text is the inspired Word of God in its totality and the gospel of John will be approached entirely in this regard: in the spirit of humility of one trying to listen and learn from it, not the arrogant air of assumed wisdom beyond that of a simple fisherman from a primitive society. For this reason also the Bible will be regarded as the only source of truth and the only appropriate authority for its (self-) interpretation. [2]

This study is concerned with these broader underlying concepts, and with the question of whether there is some 'bigger picture' underpinning John's gospel whereby we might come to a deeper understanding of its message. A pattern, which resembles the six days of creation, stretching throughout the gospel is proposed. This pattern is comprised of the spiritual equivalents of the components of the natural creation, which is seen as the precursor introduction of the Bible's 'spiritual creation.' It is tremendously exciting to perceive a new structure underlying the surface accounts that have always been visible. For one thing this allows all the 'surface' material to be understood in a wholly new light: itself a very alluring prospect! Yet it is important to realize that this work forms a proposal and not a dogmatic pronouncement of certainty. The reader is left to determine the veracity of the proposal from the evidence that will be presented.

The task of presenting this creation model in John's gospel is as difficult as it is exciting. This study has taken a long time to reach this point, as well as taking many unexpected changes in interpretation along the way. For a while it even reached such an impasse (concerning the nature of Day 5) that it lay beached on a high shelf gathering dust for three years (between 1989 and 1992), before finally being recalled to realize, with the Father's blessing, the state in which it appears here. Even then there can

---

[2] Biblical quotations included here are taken from a variety of translations. The New International Version (NIV) is used as default purely for its clarity of modern English and idiomatic expression; nevertheless other translations are also quoted. In any event, the thoughts developed here will prove independent of the translation of the Bible employed. Quotations are marked parenthetically by book, chapter and verse, except in the case of quotations from John's gospel, where only chapter and verse are detailed.

be no doubt that it does little more than scratch at the surface of the rich veins of truth and beauty embedded in John's gospel.

The value of this proposed creation model is twofold. Firstly, it will explain why certain events and conversations appear in the gospel of John, why they appear in the sequence they do and what gravity they hold on the underlying spiritual level. Secondly, the spiritual creation in John provides us with unique insights into the nature of both the Lord Jesus Christ and the Kingdom of God.[3] As we work through John's gospel with this pattern in mind each layer is gently peeled away to reveal the truths beneath, with the removal of each successive layer contributing to our ever-growing understanding of the richness and complexity of the whole.

Finally, this book has been written, quite simply, to strengthen the faith of those who already believe; for that is invariably what happens when another new and profoundly meaningful pattern is seen within the scriptural pages, consolidating the reader's conviction of the Bible's divine veracity and value. Thus if the work we embark upon here is able to strengthen the faith in the existence of God as a loving and caring Father in the mind of even one reader; then it will have enjoyed immeasurable success.

With these things in mind this study opens, hoping to reveal the presence of the spiritual creation in John's gospel and then proceeding through John with this pattern in mind, both to test

---

[3] The value of this spiritual creation model we shall be exploring is certainly not to merely achieve a structure by which the existing information in John might be mentally categorized. Nor is this model exclusive: the pattern presented here does not preclude other patterns that may pervade this remarkable book.

it, and to use it as a new standpoint to regard the marvels John, guided by the Divine Hand, reveals to us. This is the journey on which we are about to embark, and on which you, the reader, are invited to participate.

This is John's Creation…

INTRODUCTION
                                                           Page

α.1 John: The Different Gospel	1
α.2 In the Beginning…	4
α.3 The Natural Creation	5
α.4 The Spiritual Creation	9
α.5 The Gospel of John	20

JOHN'S CREATION

DAY 1   *John 1:1 – 3:21*

Exposition: Seeing the Light

1.1 Natural Light and Spiritual Light	24
1.2 Jesus Christ: The Light	26
1.3 Israel: The Darkness	27
1.4 Discipleship: Seeing the Light	30
1.5 The Wedding at Cana	31
1.6 Conclusions from Day 1	40
Exhortation: God of the Second Son	42

DAY 2   *John 3:22 – 5:47*

Exposition: Waters Above

2.1 Waters of Life: Reappearance of the Baptist	59
2.2 The Work of Jesus: Raising Above	60
2.3 Encounter at Jacob's Well	61
2.4 'Come' and 'Go'	69
2.5 Resurrection	72
2.6 Conclusions from Day 2	73
Exhortation: To See the Face of the King	75

DAY 3   *John 6:1 – 6:71*
    Exposition: Bread of Heaven

3.1 Passover – whose Passover?	90
3.2 Bread from Heaven, Bread of Heaven	92
3.3 Times and Seasons	94
3.4 Gathering Fragments	96
3.5 The Spiritual Physique	98
3.6 Conclusions from Day 3	99
Exhortation: Beyond the Water	100

DAY 4   *John 7:1 –13:38*
    Exposition: Light to Rule

4.1 The Light to Rule	113
4.2 Absolute Authority	114
4.3 Judgment from the Ruling Light	117
4.4 To See or Not to See?	119
4.5 Conclusions from Day 4	125
Exhortation: The Mark of Blood	127

DAY 5   *John 14:1 – 19:42*
    Exposition: Waters Beneath

5.1 The Serpent Stirs: Division	143
5.2 Lifted Up, Brought Low	144
5.3 The Serpent Strengthens: Desertion and Denial	147
5.4 Worship of the Beast	148
5.5 The Serpent Strikes: Death	152
5.6 Son of Man: Brokenhearted	155
5.7 Son of God: Victorious	157
5.8 Conclusions from Day 5	158
Exhortation: Stripped of All	160

DAY 6   *John 20:1 – 21:25*
    Exposition: The New Man, The Premier
6.1 Names Above Names	178
6.2 The Keyholder	180
6.3 The Three Appearances of the Lord of Heaven, Sea and Earth	185
6.4 Beginning and End	187
6.5 Conclusions from Day 6	190
6.6 Enfin	191
Exhortation: Gods	193

DAY 7   *doesn't appear*
    Exposition: The Absent Day
7.1 Silent Witness	209
Exhortation: The Beautiful Woman	212

CONCLUSIONS
Ω.1 Perceiving the Creation Sequence in John's Gospel	228
Ω.2 Comparing 'John's Creation' with Other Expositions	235
Ω.3 The Value of the Creation Sequence in John	240
Ω.4 Letters to the Seven Churches	246
Ω.5 Guides to Discipleship from John's Creation	255
Ω.6 And Last	265

Appendix A: The Uniqueness of John's Gospel
A.1 Comparing Parables in the Four Gospels	269
A.2 Comparing Healing Miracles in the Four Gospels	273

Appendix B: Creation in John's Gospel Summary
B.1 The Science of Pattern Perception	279
B.2 Constructing a Summary of John's Gospel	282
B.3 The Creation Sequence in John's Summary	285

Appendix C: The Nature of Jesus Christ
C.1 The Essence of Obedience and Submission	288
C.2 The Nature of Jesus Christ as Creator and Creation	292

INTRODUCTION

α.1 John: The Different Gospel

John's gospel arouses much interest because it differs so strikingly from the other three records of Matthew, Mark and Luke. At first glance the gospels of Matthew, Mark and Luke (which are often referred to as the 'synoptic' gospels, simply because they appear the same), provide a generally common, chronological diary of the events of the ministry of the Lord. In comparison, John's gospel is bizarre. We are provoked to wonder what John's motivation was, under the guidance of the Divine Hand, in choosing the very unique events with which he relates the life and ministry of Jesus Christ. What facet was he trying to present, what dimension exposit, in his unusual presentation of the Son of the Living God?

The uniqueness of John's gospel is commonly agreed, nevertheless for completeness we will demonstrate the point. The remarkable extent of the difference is highlighted in an exhaustive study of the parables and healing miracles of the Lord, (selected because they are common and easily identifiable features of the Lord's ministry), which is appended to avoid impeding the main flow of the argument (Appendix A). This study reveals two distinct facts distinguishing John: firstly parables and healing miracles are comparatively rare features in John, and secondly

Introduction

there is *no overlap whatsoever* between the few parables and healing miracles occurring in John with any of those in the synoptic records (Appendix A). Since the Bible is the inspired Word of God these differences cannot be inaccuracies and discrepancies: rather they are deliberate and therefore have meaning.

The signature differences in John's gospel should be seen in the light of the close relationship between John the apostle and the Lord Jesus. Five principal points attest to especial closeness between the Lord Jesus and the apostle John:

1. Amongst the twelve apostles there is evidence of a 'closer three' of Peter, James and John. This is highlighted when Jesus chooses to limit the audience of a particular revelation or miracle. In these cases he restricts the chosen twelve, the apostles, to just three: invariably Peter, James and John.

a)   At the raising of Jairus' daughter:
He did not let anyone follow him except Peter, James and John the brother of James. (Mark 5:37)
b)   At the point of transfiguration:
After six days Jesus took Peter, James and John with him and led them up a high mountain, where they were all alone. There he was transfigured before them. (Mark 9:2)
c)   In Gethsemane:
He took Peter, James and John along with him, and he began to be deeply distressed and troubled. (Mark 14:33)

2. John was 'that disciple whom Jesus loved,' as attested to in his own gospel (13:23, 19:26, 20:2, 21:20).[1] This is not a description to take lightly. The most graphic illustration of this bond is seen during the Last Supper, where John reclines on the breast of the Master whom he loves, and, more importantly, by whom he is loved (13:23-25).

---

[1] This revelation is made in the final chapter of John's gospel (21:24) which some scholars believe to be apocryphal. This author is not qualified to determine whether or not this is the case and so in this work the entire text of John is taken as the inspired Word of God.

Introduction

3. 'That disciple whom Jesus loved,' taken here to be John, was the only disciple we know who stayed with Jesus up to the point of the crucifixion (19:26). This testifies to a close and loving bond that John would risk exposure, arrest, possibly crucifixion also, to be at his Master's feet at the darkest hour.

4. Reciprocally, Jesus commends his mother Mary into the care of this disciple (19:27). Doubtless this is not because John is the only disciple there present, for Jesus could have instructed him to take his mother to another man's home. Jesus has chosen John explicitly to be the one to care for Mary and this is strong testimony to the especial bond of closeness between John and the gentle Son of Man.

5. Finally, John was the recipient of the apocalyptic vision the Revelation of Jesus Christ. John was deemed the apostle whom God allowed to live long enough to receive the library of powerful visual prophecies in which is encoded the future purpose of God. [2] He is the one selected to hear the ultimate destruction of sin and death; the creation of New Jerusalem; the means by which God will unite Himself with His creation. That John should receive this burden, and this privilege, is further evidence of his superlative standing in the spiritual understanding of the work of his (and our) Master.

These references attest to the closeness of the relationship between the Lord Jesus and John. This is not to suggest that the Lord did not have very close relationships with other apostles and disciples, of whom Peter is a prime example, but it testifies to the especial closeness between John and the Lord Jesus. This is

---

[2] Some argue John received the revelation purely because he was probably the only apostle left alive at the point the Revelation was given (~ AD 90). More likely the reverse is true! Since God's will is not molded by the vagaries of time and chance most probably John remained alive this long precisely *because* God had destined the time of the revelation and the specific man, John, to receive it.

Introduction

relevant to any consideration of John's gospel since it bespeaks the remarkable closeness of the spiritual witness we will find therein of the character, wisdom and person of the Lord Jesus Christ. Who is more likely to provide the most revealing testimony of the Lord Jesus Christ than the disciple closest to him? Furthermore, it is wholly reasonable that such a spiritually insightful document will be imbued with levels beyond the superficial text in which God's Hand can be perceived. Since God is a God of order and not of chaos (1 Corinthians 14:33), this evidence is likely to be seen as an ordered structure or pattern. Thus one concludes the likelihood that John's gospel contains some pattern in which the reader, through careful study and prayer, might better see the Hand of God in the witness John gives. With these thoughts we approach this gospel with additional caution – and additional excitement!

α.2 *In the Beginning…*

In the beginning was the Word, and the Word was with God, and the Word was God. He was with God in the beginning. Through him all things were made; without him nothing was made that has been made. In him was life, and that life was the light of men. The light shines in the darkness, but the darkness has not understood it. (1:1-5)

John opens his gospel by echoing the Genesis creation. Whilst this does not in itself necessitate that John will hold to this pattern for the remainder of his gospel, this beginning does prime us to be sensitive to this particular comparison. This is therefore a convenient point to outline the hypothesis for the presence of the spiritual creation in John's gospel and the form in which we shall encounter it.

Hypothesis for John's Creation
The material presented in John's gospel is arranged to reflect, or celebrate, the creation sequence from Genesis. John's gospel flows through six developmental stages, each one representing, in order, the spiritual counterpart of the respective creative Day.

Introduction

This is a bold claim to stake, especially since we have not yet presented the evidence on which it rests, nor have we identified a profitable reason for the gospel to be ordered in this way, even if the hypothesis is true. As necessary introduction we will revisit the scriptural record of the natural creation sequence, paying special attention to the overall structure of the pattern and the principal feature of each creative day.

α.3 *The Natural Creation*
<u>Natural Day 1: Light</u>
> And God said, "Let there be light," and there was light. God saw that the light was good, and he separated the light from the darkness. (Genesis 1:3-4)

Light. Day 1 of creation is centered on light.

<u>Natural Day 2: The Drawing Above of Water</u>
> And God said, "Let there be an expanse between the waters to separate water from water." So God made the expanse and separated the water under the expanse from the water above it. And it was so. (Genesis 1:6-7)

Day 2 is centered on an action, rather than an object. Nothing is created on Day 2: the 'furniture' that already exists is merely rearranged, although it is relevant that the central feature of the day is water. What is 'new' is that there is now water *above* (set apart from the water below, with a divide between). God has taken something from 'beneath' and drawn it from the earth to be 'above.' Additionally there is now an expanse – a gulf fixed – between that which is newly 'above' and that which remains 'below.'

<u>Natural Day 3: Food on Earth</u>
> And God said, "Let the water under the sky be gathered to one place, and let dry ground appear." And it was so. God called the dry ground "land," and the gathered waters he called "seas." And God saw that it was good. Then God said,

Introduction

> "Let the land produce vegetation: seed-bearing plants and trees on the land that bear fruit with seed in it, according to their various kinds." And it was so. The land produced vegetation: plants bearing seed according to their kinds and trees bearing fruit with seed in it according to their kinds. (Genesis 1:9-12)

Day 3 concerns the revelation of the earth, and the creation of all vegetation. Since man is initially vegetarian, Day 3 is the source of all human sustenance (food).

> Then God said, "I give you every seed-bearing plant on the face of the whole earth and every tree that has fruit with seed in it. They will be yours for food." (Genesis 1:29)

So the principal feature of Day 3 is the introduction of food and the exposure of the land from which that food was grown.

<u>Natural Day 4: Lights to Rule</u>
> And God made two great lights; the greater light to rule the day, and the lesser light to rule the night: he made the stars also. (Genesis 1:16)

Day 4 details the creation of sun, moon and stars. Word choice in scripture is very important and here the detail of the phrasing is instructive. The sun and moon are not explicitly referenced by name, rather they are described as: "the greater light to rule the day" and "the lesser light to rule the night." Emphasis is brought to the reader's attention that the heavenly bodies are lights designed to rule.

Day 4 creates a *population*. We will see that repeated in Days 5 and 6. Equally importantly, the text establishes a link between Day 4 and Day 1, in the repetition of focus on light. Day 4 incorporates light, just as Day 1, but the light is developed, refined in a specific way. The language brought to the reader's attention has a twofold flavor: Light, combined with Rulership.

Natural Day 5: Population below the Waters Above

And God said, "Let the water teem with living creatures, and let birds fly above the earth across the expanse of the sky." So God created the great creatures of the sea and every living and moving thing with which the water teems, according to their kinds, and every winged bird according to its kind. And God saw that it was good. (Genesis 1:20-21)

Day 5 also creates a population. Furthermore Day 5 partners Day 2, just as Day 4 partners Day 1, because the populace created in Day 5 is placed in areas created on Day 2. The nature of the link between Day 5 and Day 2 is that they contrast each other. Day 2 was concerned with waters being drawn *above*, whilst Day 5 populates the region left *below*. The sea where the great whales and fish swim is *below* the waters above. Even the 'firmament' (expanse, sky) where the birds fly is also *below* the 'waters above.'

One notable feature is the presence of 'tanniyn' (Hebrew), translated as 'great creatures of the sea,' (NIV) or 'great whales' (KJV). This creature is placed first in the list of those mentioned; and we shall expand upon his significance later. An additional point we shall return to later is that Day 5 has no ruler. Sun and moon are named 'rulers' of day and night in Day 4 and in Day 6 Adam will be set in authority over all the animals created on both Days 5 and 6. Day 5 itself is devoid of a ruler: the 'Throne' of Day 5 stands empty.

Natural Day 6: The New Man to Rule the Earth

And God said, "Let the earth bring forth the living creature after his kind, cattle, and creeping thing, and beast of the earth after his kind:" and it was so. And God made the beast of the earth after his kind, and cattle after their kind, and every thing that creepeth upon the earth after his kind: and God saw that it was good. And God said, "Let us make man in our image, after our likeness: and let them have dominion over the fish of the sea, and over the fowl of the air, and over the cattle, and over all the earth, and over every creeping thing that creepeth upon the earth." So God created man in

Introduction

> his own image, in the image of God created he him; male and female created he them. (Genesis 1:24-27, KJV)

Day 6 couples with Day 3. Day 6 populates the dry land that was revealed on Day 3, with the creation of all land animals and man. Adam, the new man, is the principal element of Day 6. He is given dominion over everything created on Day 6 and Day 5.

<u>Natural Day 7: Harmony with the Creator</u>

> And on the seventh day God ended his work which he had made; and he rested on the seventh day from all his work which he had made. And God blessed the seventh day, and sanctified it: because that in it he had rested from all his work which God created and made. (Genesis 2:2-3)

God rests (Genesis 2:2-3), and there is a reason *why* God rests: all the work has been completed, and all is 'very good.' This is the final portion of the creation sequence: harmony between the Creator and his creation, flawless natural beauty empowered and enlivened by the presence of the Almighty walking amidst it in the cool of the day. A heavenly rest on Earth.

<u>Structure in the Natural Creation</u>

The overall framework these days evidence is also important for our study. There is symmetrical structure in these six creative days: they are arranged in two cycles of three days. The creative acts of Days 1-3 are performed in Heaven, Waters and Earth respectively. The creative acts of Days 4-6 populate these respective areas. Days 1-3 establish a cycle that Days 4-6 repeat and enhance.

It follows that Days 1 and 4 are partnered, being associated with the 'Heaven' portions of creation; Days 2 and 5 are partnered in the 'Waters' zone; and Days 3 and 6 are partnered in the 'Earth' zone (Figure α_1).

The duration of the creation process – six days – is paramount. Why did creation last for six days? Since the power of the Creator is unlimited, it is obvious that the whole creation

Introduction

could have been created instantaneously should God have so willed. The careful division of the creation process over six separate periods suggests God deliberately draws our attention to the divisions. He has planted a deliberate pattern within the process (an observation upon which comment is seldom made), and a pattern from which we are doubtless supposed to draw education; and edification. We propose this Biblical conundrum a rich vein of learning; and one which we intend to mine assiduously.

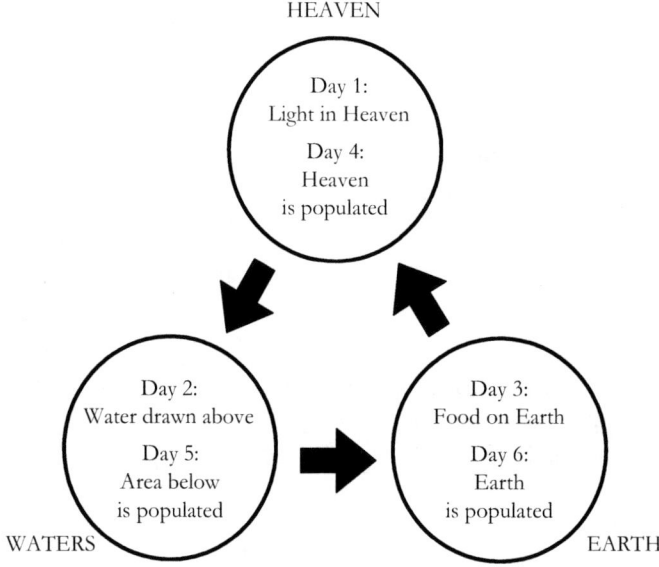

Figure α_1: Illustration of the dual cycle within the six days of creation.

$\alpha.4$ *The Spiritual Creation*

Yet this physical dispensation of creation is not the only order of God's world which His Word declares to us. Behind the mask of the physical world, and equally within it and throughout it, lies the spiritual realm of God's creation. The Bible frequently alludes to this spiritual creation: Paul writes about it explicitly to no fewer than four of the churches. Paul always couches the spiritual creation in the context of its formation by the Lord Jesus and in particular his sacrifice:

Introduction

> For Christ's love compels us, because we are convinced that one died for all, and therefore all died. And he died for all, that those who live should no longer live for themselves but for him who died for them and was raised again. So from now on we regard no one from a worldly point of view. Though we once regarded Christ in this way, we do so no longer. Therefore, if anyone is in Christ, he is a new creation; the old has gone, the new has come! (2 Corinthians 5:14-17)
> (see also Isaiah 65:17 & 66:22; Ephesians 4:17-24, Galatians 6:14-15, Colossians 3:9-10; Revelation 21:1)

This impacts our view of John's gospel. The gospel is a declaration of the person of Jesus Christ and we have already seen John open this declaration in direct parallel with the origin of creation's sequence. To this we add the understanding of a spiritual creation revealed in scripture which originates in the Lord Jesus. Our next step therefore is to revisit the components of the natural creation introduced in Genesis and learn the spiritual metaphors they form in scripture. By doing this we hope to have a better understanding of the form which (at least one projection of) this spiritual creation might realize in the scriptural pages. Once we have formulated some conception of the components of the 'spiritual creation' we will be well placed to open our analysis of the gospel of John.

Spiritual Day 1: Illumination

At a simplistic level light represents things that are 'good' and darkness represents things that are 'bad.' There are many supporting texts for this notion, all appealing to the concept that light describes something godly, whilst darkness is the ungodly counterpart.

> For you were once darkness, but now you are light in the Lord. Live as children of light (for the fruit of the light consists in all goodness, righteousness and truth) and find out what pleases the Lord. Have nothing to do with the fruitless deeds of darkness, but rather expose them. For it is shameful

Introduction

even to mention what the disobedient do in secret. But everything exposed by the light becomes visible, for it is light that makes everything visible. This is why it is said: "Wake up, O sleeper, rise from the dead, and Christ will shine on you." (Ephesians 5:8-14) (see also Acts 26:16-18, Romans 13:11-14)

This concept has firm footing in the original appearance of light and darkness, where God made an explicit separation of the one from the other (Genesis 1:4).

Nevertheless this thinking is not sufficient to explain all instances. To understand the spiritual equivalent of light we should consider it alongside its necessary counterpart: darkness. For example, the Bible also records:

The LORD said that he would dwell in the thick darkness. (1 Kings 8:12)

This is contrary to the simple understanding of darkness representing all things bad, because in God there is no sin, nor any impure thing. Can we at least say that because man is evil, and the temple of the Lord was centered among mankind, that God was dwelling in the evil? Indeed we cannot: at no point does scripture associate God with sin, whether in the sense of a common dwelling place or another manner. Since the Fall in Eden God does not make his dwelling place with men (e.g. Psalm 115:16) indeed He cannot, lest man be instantly destroyed by His presence (e.g. Exodus 19:12-13). Only at the end, where Christ and his faithful have filled the Earth with the glory of the Lord, can harmony between the Creator and the created truly be established (Revelation 21:3). Translating the Lord 'dwelling in thick darkness' as any version of God dwelling amidst sin, in however tentative a connection, is frankly untenable. This requires our understanding of the Biblical terms 'light' and 'darkness' to be enhanced.

Synonyms are helpful to decode the meaning of a word, because they immediately supply an alternative understanding of God's usage of the word. There are two ways to find synonyms:

Introduction

either by finding the term in a parallelism (a literary construct of two parts written to necessarily equate with each other); or by consulting different translations to obtain a different rendering of the word. Here are some examples of parallelisms and different translations of the word 'darkness:'

> (1a) I will open my mouth in a **parable**: I will utter dark sayings of old… (Psalm 78:2, KJV)
> (1b) I will open my mouth in parables, I will utter **hidden things**, things from of old… (Psalm 78:2, NIV)
> (2a) The proverbs of Solomon the son of David, king of Israel; To know wisdom and instruction… To understand a proverb, and the interpretation; the **words of the wise**, and their dark sayings. (Proverbs 1:1-2, 6, KJV)
> (2b) The proverbs of Solomon son of David, king of Israel: for attaining wisdom and discipline…for understanding proverbs and parables, the sayings and **riddles** of the wise. (Proverbs 1:1-2, 6, NIV)

Using all the synonyms above we have four equivalents for the scriptural term 'darkness': (1a) 'parables,' (1b) 'hidden things,' (2a) 'words of the wise,' (2b) 'riddles.' We thus solve the deeper meaning, without in any way contradicting the simpler one: the scriptural component 'darkness' is best interpreted as *not understanding* and, by implication, light is interpreted as 'understanding.' Thus 1 Kings 8:12 above is an insight into the relationship between man and God: God is explaining to Solomon that when the feeble torchlight of mortal understanding is pointed in the direction of the Almighty it is swallowed in the huge gulf of darkness that is our unknowable God! We look towards God, as if to behold the Almighty, but we see only darkness, for we cannot hope to understand the enormity of what we behold.

> Who has understood the mind of the LORD, or instructed him as his counsellor? (Isaiah 40:13)

Introduction

> O the depth of the riches both of the wisdom and knowledge of God! how unsearchable are his judgments, and his ways past finding out! (Romans 11:33)
>
> For now we see through a glass, darkly; but then face to face: now I know in part; but then shall I know even as also I am known. (1 Corinthians 13:12)

This latter verse confirms the idea of darkness representing lack of understanding: the Greek word translated 'darkly' is 'enigma,' [3] which transliterates into the English language as something unknown. Thus we conclude the scriptural components of 'light' and 'darkness' are interpreted in the fullest sense as 'understanding the things of God' and 'not understanding the things of God.' The metaphor is intuitive: it makes sense to represent things which are difficult to perceive mentally with things difficult to perceive visually; i.e. that things not understood should be said to be 'unseen,' to be in darkness. The phrase 'to be in the dark' exists in modern parlance as a metaphor for not understanding something, likewise the phrase 'to see the light' is a common metaphor for coming to the point of understanding.

Jesus uses the idea of light as a figure for communicating understanding in teaching the gospel to others (Matthew 5:14-16). The metaphor he chooses for transmitting the understanding of his gospel is the idea of a light being set in a prominent position: on a candlestick. The light then shines all around and those who see it come to an understanding of God's goodness and praise Him.

Spiritual Day 2: Life Drawn up out of Death

On Day 2 there was a 'drawing up' from the Earth to a new position above it and this drawing up was achieved with water. Furthermore a discrimination is made between the two states of

---

[3] Wilson B., 'The Emphatic Diaglott', 1942, Watch Tower Bible and Tract Society, Cambridge, UK, p 588

Introduction

above and below with a fixed divide. This is a perfect description of baptism in all points! We begin 'below,' 'of the Earth,' 'earthly': it is our initial state. Through God's action we are 'drawn above' and between our new state and the old is the divide between life and death. To emphasize the comparison, the vehicle through which God performs this miracle is water. The spiritual act of baptism echoes well the components of Day 2: something dead is drawn up to new life, enacted in the physical world through water.

Spiritual Day 3: Bread from Heaven

The third day saw the provision of food. In Western European culture, to which this author belongs, 'bread' is a metaphor for all food, or sustenance, as any dictionary definition will ratify. More importantly this metaphor was also true in Israel at the time of Christ. An expert in near-Eastern Aramaic culture writes:

> "In the Near East, bread is the main and most essential food no matter what else may be offered. Even if a family has an abundance of all kinds of food but has no bread, people consider that family to be poor. Men gain fame and are highly spoken of if their families are noted for their plentiful bread. In certain areas where old customs and manners are still carried out, very little is known about growing vegetables. When wheat crops fail, people face starvation." [4]

So, scripturally the word 'bread' stands as a metaphor for all food on the natural plane, and on the spiritual plane bread stands as a metaphor for the Word of God. These metaphors pervade the law, prophets and gospels:

> The tempter came to [Jesus] and said, "If you are the Son of God, tell these stones to become bread." Jesus answered, "It

---

[4] Errico R. A., Lamsa G. M., "Aramaic Light on the Gospel of John," 2002, Noohra Foundation, Smyrna, GA, p 98

Introduction

is written: 'Man does not live on bread [5] alone, but on every word that comes from the mouth of God.' " (Matthew 4:4 quoting Deuteronomy 8:3)

As the rain and the snow come down from heaven, and do not return to it without watering the earth and making it bud and flourish, so that it yields seed for the sower and bread for the eater, so is my word that goes out from my mouth: It will not return to me empty, but will accomplish what I desire and achieve the purpose for which I sent it. (Isaiah 55:10-11)

Spiritual Day 4: Lights to Rule

Day 4 marks the beginning of the second cycle (Figure α_1), and thus links with Day 1. Day 4 is a development of Day 1: it furthers a process begun there. In Genesis we see this as the development of the general "light" is refined into the celestial bodies of the sun, moon and stars, and these bodies are invested with authority to rule:

God made two great lights--the greater light to govern the day and the lesser light to govern the night. He also made the stars. (Genesis 1:16)

In scripture sun, moon and stars are commonly used as symbols of governments and ruling bodies (Table α_1).

Frequently the allusion of sun, moon and stars being darkened comes when God is pronouncing judgment against rulers in human kingdoms. Doubtless the metaphor arises because political authorities are elevated above the majority of the people and govern the days and nights of those beneath them; as the sun and moon were set to govern the days and nights in Genesis 1. Therefore prophecies describe them as heavenly bodies and, when speaking of judgment coming upon them,

---

[5] The context confirms Jesus is not referring to bread as one foodstuff amongst many, but as a general metaphor for all physical food.

Introduction

employ the metaphor of God dousing the lights of the heavens, as He extinguishes the ruling light they held.

Kingdom	Scriptural representation as sun, moon and stars
Babylon	An oracle concerning Babylon that Isaiah son of Amoz saw… The LORD Almighty is mustering an army for war… to destroy the whole country… See, the day of the LORD is coming --a cruel day, with wrath and fierce anger-- to make the land desolate and destroy the sinners within it. **The stars of heaven and their constellations will not show their light. The rising sun will be darkened and the moon will not give its light**… Whoever is captured will be thrust through; all who are caught will fall by the sword. (Isaiah 13:1-15) …you will take up this proverb against the king of Babylon, and say… "How you are fallen from heaven, **O Lucifer, son of the morning!** How you are cut down to the ground, you who weakened the nations!" (Isaiah 14:4, 12)
Egypt	"Son of man, take up a lament concerning Pharaoh king of Egypt and say to him: '…I will drench the land with your flowing blood all the way to the mountains, and the ravines will be filled with your flesh. **When I snuff you out, I will cover the heavens and darken their stars; I will cover the sun with a cloud, and the moon will not give its light. All the shining lights in the heavens I will darken over you; I will bring darkness over your land**, declares the Sovereign LORD'" (Ezekiel 32:2-8)
All nations	Let the nations be roused; let them advance into the Valley of Jehoshaphat, for there I will sit to judge all the nations on every side… For the day of the LORD is near in the valley of decision. **The sun and moon will be darkened, and the stars no longer shine.** The LORD will roar from Zion and thunder from Jerusalem; the earth and the sky will tremble. (Joel 3:12-16) "But in those days, following that distress, **the sun will**

> be darkened, and the moon will not give its light; the stars will fall from the sky, and the heavenly bodies will be shaken. At that time men will see the Son of Man coming in clouds with great power and glory." (Mark 13:24-26)

Table α_1: Scriptural examples of governing bodies of men being described metaphorically as the astronomical bodies of sun, moon and stars. [6]

Spiritual Day 5: Below the Waters Above

Day 5 is the counterpart to Day 2. Since we have interpreted Day 2's 'waters above' as the action of baptism, this gives an ominous flavor to the position of those things 'below.' And Day 5 is very clearly concerned with the area 'below' the waters of

---

[6] A final intriguing example of sun moon and stars as governing bodies is seen in the book of the Preacher. The final chapter of Ecclesiastes begins with a poetic description of the features of old age. Failing eyesight is represented as the view through the window growing dim (v3), dulled hearing as the 'sound of the grinding' fading (v4), failing vocal power as the birdsong growing faint (v4), and the overall diminution of strength and posture is depicted as the strong man stooping (v3). But the principal element of advancing mortality, the first item listed is the darkening of sun, moon and stars.

> Remember your Creator in the days of your youth, before the days of trouble come and the years approach when you will say, "I find no pleasure in them"--**before the sun and the light and the moon and the stars grow dark**... (Ecclesiastes 12:1-2)

The Preacher describes the advancement into old age primarily bringing a darkening of the sun, moon and stars. It is sometimes suggested the Preacher is referring to failing eyesight. There are problems in logic with this interpretation, for the verse describes a failing transmitter, not a failing receiver – and the eyes are receivers that detect incoming signals, not transmitters that send any forth. Furthermore we already have a description of the eyes' demise in verse 3. Rather this poetry is wholly commensurate with the scriptural pattern (Table α_1): it is the *authority* of the elderly that wanes. A father rules his household throughout his younger and middle years. As he advances to old age, and the body fades, he cannot be the ruler in the house any longer, but rather number among those for whom care is taken. His sun and moon have dimmed and the authority of the household must pass to a younger and brighter star.

Introduction

Day 2. Day 5 populates the sky and sea – both these areas are below the 'waters above' of Day 2. Indeed by this analogy anything residing below the waters of baptism is, quite simply, dead. So already we are finding an association between Day 5 and death.

With this in mind we focus on the creature named first in the list of those created on Day 5: the 'great whales' (KJV) or 'great creatures' (NIV). The Hebrew word is "tanniyn." Scripture teaches us a fascinating thing about this creature "tanniyn": he is synonymous with Eden's serpent! The Hebrew word for Eden's serpent is "nachash," which is not explicitly listed in the creation sequence. But the equivalence of the two Hebrew words is shown by Isaiah:

> In that day, the LORD will punish with his sword, his fierce, great and powerful sword, Leviathan the gliding serpent [**nachash**], Leviathan the coiling serpent [**nachash**]; he will slay the monster of the sea [**tanniyn**]. (Isaiah 27:1)

This equivalence is corroborated and expanded upon by other scriptures (Table α_2).

The table demonstrates the Biblical relation between "nachash" (Eden's serpent) and "tanniyn": both words describe the same family of creatures. This family is reptilian: i.e. their behavior is hybrid between land-based and sea-based, which is why either term can describe either form.

This family includes Eden's serpent ("nachash"), which particularly alerts our interest, because the Bible demonstrates a link between the serpent of Eden and death through the cross of Jesus Christ, through the covenant of Genesis 3:15. [7] This

---

[7] The link between the curse of the serpent and the crucifixion of Christ is not trivial to establish. Hebrews 2:14-18 and Galatians 3:16-29 are principal in establishing the interpretation, though it is not an obvious proof. Nevertheless since the vast majority of Christianity is agreed on the veracity of the interpretation we shall not engage in any lengthy exposition of the point here.

establishes a relation between creation's Day 5 and the crucifixion of Christ.

	Hebrew: Tanniyn	Hebrew: Nachash
Land creature	"I will make Jerusalem a heap of ruins, a haunt of jackals; [**tanniyn**] and I will lay waste the towns of Judah so no one can live there." (Jeremiah 9:11)	There be three things which are too wonderful for me, yea, four which I know not: The way of an eagle in the air; the way of a serpent [**nachash**] upon a rock; the way of a ship in the midst of the sea; and the way of a man with a maid. (Proverbs 30:18-19)
Sea creature	"But you, O God, are my king from of old; you bring salvation upon the earth. It was you who split open the sea by your power; you broke the heads of the monster [**tanniyn**] in the waters." (Psalm 74:12-13)	"Though they hide themselves on the top of Carmel, there I will hunt them down and seize them. Though they hide from me at the bottom of the sea, there I will command the serpent [**nachash**] to bite them." (Amos 9:3)

Table α_2: A family of creatures, some that live on land and some in the sea, which family includes Eden's serpent, described by the words "tanniyn" and "nachash."

Finally, we also note that Day 5 is devoid of a 'ruler.' Days 4 and 6 both specify rulers of their populations: Day 5 has none of itself. Day 5's throne remains empty until Day 6, when its rightful ruler arrives (Genesis 1:26). This 'absent Throne' also provides a strong realization of the 'death' theme, as we shall see all too clearly as the gospel unfolds…

Introduction

Spiritual Day 6: The New Man, The Premier

Day 6 is partnered with Day 3: it provides a population (animals and man) for the zone which Day 3 established. Although there are myriad creatures formed on Day 6 there is only one of singular importance: the man Adam. The spiritually pertinent fact of Day 6 is the introduction of man: commissioned with authority to govern all creatures of land, sea and air.

What do we take here for the spiritual creation? That Day 6 concerns the introduction of the ruler of all the living components of the spiritual creation, just as natural creation's Day 6 introduced Adam, the ruler of all the natural creation.

Spiritual Day 7: Harmony with the Creator

The spiritual parallel to the natural seventh day is obvious, powerful and beautiful. The 'seventh day' bespeaks a time when the Creator lives in harmonious union with all of His creation.

$\alpha.5$ *The Gospel of John*

We are now well prepared to study John's gospel. The study presented in this work is divided into seven sections, each attributed to a sequential creative day. The proposed division of the gospel, in which this creation model will be most readily perceived, is given in Table α_3.

This structure is to aid the interpretation of the gospel in the light of the spiritual creation sequence, *though the interpretations themselves are not constrained by this thought*. A separate section included in the concluding chapter of this work will discuss whether reading the ministry of Jesus Christ in John's gospel in the light of a spiritual creation sequence model is justifiable in the light of the expositions we have encountered (Section $\Omega.1$). Regardless of this outcome, the consideration of scripture in the light of a new model is inherently valuable in opening whole new avenues for mental exploration. A well known account considered at a new angle will often yield new treasures, new gems to be mined from the infinite mind of the Maker, whether one is reflecting upon the broadest conceptual form or in the smallest act or phrase. So often in the Bible beauty is in the detail.

Introduction

'Day' of spiritual creation in Christ's ministry	Section of John's gospel
1	John 1:1 – 3:21
2	John 3:22 – 5
3	John 6
4	John 7 – 13
5	John 14 – 19
6	John 20 – 21
(7: Day of Rest)	*doesn't appear*

Table α_3: Proposed breakdown of the gospel of John according to the six-day model of creation. The justification for the placement of 'day' divisions will transpire as we expound each section and is summarized in the concluding section of this work.

Each 'Day' of this following study comprises a section of exposition, where the relevant portion of John's gospel is examined. Each expository section is complemented with an exhortation, drawn either from the particular portion of John associated with that Day, or from a general reflection of the Day's theme. It seems proper that scriptural study should be brought to the fruition of exhortation to encourage the disciple that the gospel message is living and impactful in one's life: this is not purely an intellectual exposition. This couplet of exposition and exhortation is repeated seven times, for each of the spiritual days we explore.

The work concludes with consideration of the bigger picture in posing the questions:

1 Having considered the evidence, can we conclude that John's gospel presentation of the person and ministry of Jesus Christ is patterned according to a spiritual creation sequence?

2 Why would the creation pattern be employed in a gospel narrative?

Introduction

- What is gained for the glory of the Father and Son from a gospel structured as the creation sequence?
- Are there other parts of scripture structured according to creation's six days and how are we edified from seeing them this way?
- How does perception of John's spiritual creation help us be better disciples of Christ?

The final chapter of conclusions addresses these 'big picture' questions of overall conceptual format to ensure that we have not 'missed the forest for the trees.'

DAY 1 *John 1:1-3:21*

EXPOSITION:
Seeing the Light

From the model we have seen 'light' used in the Bible to represent 'illumination': a state of understanding (Section $\alpha.4$). 'Light' is also the predominant concrete noun in the opening portion of John (Appendix B).

We therefore anticipate light will be the central element of Day 1 of John's spiritual creation. For each day we begin by stating the basic premise that arises from the model; for Day 1 this becomes:

Basic premise

In this section of John's gospel we anticipate the gospel message to be portrayed in terms of the creative element 'Light,' with Jesus at the center of that message as the Light of the World. We particularly expect that the contrast between 'Light' and 'Darkness' will be evidenced in terms of who *understands* Jesus, and who does not, with Jesus portrayed primarily as the one who both understood God's plan, and enables others to understand it.

Day 1 Exposition: Seeing the Light

1.1 *Natural Light and Spiritual Light*

We have previously introduced this study of John's gospel as a description of the spiritual creation, in a comparative way to the natural. But John is presenting *more* than just a parallel between the spiritual creation and the natural creation, for to simply equate the two would be to misunderstand the essential supremacy of the spiritual over the natural. The spiritual light (understanding Christ) is not merely *equal* to the natural light of creation: rather it is *far superior*. What is especially satisfying from John's excellent presentation of the spiritual creation sequence is he explains *why* the spiritual light is better than the natural light.

Consider the natural creation:

And God said, "Let there be light," and there was light. (Genesis 1:3)

But the *words* God spoke to create the light, i.e. the manifestation of His intended will, faded away and were heard no more. The light they created still exists, but it is non-sentient [i.e. it does not think for itself, it has no capacity for reasoning or independent thought]: bouncing around the universe unaware of its own Creator or purpose, being governed wholly by the laws of physics in its movements and attributes.

In John we are shown the superiority of the spiritual creation:

In the beginning was the Word, and the Word was with God, and the Word was God. He was in the beginning with God. All things were made through Him, and without Him nothing was made that was made. In Him was life, and the life was the light of men… And the Word became flesh and dwelt among us, and we beheld His glory, the glory as of the only begotten of the Father, full of grace and truth. (1:1-4, 14, NKJV)

Once again God speaks, with His Word, and the Light (Christ) comes into the world. But in the spiritual creation John takes care to describe the provision of Jesus simultaneously as the Light of the World *and* as the embodied Word of God (1:14). So

Day 1 Exposition: Seeing the Light

in the second creation, the spiritual, it is not only the light that endures but *also* the purpose (Word) with which God created it![1] Thus the spiritual light (Christ) is far superior to the natural light for an explicit reason: Christ retains the express purpose of the Almighty within him, thus he makes sentient decisions about where he shines and whom he illuminates! An example is when Jesus meets Zacchaeus, who has climbed the tree to get a better view of him.

> When Jesus reached the spot, he looked up and said to him, "Zacchaeus, come down immediately. I must stay at your house today." So he came down at once and welcomed him gladly. (Luke 19:5-6)

Jesus stops, changes direction (looks up into the tree), and *chooses* where he will shine next. This is the difference between the spiritual light and the natural light. If natural light entered Zacchaeus' house that day, it did so purely because the principles of refraction and reflection bounced it in there, with no sentient decision on the part of the light itself. By contrast Jesus emphasizes that he has sought out Zacchaeus deliberately: "For the Son of Man came to seek and to save what was lost." (Luke 19:10) This is the idea we are introduced to in John's Creation. It is a stunningly simple yet profound introduction to Jesus Christ, the one man who had the very will of God embedded in his heart and mind, and so shined in the dark world of men selectively and intelligently, illuminating whom he would.

There is another thought on light within the natural creation that we are edified to consider. Light, we have reasoned, is employed in the Bible as a metaphor for understanding. How fascinating (and humbling) it is therefore to realize that in all the realm of science light remains an entity whose composition and structure, (though universally described using the term 'photon,')

---

[1] A more detailed exposition of John 1:1-14, pertaining to the nature of Jesus Christ John presents, is given in Appendix C.

Day 1 Exposition: Seeing the Light

is still fundamentally unknown! The Nobel Laureate physicist Albert Einstein, whose theories still underpin the contemporary physical understanding of light, said:

> "Every physicist thinks that he knows what a photon is. I spent my life to find out what a photon is and I still don't know it." [2]

God has given us light (illumination) so we might see and understand the natural world around us. We have also seen from scripture that light itself is used as a metaphor for spiritual understanding. Yet how beautifully and powerfully is the supremacy of Almighty God maintained, for the very metaphor of understanding – light – remains a thing man cannot understand! The author suggests that the importance of this scriptural lesson is profound, and should not escape the reader.

1.2 Jesus Christ: The Light

Read the opening 14 verses of John 1. The gospel opens with an introduction of Jesus Christ using the metaphor of light. [3] Specifically three statements are made:

> In him was life, and that life was the light of men. (1:4)
> The light shines in the darkness, but the darkness has not understood it. (1:5)
> The true light that gives light to every man was coming into the world. (1:9)

We interpret these verses using 'understanding' as the element which light represents to obtain their full meaning. Ultimately it is 'understanding' which brings life (1:4), because it enables us to respond in the appropriate way to God's love.

---

[2] Einstein A., in Hecht E., "Optics" 2nd Ed., 1987, Addison-Wesley, Reading, USA, p 9

[3] These verses also form a critical exposition of the nature of Jesus Christ, which is detailed in Appendix C.

Day 1 Exposition: Seeing the Light

Consider the saving act of baptism: we could not have guessed that being immersed in water could possibly bring us eternal life except Christ had taught us. In fact immersion in water cannot bring salvation *except* it is performed with full understanding that one is enacting an imitation of death as Christ also died, making a conscious decision to 'kill' the natural man in an attempt to live in the Spirit, and not after the flesh. Without this understanding (enlightenment) baptism is merely the act of getting very wet, and achieves no useful function.

In the same way we understand 1:5 and 1:9. Understanding has always struggled against the risk of being lost amidst ignorance (1:5) – how appropriate is the metaphor of light here! It calls to mind the image of a fragile candle flame, which has a complexity and a beauty unmatched by the blank void, its ignorant counterpart. There is perpetual risk of losing the flame to that darkness, snuffed out in its cold embrace.

Likewise it is necessary to obtain this light, this understanding, from Jesus himself (1:9). Often the thought is voiced that there are 'many paths to truth,' with the Bible, even Jesus himself, as only one available route, with other routes to truth open through different religions, or acts of meditation, or studies of science. How thoroughly these thoughts are contradicted by this opening lesson in John! This careful metaphor of light in the opening verses of John unambiguously paints the picture where there is no other source by which we might be ignited in the understanding of God than by the Light of Jesus Christ. Hence truly the gospel message of Jesus is the light that brings life (1:4), from which we can overcome the darkness (1:5) and receive that light ourselves (1:9).

1.3 Israel: The Darkness

In deliberate contrast to the light of the world, John introduces those to whom Jesus was sent: the House of Israel. John represents the Israelites as the darkness and it is easy to see why: the text is composed of a stream of questions, an obvious indication that they understood nothing of what was going on (Table 1_1).

Day 1 Exposition: Seeing the Light

The Pharisees' lack of understanding of all the things that either John the Baptist, or Jesus, have come to do (Table 1_1), culminates in Nicodemus' final, bewildered comment: "How can these things be?" (3:9). Particularly indicting is that these questions are coming from the Pharisees and Sanhedrin: the religious leaders of God's people, those whose *knowledge* of the scriptures was the greatest, and yet who still *understood* nothing of them. Truly man without Christ is in utter darkness, (and notice how this point is underscored by the attractive detail that Nicodemus came to Jesus *at night* (3:2)).

1	"Who are you?"	(1:21)
2	"What then?"	(1:21)
3	"Are you Elijah?"	(1:21)
4	"Are you the Prophet?"	(1:21)
5	"Who are you, that we may give an answer to those who sent us?"	(1:22)
6	"What do you say about yourself?"	(1:22)
7	"Why then do you baptize if you are not the Christ, nor Elijah, nor the Prophet?"	(1:25)
8	"What sign do you show to us, since you do these things?"	(2:18)
9	"It has taken forty-six years to build this temple, and you will raise it up in three days?"	(2:20)
10	"How can a man be born when he is old?"	(3:4)
11	"Can he enter a second time into his mother's womb and be born?"	(3:4)
12	"How can these things be?"	(3:9)

Table 1_1: Twelve questions posed by spiritual rulers amongst the Israelites to John the Baptist and Jesus upon encountering the ministry and person of Jesus Christ. The number of questions varies with translation: this list is compiled from the Greek text. [4]

This lack of understanding is not a mere misfortune for the Israelites; rather it constitutes a serious failing on their part. They

---

[4] Wilson B., *Op. cit.*, pp 314-320

have been commissioned by God to be His witnesses, to declare His Name to the nations and proclaim the coming of the Messiah.

> "You are my witnesses," declares the LORD, "and my servant whom I have chosen, so that you may know and believe me and understand that I am he. Before me no god was formed, nor will there be one after me. I, even I, am the LORD, and apart from me there is no Savior." (Isaiah 43:10-11)

The Israelites were to be lights to the surrounding peoples, illuminating the Gentile nations in darkness. The Pharisees were not only failing in that task, but also hindering those who might otherwise have succeeded (Luke 11:52). Therefore John teaches that not only were the Pharisees *in* darkness, but also that they *constituted* the very darkness against which the light was struggling. This metaphor brings this deeper understanding of their culpability in failing to respond correctly to the Light of Jesus Christ.

However, lest we judge them carelessly, we should recognize that this same commission to 'understand' God's purpose falls upon ourselves, not just the Pharisees of old. The proverb declares:

> Evil men understand not judgment: but they that seek the LORD understand all things. (Proverbs 28:5, KJV)

This is more of a commission than an observation, for it describes a state we press towards, not one we can ever achieve. But it is a commission by which all who claim to be followers of Christ are bound. Truly we are in no place to condemn the shortfalls of others' understanding, but merely learn from them in all humility.

Day 1 Exposition: Seeing the Light

1.4 Discipleship: Seeing the Light

Read John 1:35-51. Here John describes the earliest bonds of discipleship through the calling of Andrew, Philip and Nathanael. Again we witness the metaphor of illumination, although the association is subtle this time. As Andrew enquires where Jesus resides, Jesus replies (and this is Jesus' first direct statement recorded in John):

> "Come," [Jesus] replied, "and you will see." (1:39)

This statement constitutes a fascinating insight to the nature of discipleship! Here is the light of the world, introduced to the children of Israel, and he is inviting them to follow him so that they will see. This completes the picture of light and darkness we have considered, because clearly there are two available responses to the invitation. One is described by the earlier verse:

> The light shines in the darkness, but the darkness has not understood it. (1:5)

In terms of what we have deduced about light and darkness as scriptural metaphors; this verse (1:5) is no longer merely a commentary: it is now a *definition*. It is *by definition* that those who understand are in the light, and those who do not understand are in darkness. This latter position describes the Pharisees. In the translation of 1:5 the NIV offers "the darkness has not overcome" the light whilst the KJV has the darkness "comprehended it not." Perhaps by combining these two similar renditions we obtain the most powerful understanding. The interpretations, taken together, present both the idea of a conceptual overcoming, and a raw physical overpowering. Perhaps 'grasped' is therefore the best English word to use, since both interpretations are maintained within it. It is possible to grasp something intellectually, in the mind, or physically, with the hands. The section above demonstrates the Pharisees' inability to grasp Jesus intellectually. Yet interestingly John's gospel also cleverly includes detail of the failure of the Pharisees to grasp

Jesus physically (in Day 4, where the aspects of the spiritual light recur of Day 1 recur):

> At this they tried to seize [Jesus], but no one laid a hand on him, because his time had not yet come. (7:30)
> Again they tried to seize [Jesus], but he escaped their grasp. (10:39)

Yet the response of a few, a chosen few, was not characterized by the darkness' inability to grasp the light. The hearts of these few were enlightened by Jesus' presence, and John's gospel shows us that they knew, and grasped, what they had found:

> Andrew: "We have found the Messiah" (1:41)
> Philip: "We have found the one Moses wrote about in the Law, and about whom the prophets also wrote – Jesus of Nazareth" (1:45)
> Nathanael: "Rabbi, you are the Son of God; you are the King of Israel." (1:49)

Here in Day 1 of John's Creation we witness faithful men finding the Light of the World, who gives light to every man, even as we find him ourselves in the pages of John's gospel opening before us. "Come with me," Jesus says, "and I will make you see."

And that, of course, is exactly what we hope to do.

1.5 The Wedding at Cana
The Prime Miracle

The events at Cana are central to the opening message John's gospel communicates about understanding and not understanding. Read the first eleven verses of John 2: the miraculous transformation of water into wine performed by Jesus at the Wedding at Cana. Notice the comment at the end of the miracle:

Day 1 Exposition: Seeing the Light

This, the first of his miraculous signs, Jesus performed at Cana in Galilee. (2:11)

The Greek word translated 'first' is 'arche' [5] but, lest we understand this to mean solely that the miracle at Cana was the first chronologically in the ministry, it is worth noting the full breadth of this word's meaning. 'Arche' is perhaps better translated 'prime': note its presence in existing English words such as: arch-enemy, archetypal, Archbishop. The presence of 'arche' in each of these words denotes a primary sense of rank rather than mere chronology. Thus we do best to understand John 2:11 as saying:

This *primary* miraculous sign Jesus performed in Cana of Galilee. He thus revealed his glory, and his disciples put their faith in him (2:11, author's paraphrase)

Our interest is piqued to hear the miracle described as the *prime* declaration of Jesus' glory. Our puzzlement is equally heightened when we stop to consider the details of this miracle itself. A miracle showing Jesus replenishing the alcohol supply at a celebration event is said to comprise the prime declaration of the glory of the Son of God: this is frankly astounding! This makes the miracle all the more intriguing; and deserving of our closest attention.

Sign of the Woman

Now to the events of the wedding feast proper. The first point of interest comes in verse 3, when the wine runs out. Mary brings this matter to the attention of Jesus, whereupon the Lord gives a most astonishing reply:

And when they wanted wine, the mother of Jesus saith unto him, "They have no wine." Jesus saith unto her, "Woman,

---

[5] Wilson B., *Op. cit.*, p 318

Day 1 Exposition: Seeing the Light

what have I to do with thee? mine hour is not yet come." His mother saith unto the servants, "Whatsoever he saith unto you, do it." (2:3-5, KJV)

It seems a bizarre response by the Lord; indeed at surface level it appears disrespectful! John teaches us to pay special attention to details that appear counter-intuitive. Furthermore it is clear from the quote that Mary understands that Jesus has spoken with meaning. Firstly Jesus refers to his mother as "Woman." This is doubtless not a disrespectful form of address within the culture of the day; indeed the NIV attempts to communicate this point using the translation "Dear woman." Word choice is important in scripture, and so we must challenge ourselves to spot the association. "Woman" calls to mind the events of Eden, because that is where we first meet a character initially called only by that name. This "woman" is a very important scriptural concept and character. The covenant relationship between God and mankind was enacted through "woman": the serpent would bruise the heel of the woman's seed, and the woman's seed would bruise the serpent's head (Genesis 3:14-15). This speaks explicitly of Christ. Additionally this connects directly to wine, because Christ, the seed of the woman, will destroy the serpent by the provision of his life's blood, (19:34), which the Word of God symbolizes with wine (Matthew 26:27-29).

So it is a matter of considerable import that as Jesus is in Cana, giving a prime declaration of his purpose and destiny, the "woman" asks him to provide "wine." Now we have an insight into Jesus' answer. Within the spiritual creation Jesus' response is compelling. "Woman, what have I to do with thee?" is not simply rhetorical; rather it explicitly provokes memory of the Eden covenant: that the seed was to save the woman by destroying the serpent. Jesus continues: "mine hour is not yet come," and we know this "hour" refers to his crucifixion (see 12:23 & 12:27). Thus we can paraphrase Jesus' answer as: "Remember the covenant? I am indeed the Seed [Woman, what have you to do

Day 1 Exposition: Seeing the Light

with me?]; and I will save you with the provision of wine, but that will only come when I am crucified [mine hour is not yet come]."

Fascinatingly, the patterns in John's gospel are so deep-woven that the matter is not concluded there. We peek forward from Day 1 to Day 5 of John's Creation to see the conclusion of this pattern. Standing at the foot of the cross, alongside the gospel witness John, we hear Jesus utter these words:

"Woman, behold your son!" (19:26)

Firstly an important disclaimer: There is no doubt from the immediate context that this is a formal introduction by Jesus of his mother to the apostle John. This is an act characteristically unselfish (indeed incredible) that Jesus, even as he hangs dying on the cross, is making arrangements for the care of others. But, with that established, we would very much like to suggest a second meaning for this remark, which attaches directly to the Wedding at Cana. Indeed we suggest that this is a continuation of Jesus' reply to Mary in Cana. The justification of relating the crucifixion moment to Cana is twofold: first, Jesus refers directly to his crucifixion "hour" at Cana; and second, the signature keyword "Woman" arises in both places, provoking the reader to link the two events. At Cana Jesus is asked to provide wine; at Golgotha the wine of the covenant is revealed. During that grisly crucifixion, as Jesus hangs on the cross, he says these words [the grammar has been changed by the author to emphasize the argument]:

"Woman: Behold! Your son!" (19:26, author's paraphrase)

Remember Jesus was bleeding as he spoke these words. This is not stated for melodrama, rather the pertinent point is that the very substance of the wine of the new covenant was issuing from his body at the precise moment he instructs the "woman" to look at him; to "behold" her son. Now we understand why the keyword "woman" is so appropriate at Cana, for Cana is the prime declaration of Jesus' ministry (2:11). It naturally links to

Day 1 Exposition: Seeing the Light

both Eden and the crucifixion, because the word "woman" is deliberately prominent in both of those places too. We propose Figure 1_1 as the complete answer to Jesus' erstwhile baffling comment in Cana. It is on the cross that Jesus' ministry, prophesied in Eden and announced in Cana, is completed: The wine (blood) finally comes and the woman (Eve: mother of all living/Mary: mother of the Living) has been saved from the power of the serpent (death).

> I will put enmity between you and the **Woman**... he shall bruise your head and you shall bruise his heel
> *Genesis 3:15*

> O **Woman**, what have you to do with me? My hour has not yet come
> *John 2:4*

> **Woman**, Behold your son!
> *John 19:26*

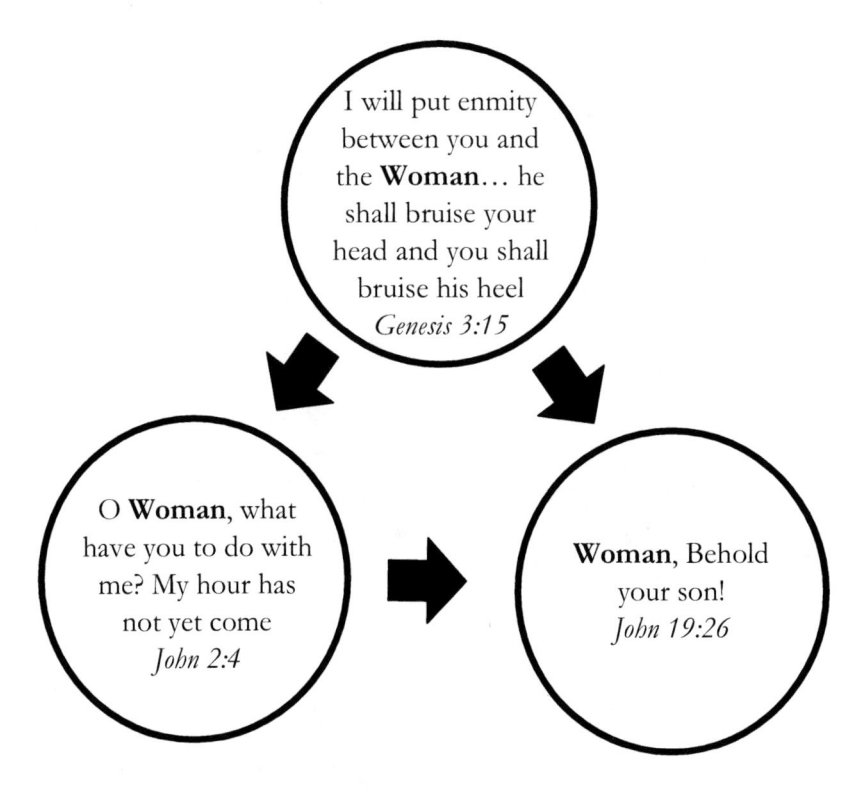

Figure 1_1: Sign of the Woman. The link, based on the word "Woman," between the covenant made in Eden; the introduction of Jesus' ministry in Cana; and its completion on the cross.

Stone Waterpots: Fulfilling the Law

> Nearby stood six stone water jars, the kind used by the Jews for ceremonial washing, each holding from twenty to thirty gallons. (2:6)

Day 1 Exposition: Seeing the Light

Our interest in these water jars is provoked because John tells us far more detail about them than we (seemingly) need to know. We are told:

(a) Their constituency: Stone.

(b) Their purpose: For ceremonial cleansing of the Jews (KJV: purification).

(c) Their volume: 6 jars at 20-30 gallons per jar ≈ 150 gallons total.

(d) Jesus finds them in need of replenishment and fills them up.

What are these jars supposed to signify? To understand seemingly innocuous details in the gospel of John it is paramount to keep our minds trained on the spiritual equivalents of physical things. Consider the first three physical parameters of the jars on the spiritual plane: i.e. something contained in stone, which the Jews used for purification, which is now empty. This is a perfect description of the Mosaic Law in all three counts! The Law was written on two tables of stone (Exodus 31:18), had the purpose of purifying the Jews (1 Chronicles 23:28), but was now empty and ready to pass away (Hebrews 8:13). So John is using the water jars as a representation of the Mosaic Law showing us is that the old, 'stone-based' way in which the Jews used to clean themselves is now empty, devoid of power to make clean (Table 1_2).

Jesus' arrival hails a fundamental transformation. Jesus fills full (fulfills) the water jars: a perfect enactment of his role! This is how the miracle acts as a prime declaration of his glory in fulfilling God's will (2:11) because it graphically illustrates how the life of the Lord Jesus wholly enclosed the Mosaic Law: he was come to fulfill it, and thus radically and permanently transform the covenant relationship between every man and his God (Table 1_2).

Day 1 Exposition: Seeing the Light

	Waterpots at Cana	Tablets of Mosaic Law
Constituency: Stone	"And there were set there six waterpots of stone…" (2:6)	"When the LORD finished speaking to Moses on Mount Sinai, he gave him the two tablets of the Testimony, the tablets of stone inscribed by the finger of God." (Exodus 31:18)
Purpose: Purification	"…after the manner of the purifying of the Jews…" (2:6)	"The duty of the Levites was to help Aaron's descendants in… the purification of all sacred things…" (1 Chronicles 23:28)
Jesus effect on them: To fulfill (fill full)	"Jesus said to the servants, "Fill the jars with water"; so they filled them to the brim." (2:7)	"Do not think that I have come to abolish the Law or the Prophets; I have not come to abolish them but to fulfil them." (Matthew 5:17)

Table 1_2: Comparison of defining parameters of the water jars at Cana and the two tables of testimony of the Mosaic Law bearing the Ten Commandments.

Water into Wine

Even considering the weighty symbology of the stone jars, we are yet to touch upon the central feature of the miracle: water was transformed into beautiful wine. Note the quantity: 6 water jars containing between 20-30 gallons would generate 700-1 100 bottles of wine!! Doubtless this represents the abundance of mercy we receive at the Hand of the Almighty.

And with God's miracles there is always blessing upon blessing. Jesus did not only refill the jars with water, returning them to their former state, but also transformed their entire content, from water to wine – and not just wine, but the best wine any had tasted (2:10). Thus the last state of the jars was far greater and more beneficial than any state they had enjoyed

Day 1 Exposition: Seeing the Light

before: another perfect parallel with the former covenant of Moses and the latter covenant in Christ.

A central feature of the miracle is the difference of operation of the water and the wine. The water was washing water, not drinking water. That water only ever touched a man on the outside, whereas wine is necessarily drunk, fully ingested inside the body. The changes wine effects upon the human body operate from within, whilst washing water can only touch the exterior. What an excellent parallel this forms for our understanding of the two covenants! Ultimately the law could only clean a man 'from the outside,' or declare him guilty if he remained unclean. But the love of Christ operates upon the heart and cleans the man who embraces it from within.

This instructs us that the covenant relationship with our Father we enjoy through the Lord Jesus is closer and more powerful than anything experienced under the Mosaic Law. It is not just a different covenant, it is a much *better* covenant: that which was water has now been made wine and it is ingested deep within us. Truly we stand no longer at Mt Sinai, the Mount of Judgment, smoldering with the fire and brimstone of the awesome power of the Mighty One. We are called to stand before Mt Zion, to behold the living water (made wine) and the loving mercy of so caring and patient a Father. Truly spiritual Zion reaches so much higher than Sinai, (and beautifully the reverse is true in the physical world), because at Zion we are finally enabled to find the freedom from the bondage long held, to taste the wine of the new covenant, and to be gently touched by the crippling body-blow that is the understanding of total forgiveness. It is this Zion we first glimpse in John's recount of the miracle of Jesus Christ on that wedding day in Cana.

Seeing the Light: Understanding the Miracle

> He thus revealed his glory, and his disciples put their faith in him. (2:11)

The transformation of water into wine is the heart of the miracle, and truly the glory of the Lord was revealed on this Day

Day 1 Exposition: Seeing the Light

to those who 'saw the light.' But since 'understanding' is the overriding concept of Day 1, we anticipate that the gospel writer will pay particular attention to how much the witnesses of the miracle actually understood of what they saw. The narrative concludes, indeed culminates, with exactly this point. Jesus instructs the servants to bear the water made wine to the wedding guests:

> They did so, and the master of the banquet tasted the water that had been turned into wine. He did not realize where it had come from, though the servants who had drawn the water knew. (2:8-9)

The detail that the servants knew where the wine came from is a (seemingly) superfluous piece of information: it is glaringly obvious that the servants are aware of the wine's origin, for they are the very people who filled the water jars in the first place! (Remember these jars held ~ 150 gallons in total, so this was no small task readily forgotten!) John is emphasizing the servants' understanding in deliberate contrast to the master of the banquet, who did *not* know the wine's origin. The spiritual interpretation within John's spiritual creation is simple. The wine represents the new covenant in Christ (Matthew 26:27-29). John shows us the "masters of the banquet" in Israel (i.e. the Pharisees and rulers) did not understand the origin of the wine, whereas the servants (i.e. the common people) did (see Table 1_3).

John concludes the miracle by focusing on who *understood* the source of the miracle and who did not; who had seen the light as to where the wine had come from, and who remained in the darkness (Table 1_3). Ultimately those who were in positions of social and religious authority rejected Jesus' teaching, but it was a common fisherman who confounded them all with the declaration:

> "You are the Christ, the Son of the living God." (Matthew 16:16)

Day 1 Exposition: Seeing the Light

	Upon witnessing the miracle at Cana	Upon witnessing Jesus' ministry
Those with high social status	"…the master of the banquet tasted the water that had been turned into wine. **He did not realize where it had come from…**" (2:9)	"Then they [the Pharisees] hurled insults at him and said… We are disciples of Moses! We know that God spoke to Moses, but as for this fellow [Jesus], **we don't even know where he comes from.**" (9:28-29)
Those with low social status	"…though the servants who had drawn the water knew." (2:9)	"And the common people heard him gladly." (Mark 12:37)

Table 1_3: Comparison of the reactions of those in high social standing and low social standing upon receiving the wine at Cana and the teachings of Christ.

Truly it was the servants at the Feast who understood the origin of the water made wine, whilst the rulers never grasped its source. In this way a simple Jewish wedding feast is transformed into a profound prophecy and revelation of Christ's ministry.

1.6 Conclusions from Day 1

We observe a pervasive presence of light in the beginning of John's gospel, both as a physical word and as a spiritual metaphor for understanding.

Christ is represented as a shining Light, and John focuses the reader's attention on the *responses* of all who were 'shined upon': whether they were truly illuminated and understood Jesus' message; or whether they adhered to the darkness by failing to understand it. The metaphor itself is particularly attractive because in all man's excellence of scientific understanding, natural light is one basic material whose nature remains fundamentally inexplicable. So beautifully is the superiority of Almighty God

Day 1 Exposition: Seeing the Light

maintained, that man cannot understand the very element God has chosen as His metaphor for 'understanding.'

Day 1 of John's gospel underscores how the spiritual creation stands in excellence above the natural. In the natural creation the sun rises on the evil and the good and the rain is sent on the just and on the unjust (Matthew 5:45). The superlative nature of the spiritual creation accounts for *why* this is true. Sunshine and rain in the natural creation do not retain the creative words and purpose of God within them, they therefore act indiscriminately. By contrast John's gospel reveals that the spiritual Light (Christ) retains the (creative) Word of God within him, meaning that he makes sentient decisions about where, and upon whom, he shines. Thus spiritual Day 1 (in John) excels natural Day 1 (in Genesis) and, in good accordance with a common scriptural prerogative, (which we shall explore in detail in the following exhortation), the chronological latter excels the former.

EXHORTATION 1:   *John 2*
God of the Second Son

He was the first son. Not just the firstborn son, you realize, but the first son ever born to man. The precedental firstborn. And his name was Cain.

The events unfolding for Adam and Eve at the birth of Cain were doubtless both exhilarating and traumatic, as they witnessed – indeed performed – the first ever human reproduction of life. The importance of this event is evident in the scriptural record: there are no fewer than four details given in association with Cain's birth: copulation, conception, birth and triumphal announcement.

> Adam lay with his wife Eve, and she became pregnant and gave birth to Cain. She said, "With the help of the LORD I have brought forth a man." (Genesis 4:1)

Compare this to the record of the second son's arrival:

> Later she gave birth to his brother Abel. (Genesis 4:2)

Day 1 Exhortation: God of the Second Son

The trump and fanfare has passed by the second birth. As is logically deductive, the pride, joy and excitement from the arrival of the firstborn child are muted by the arrival of the second and the record here in Genesis bears that out, as does human behavior. So often it is the firstborn child who bears the pride of the parents, and in Old Testament times, where males had precedence over females, this translated into the pride of the father being instilled in the firstborn son. But the precedental firstborn is Cain: and Cain is a murderer. By contrast the second son, over whose arrival no human fanfare is voiced, is a righteous man. This is the precedent that the Bible sets for brothers in scripture.

God of the Second Son: First and Second Sons of Men

Consider how globally this principle applies throughout scripture. The firstborn bears the pride of the (human) father, and is a failure in spiritual terms, whereas a younger son finds the favor of his Heavenly Father. The evidence is overwhelming. Consider Abraham: the primary patriarch of all Israel through whom all the nations of the Earth receive a blessing. He is not the firstborn: it is Nahor or Haran who is the eldest. (It requires a little detective work between Genesis 11:26-12:4 to establish this.)

Then there is Isaac. First in line to God's promises he may be, firstborn he is not. He again is a second son, a subsequent child to Abraham's firstborn: Ishmael. The Bible shows us how Abraham, the human father, places his hopes in Ishmael, for when Abraham is told that he will father a great nation he replies:

"O that Ishmael might live before thee!" (Genesis 17:18, KJV)

But God is keen to accentuate that it is Isaac, the second son, in whom the blessing will be established.

Then God said, "Yes, but your wife Sarah will bear you a son, and you will call him Isaac. I will establish my covenant with him as an everlasting covenant for his descendants after him.

43

Day 1 Exhortation: *God of the Second Son*

And as for Ishmael, I have heard you: I will surely bless him; I will make him fruitful and will greatly increase his numbers. He will be the father of twelve rulers, and I will make him into a great nation. But my covenant I will establish with Isaac" (Genesis 17:19-21, see also Genesis 21:9-12)

Following Isaac, the trio of the patriarchal line is completed with Jacob: the father of the twelve tribes of Israel. Once more Jacob is a second son: Esau is the elder brother (Genesis 25:25-26). Here the scripture is strikingly clear in God's feelings towards the two sons:

Jacob I loved, but Esau I hated. (Romans 9:13, quoting Malachi 1:2-3)

How stark the statement! But what reinforcement this gives of the scriptural pattern of the second son finding favor in the eyes of the Almighty, whilst the firstborn's actions are not right before God. The Bible also reinforces the other half of the principle: that the firstborn son is the favorite of the human father. Esau becomes a skilled hunter, and Isaac, with the satisfaction of his stomach firmly to the fore, favors him (Genesis 25:28).

The line of the three consecutive patriarchs who defined the origins of God's people: Abraham, Isaac and Jacob are all second sons.

The pattern doesn't stop here. The man chosen to lead God's people out of Egypt was Moses: once again a second son, some three years the junior of his brother Aaron (Exodus 7:7). Yet God insists Moses, the second son, must be His mouthpiece to the children of Israel. God is even angered when Moses suggests that someone else should take the role (Exodus 4:13-14). Notice especially that, even though the Lord relents to Moses' constant objections to qualify as God's witness, and Aaron is sent to be the direct mouthpiece to Pharaoh, God is still insistent on the superiority of the younger over the elder:

Day 1 Exhortation: *God of the Second Son*

"What about your brother, Aaron the Levite? I know he can speak well... He will speak to the people for you, and it will be as if he were your mouth and as if you were God to him." (Exodus 4:14, 16 – see also Exodus 7:1)

Later still Israel becomes a monarchy, and God chooses a king to lead them: a man after His own Heart: David, a forerunner of Jesus Christ. The principle of brothers is reinforced. Samuel, the prophet, is sent to Jesse (David's father) to anoint one of his sons, and Samuel, responding more as a human man than the divinely appointed prophet he was called to be, is impressed by the sight of the firstborn son Eliab. But God, who sees so very differently, chooses the younger brother.

Samuel saw Eliab and thought, "Surely the LORD's anointed stands here before the LORD." But the LORD said to Samuel, "Do not consider his appearance or his height, for I have rejected him. The LORD does not look at the things man looks at. Man looks at the outward appearance, but the LORD looks at the heart." (1 Samuel 16:6-7)

These passages have firmly established the principle in scripture. Where brothers appear, there is invariably a spiritual superiority of the younger over the elder. We have not exhausted the list of examples either, consider also: Shem over Japheth (Genesis 10:21; Luke 3:36) although there is uncertainty here over who is the eldest; Judah over Reuben (Genesis 49:3-4, 8); Ephraim over Manasseh (Genesis 48:14); and Solomon over Amnon (2 Samuel 3:2; 12:24). Indeed the pattern is so pervasive that it is difficult to name even one righteous man in scripture who is presented in the role of one amongst brethren, and noted by scripture to be the eldest. Of the few cases where righteous men in scripture are firstborn sons: Samuel, John the Baptist, and possibly also Samson and Jonathan, the Bible seems careful not to present them as one amongst brethren, but simply men alone. In these cases if they have brothers, as some of them do, those brothers do not appear in the scriptural record alongside them.

Day 1 Exhortation: God of the Second Son

The reason we consider the superiority of the second son over the firstborn in scripture is to advance our thinking to spiritual parallels of the same pattern, which are powerful and exhortational. In all there are four different levels on which this same pattern operates (explanation of the relationships follows): the Kings of Israel (Firstborn = Saul, Second son = David); Sons of God (Firstborn = Adam, Second son = Jesus); The covenants (Firstborn = Old Testament, Second son = New Testament); and ourselves (Firstborn = physical birth, Second son = born of water and the spirit).

God of the Second Son: First and Second Kings of Israel

The first king, Saul, was a failure: indeed the establishment of the monarchy itself was tantamount to a rejection of God (1 Samuel 8:6-7). Saul was chosen deliberately to represent the things that humans choose: a man with an exceptional physique, (1 Samuel 9:2). But the second king was chosen to match the spiritual characteristics God sought for His people: a man whose heart was right with God (1 Samuel 13:14).

There is a further point to notice in David's case. He is not the second son of Jesse, he is the eighth (1 Samuel 16:10-11). Some may feel this weakens the pattern, now the eighth son is chosen and not the second. More likely the reverse is true, that the pattern is strengthened! Given that scriptural patterns are often completed in sevens (e.g. days of the week, apocalyptic judgments, etc) it is understandable to view the 'eighth' as a repeat of the 'first': the start of a new cycle. (The first day of the week is also the eighth day, counting from the beginning of the previous week.) In this sense therefore, we can view the 'eighth son' as the 'second firstborn.' This feature of being a 'second firstborn' is very relevant to the Lord Jesus Christ, in whom this pattern is ultimately culminated, and of whom King David, the eighth son, was a shining scriptural precedent.

God of the Second Son: First and Second Sons of God

Jesus is the Son of God, indeed the gospel of John describes him as the only Son of God, and therefore necessarily the

Day 1 Exhortation: *God of the Second Son*

firstborn, several times (1:14; 1:18; 3:16; 3:18). Paul also refers to Christ explicitly as the firstborn of the new creation (Colossians 1:15). Nevertheless without all contradiction we also find an irrefutable pattern in scripture by which Jesus is the *second* son of God, for there is another man who is referred to as the son of God, and who preceded all others chronologically: the man Adam (Luke 3:38). This relation perfectly encapsulates the whole spirit of the scriptural relationship of brothers. In the firstborn son is the pride of man, with the spirit that grasps at equality with God, just as Adam grasped at the fruit of the knowledge of good and evil, believing it would bring equality with God (Genesis 3:5-6). The second son, Jesus, is presented in deliberate contrast to the Eden account as the one with humility, who would not consider equality with God something to be grasped (Philippians 2:6). How perfectly this theme, so commonly enacted with scriptural pairs of brothers, is brought to fruition between the 'brothers' of Adam and the Lord Jesus! Appreciate the additional weight it lends to this thought:

> For since death came through a man, the resurrection of the dead comes also through a man. For as in Adam all die, so in Christ all will be made alive. (1 Corinthians 15:21-22)

How neatly this pattern ties these two characters in these verses together! Adam and Christ are not two random characters in history, one that brought death into the world and one that brought life. They are brothers! The firstborn realizes all that the human spirit can achieve (death and destruction) whilst the second son, over whom there is no human fanfare made nor any human desire aroused (Isaiah 53:1-3), displays the fruit borne of the divine Spirit, the perfect will of God: Life. This deepens our understanding and is also an important development of our pattern. Whereas before we only had the notion of seniority of the second son over the firstborn, now we have a direct association of Death with the firstborn, and Life with the second son.

Day 1 Exhortation: *God of the Second Son*

We step up a gear in our thinking to determine what new revelations from scripture this pattern supplies. Consider one conversation Jesus has with the Sadducees. The Sadducees did not believe in the resurrection. In an attempt to demonstrate that the doctrine was nonsense they created a story in which a woman had several husbands (legally) through successive deaths. They questioned Jesus as to whose wife she would be in her resurrected state (Matthew 22:23-28). Here is the latter part of Jesus' reply:

> "But about the resurrection of the dead--have you not read what God said to you, 'I am the God of Abraham, the God of Isaac, and the God of Jacob?' He is not the God of the dead but of the living." (Matthew 22:31-32)

An extraordinary response! On the face of it, the logic seems laughable! The evidence Jesus gives that 'God is a God of the living' is that he is the God of Abraham, Isaac and Jacob: three people who are all long dead! By human logic: if God is the God of Abraham, Isaac and Jacob, who are all dead, this clearly demonstrates He is a God of the dead! It is not surprising therefore, that the crowds are stupefied by his reasoning (Matthew 22:33).

How then do we understand Jesus' statement? We know Abraham, Isaac and Jacob have died in faith and therefore are considered to be alive in the Eyes of the Almighty (Luke 20:38). (This is an interesting concept in itself, but we will not develop it further here.) With our model that God is the God of the Second Son, we have both the ability to solve this quote from Jesus and draw from it a new and powerful thought we may not have previously considered. God is the God of Abraham (the second son) Isaac (the second son) and Jacob (the second son). Jesus deliberately couples this statement with the teaching that He is also a God of the living, not of the dead. We have reasoned above that the first son is connected to death, whilst the second son is connected to life (1 Corinthians 15:21-22). The Sadducees are being told plainly that God is NOT the God of the firstborn

Day 1 Exhortation: God of the Second Son

(who are all dead) but the God of the Second Son (who lives). Here is the true beauty of the statement: who is telling the Sadducees all this? *Jesus: The Second Son of God!* They are being told, albeit very subtly, where the source of life is to be found: with Jesus Christ himself! With sufficient depth of understanding of their scriptures they would know God rejects the firstborn son of man and looks to the second son. But, though they consider themselves learned scholars of the Word, this powerful but subtle point is missed; they fail to see the light shining before them.

God of the Second Son: First and Second Covenants

We also see the imposition of this pattern on the covenant relationships between man and God. Not only is Jesus the second Son of God following firstborn Adam, but Jesus is also the instigator of the second covenant between all men and their Creator. Once again the link between the firstborn and death, and the second son and life is to the fore: the first(born) covenant, the Mosaic Law, brought only death, since it concerned the achievements of man, but the second covenant brought life, since it concerned the provision of God.

> Nearby stood six stone water jars, the kind used by the Jews for ceremonial washing, each holding from twenty to thirty gallons. Jesus said to the servants, "Fill the jars with water;" so they filled them to the brim. Then he told them, "Now draw some out and take it to the master of the banquet." They did so, and the master of the banquet tasted the water that had been turned into wine. (2:6-9)

We have already established that these waterpots are symbolic of the stone tablets of the Law. We also determined the central point of the miracle as the transformation of the relationship every man has with his Maker. Man is transformed from the covenant of Moses, which has run dry, into the covenant of grace in Jesus Christ, washed clean in the wine of his shed blood (Section 1.5).

Day 1 Exhortation: *God of the Second Son*

The pattern of 'God of the Second Son' extends this understanding. The firstborn son achieves only the failure of man, whilst the second brings the grace of God. In the same way the first covenant failed: not because God's provision was insufficient, but because man's response to it was insufficient – he couldn't keep the law. But, as always where man fails, God gives more grace. Therefore a second covenant was offered, wholly of grace, succeeding where the first had failed. In this second covenant man, in all his spiritual decrepitude, can find life at last, and God is pleased to set aside our failures (revealed by the Law) to provide His grace.

He sets aside the first to establish the second. (Hebrews 10:9)

Unfortunately, for some this verse yields a problem, namely, is the Law truly done away or does it still exist? (This is an aside, although a necessary one, since verses concerning the role of the Mosaic Law subsequent to the coming of Christ seem contradictory at first glance.) Consider these verses:

1) Mosaic Law: Surviving absolutely
"I tell you the truth, until heaven and earth disappear, not the smallest letter, not the least stroke of a pen, will by any means disappear from the Law until everything is accomplished." (Matthew 5:18)
2) Mosaic Law: Done away completely
By calling this covenant 'new,' he has made the first one obsolete; and what is obsolete and aging will soon disappear. (Hebrews 8:13, see also 2 Corinthians 3:7-17)

How can we harmonize understanding of these seemingly conflicting observations? To understand the transition between covenants performed by Christ we allude to the analogy of transformation occurring when a caterpillar metamorphoses into a butterfly.

The caterpillar weaves the cocoon around itself and the butterfly emerges. Is the caterpillar the same creature as the

Day 1 Exhortation: God of the Second Son

butterfly? We could say "yes" and be correct, for at all times there was only one creature, which had but a single birth. However we could also say "no" and be equally correct, for there is nothing in the butterfly, in either shape or locomotion, even vaguely resembling the caterpillar that once was. The caterpillar inched slowly with its multitudinous feet over whatever surfaces supported it, whilst the butterfly flutters swiftly and delicately from place to place through the air, born aloft of beautiful membranous wings. Is the caterpillar dead and gone? "Yes," the caterpillar is dead and gone, for his shell lies within the cocoon and neither figure nor form of caterpillar is anymore seen. However without contradiction one can equally say "no" the caterpillar is still alive, albeit in the form of a butterfly, which has a completely different shape and is much more beautiful. It is helpful to understand the transition between the covenants in this way, because it teaches us of the balance between the unity of God's purpose and the striking difference of the two covenants. It is true, within certain limits, to declare the Law both 'done away' and 'not done away,' and we understand now why we find both opinions within the scriptural record, (Matthew 5:18 and Hebrews 8:13). It is traditionally quoted that the Mosaic Law has passed 'in the letter' but is maintained 'in the spirit,' a useful description, and the metaphor of the caterpillar and the butterfly wholly maintains that theme.

Therefore to those who strenuously argue no detail of the Mosaic Law has passed we can proffer agreement, for the caterpillar and butterfly are one and the same creature; albeit given the understanding that all the features of the caterpillar have certainly vanished, for now we have a butterfly. The observations of the literal formalities of the Law have also vanished away, lying discarded in the cocoon of the empty tomb.

Likewise to those who would insist that the Mosaic Law is completely vanished we can also agree, for nothing even remotely resembling a caterpillar remains. Once again this is qualified with the understanding that the butterfly grew from the caterpillar in the cocoon: the second covenant grew from the fulfillment of the Mosaic Law in Christ. The covenant of grace, under whose

51

Day 1 Exhortation: God of the Second Son

beautiful wings we shelter, has developed wholly from Sinai's covenant, which revealed only man's failure and guilt. This is not to say that the grace of God cannot exist without the failure of man coming before, but rather that the grace of God to salvation cannot be accessed by man until his failure is firstly recognized.

God of the Second Son: The Disciple

Paul comments on the transition between the two covenants, invoking the now familiar idea of the firstborn being associated with death, and the latter with life.

> He [God] has made us competent as ministers of a new covenant--not of the letter but of the Spirit; for the letter kills, but the Spirit gives life. (2 Corinthians 3:6)

This verse allows us to develop the pattern of the second son into its final, most powerful and personal form: our lives in Christ. Every one of us has been born first (firstborn) of a woman, our mother. This first birth yields only the (fatal) achievements of man: the singular guarantee of this mortal life is that one day we will die. However, in baptism we have a chance to be born again, necessarily a 'second birth.' Our model instructs us that life is found only in our second birth, and never in our first.

But there is more. Jesus also established that God is a God *only* of the second son and *not* of the firstborn, because he is a God of the Living and not of the Dead, (Matthew 22:32). This is fundamental for our understanding of discipleship! Before we are baptized we have only been born once (i.e. physically) therefore we are firstborns. But God is not a God of the firstborn: so we do not have the right to even say that He is our God! Furthermore if He is not our God, then we cannot find true communion with Him and, even more importantly, *God will never be seen in us!* Irrespective of the works we do whilst we are not baptized, we are still not evidencing the Father, for He is not our Father if we are firstborn. If, however, we are second-born, of water and of the spirit, then God, who is God of the Second Son,

Day 1 Exhortation: God of the Second Son

becomes our God, and we have the possibility to share communion with Him and to reflect a little of His glory in our lives. This forms our understanding of the nature of the covenant in which we are privileged to share together in Christ Jesus.

The More Glorious Ministry

> Now if the ministry that brought death, which was engraved in letters on stone, came with glory, so that the Israelites could not look steadily at the face of Moses because of its glory, fading though it was, will not the ministry of the Spirit be even more glorious? If the ministry that condemns men is glorious, how much more glorious is the ministry that brings righteousness! For what was glorious has no glory now in comparison with the surpassing glory. And if what was fading away came with glory, how much greater is the glory of that which lasts! (2 Corinthians 3:7-11)

Having learned that it is only as second sons that we achieve communion with our Father and begin to show His character in our lives, these verses expand on how that can be achieved, telling of the more glorious ministry we enjoy in Christ. But let's make sure we understand the terminology first: what does Paul mean by 'glory'? Glory is certainly a very common word in religious communities, but for all it is used, it seldom seems well understood. It is a word that tends to get waved around by religious people purely because it is known to be Biblical, with the user then supposing that something profitable is being said, but, rather sadly, often without any formal understanding of the term being grasped.

Glory: Giving Evidence of Greatness

To understand the word, we must investigate its scriptural usage. Many of its uses are open to a variety of interpretations, but some are more exact, and it is from these that we can identify what "glory" means.

> The heavens declare the glory of God; the skies proclaim the work of his hands. (Psalm 19:1)

Day 1 Exhortation: God of the Second Son

> Professing to be wise, they became fools, and changed the glory of the incorruptible God into an image made like corruptible man--and birds and four-footed animals and creeping things. (Romans 1:22-23, NKJV)

Psalm 19:1 tells us a very interesting thing: non-sentient – indeed inanimate – things can express the glory of God. The skies are not alive, they cannot think and they are not self-aware: yet they can declare the glory of God. The verse from Romans adds a surprising facet of the glory of God: it can be changed (or 'exchanged' as some translations render) by men! Thus whatever meaning we develop for 'glory,' it must be able to incorporate both these facets.

The skies proclaim the work of God's hands (Psalm 19:1): they give evidence that whoever made them is great. How is this achieved? The skies visibly demonstrate enormous beauty and complexity with the scenes they often render. An object with great beauty and complexity indicates its creator is extremely skilled. For example: a watch that keeps good time is evidence that somewhere in the world there is a skilled watchmaker. In the same way the existence of the vast and often beautifully colored skies can be submitted as evidence of a designer and creator who is great indeed. Thus 'glory' is inherently connected with 'giving evidence of greatness.'

The verse in Romans is in the same vein: men have changed (or exchanged) the 'glory' of God for images of men and beasts. Paul is describing those who worship facsimiles of the created components of the Earth rather than the Creator. In olden days, this was idol-worshippers; the modern day equivalent is the proponents of the theory of evolution. To equate contemporary evolutionists with idol-worshippers of yesteryear may sound surprising at first consideration, yet philosophically their stances are the same. Evolutionists recapitulate exactly the philosophy and mannerisms of the idol-worshippers of old by attributing the existence of creation to the creation itself. Just as Aaron had the people of Israel bow down before the golden calf saying: "These are your gods, O Israel, who brought you up out of Egypt" (Exodus 32:3), so the

Day 1 Exhortation: God of the Second Son

modern evolutionist will regard a fragment of bone dug from a Tanzanian hole, or a dubious drawing penned in the science publication *du jour* and say: "You are my Maker, you are my source." In both cases the action of the true God, the one God, is removed from their mind, denied from their declarations. Observe one perfect fulfillment of the prophecy that praise would be given to the creation and not the Creator in the words of Charles Darwin:

> "When I view all beings not as special creations, but as the lineal descendants of some few beings which lived long before the first bed of the Silurian system was deposited, they seem to me to become ennobled." [1]

All these men, ancient and modern, replaced faith in the existence of God with faith in the created elements themselves. In this way they change the 'evidence' they gave of the existent creation around them. In this way, therefore, they change God's glory into images of created things.

Thus from Psalm 19 and Romans 1: 'glory' is translated as 'giving evidence of greatness.' Inanimate objects can give evidence (Psalm 19:1), even compelling evidence, just as the bloodstained earth gave compelling evidence against Cain of violence against his brother (Genesis 4:10). Man, as a living and self-aware creature, is able to give evidence of God's greatness in more overt and premeditated ways. He already gives glory to God passively by merely existing: the complexity and beauty of the human creature already evidences a uniquely and immeasurably skilled Creator. However he can also glorify God actively in meditation and silent appreciation of the beauty of the creation he witnesses, in vocal prayer and praise, in active service towards others, and in logically reasoned argument of the faith he has in the existence of his Creator. This is the process of glorifying God.

---

[1] Darwin C., "The Origin of Species" 1859, 1st Ed. reprint 1985, Penguin Classics, London, UK, p 458

Day 1 Exhortation: *God of the Second Son*

<u>Glory: Following One's Designed Function</u>

There is one more attribute inseparably linked to glory: the function of 'doing what one has been designed to do.' We return to the example case of the watchmaker and the watch. The existence of a watch that keeps accurate time gives evidence that the watchmaker has a great and delicate skill, i.e. the watch gives glory to the watchmaker. But notice that the watch glorifies the watchmaker *only whilst it works properly*. A malfunctioning watch gives no evidence that the watchmaker has a great skill: in fact the reverse is true! The malfunctioning watch is an embarrassment and an offence to the watchmaker, and the watchmaker is sensible to swiftly bring about either its repair or its destruction. In the same way God's creation only gives glory to God *whilst they correctly perform the purpose for which they were designed*: an educational concept.

We transfer that concept to the creation. A flower opening in bloom is glorifying God, because that is precisely what flowers are designed to do. Similarly across creation's spectrum: every nightingale that sings, every ice crystal that freezes, every tree that thrusts its branches skywards, every predator that stalks its prey at dusk and every bolt of lightning that shatters the very air through which it passes glorifies God: because it performs its designed function! This principle is the same with man, albeit the result is so very different. Man was designed to love and praise God (17:1-17), it was our purpose from the beginning, and remains so to this very day. Unfortunately this component of creation has proven thoroughly and appallingly dysfunctional. Man directs his life entirely according to his selfish desires, this is a matter of long established fact and this malfunction is an offence to his loving Maker. Notice how this argument deepens our understanding of the damage of sin: sins are not just our failures, which bring *us* disappointment; they are a malfunction of the purpose for which God designed us and therefore a deep offence to our Maker. Everyone who approaches bread and wine should carefully bear this in mind. Jeremiah comments:

> Even the stork in the sky knows her appointed seasons, and the dove, the swift and the thrush observe the time of their

Day 1 Exhortation: God of the Second Son

migration. But my people do not know the requirements of the LORD. (Jeremiah 8:7)

Nevertheless we take heart that these truths are the source of the words of Paul we considered above, (2 Corinthians 3:7-11): that in our baptized life in Christ we undertake a more glorious ministry, redressing the missing glory from our lives. Paul says that in our life in Christ we are better placed to give evidence of God's greatness than ever we could under the Mosaic Law. How is that true? Because we give evidence of the greatness of God's mercy in the covenant of the water made wine by responding to it in being baptized, and taking the bread and wine for the atonement it brings. We also appreciate that doing this goes hand in hand with following our designed function: as we expect, understanding the dual nature of the outworking of glory. God created man to live, and to praise Him: therefore those of us who are baptized into Jesus Christ for the forgiveness of our sins are giving glory to God: because our very salvation is the demonstration of God's great mercy, and embracing it is what we were designed to do. Glory is therefore also realized when we take bread and wine, when we show kindness to other members of our spiritual family, when we include someone who would otherwise be left out, when we pray and when we show gentleness to those around us. None of these things have we learned from our first, natural, birth. These are the actions of the second son. It is at these times we walk a more glorious path in our discipleship, the very path we were designed to take.

So then, let us take our appropriate place in God's beautiful (and glorious) creation, from which we are so far fallen. Let us be born again in the waters of baptism, for God is the God of the Second Son, and in our second birth we can make Him our Father. Let us fulfill the role for which we were designed, and thereby give evidence of His greatness in accepting and enacting the more glorious ministry. The psalmist said: "O LORD, our Lord, how excellent is thy name in all the earth!" (Psalm 8:1). Our role is to recognize that fact, and, in all the ways we interact with others, proclaim irrefutable evidence thereof.

DAY 2

John 3:22-5:47

EXPOSITION:
Waters Above

In the natural creation, Day 2 sees a divide created, with waters gathered above separated from those below. Again we compose our premise for John's Day 2 from the spiritual equivalents of this.

> **Basic premise**:
> In this section of John's gospel we expect to meet division; and division enacted through the metaphor of waters. We expect to find life (things above) drawn out of death (things beneath), with water used as the principal metaphor to convey that message. As Day 2 of the model focuses on the 'waters above' (the newly placed element) we expect this part of John to be positive, focusing on the heavenly, life-giving aspects of Christ's ministry.

Day 2 Exposition: Waters Above

2.1 Waters of Life: Reappearance of the Baptist
Read John 3:22-36.

> After this, Jesus and his disciples went out into the Judean countryside, where he spent some time with them, and baptized. Now John also was baptizing at Aenon near Salim, because there was plenty of water, and people were constantly coming to be baptized. (3:22-23)

Without the creation pattern John the Baptist's presence in John 3 would be most erratic. He has already completed his Herald role and baptism of the Messiah (1:6-36) and thus we would expect, as with the synoptic gospels, to see no further appearance of him. But within the model of John's Creation the Baptist's re-appearance is appropriate, even to be expected, at the opening of Day 2, for there is no more appropriate example of 'raising up' with water than baptism. The picture of John the Baptist tending those "constantly coming to be baptized" (3:23) is an excellent reflection of spiritual creation's Day 2.

The depth of the parallel extends further than just a mention of John the Baptist's baptismal work.

> They came to John and said to him, "Rabbi, that man who was with you on the other side of the Jordan--the one you testified about--well, he is baptizing, and everyone is going to him." To this John replied... "The one who comes from above is above all; the one who is from the earth belongs to the earth, and speaks as one from the earth. The one who comes from heaven is above all." (3:26, 31)

John replies to those asking about Jesus' work of baptism by giving a description of Jesus, understandably, since Jesus and baptism are themselves closely linked (one who is baptized is transferred 'into Christ'). John describes Jesus as "the one above" and therefore those baptized into him are likewise "drawn above" to be with him; cleverly mirroring the very act of God with the waters on Day 2.

59

Day 2 Exposition: Waters Above

2.2 The Work of Jesus: Raising Above

This picture of "drawing above" is fleshed out in the following accounts. The encounter at Jacob's Well (4:1-43) the healing of the official's son (4:46-54) and the healing of the infirm man at Bethesda (5:1-15) are all written with emphasis on the likeness of creation's Day 2. (The account of the Samaritan woman at Jacob's Well, which exemplifies this theme beautifully, is extracted to the following section.) In both other cases John details events in which a man is physically raised up from his prostrate position (the enactment of being 'drawn above'). For example:

> The royal official said, "Sir, come down before my child dies." Jesus replied, "You may go. Your son will live." The man took Jesus at his word and departed. (4:49-50)

The central feature hints at resurrection: a restoring to full health of one who is close to death. Doubtless the child lay prostrate and God's power, acting through the father's faith, acts to draw him up again. The case of the invalid at Bethesda matches the theme of raising up even more explicitly:

> Then Jesus said to him, "Get up! Pick up your mat and walk." At once the man was cured; he picked up his mat and walked. (5:8-9)

The recurring theme of water is seen amidst the healing. Here it is the pool at Bethesda, the physical water, by which the healing usually came for those who gathered at the poolside. Yet these waters are contrasted by Jesus as the spiritual water, who draws up the man from his afflicted state to the full physical abilities of one who is alive.

But why are we shown two miracles, (the official's son and the invalid at Bethesda), why does not one suffice?

There are two distinct ways in which a human ailment can be severe. It can be either chronically severe, (i.e. has been a problem for a very long time), or acutely severe, (i.e. is life-

Day 2 Exposition: Waters Above

threatening). These two miracles are not just repeats of each other therefore, but rather a discrete example of each type. The son of the official's illness is acutely severe (he is critically ill and about to die) and he is brought back from the brink of death by Jesus' act of healing. By contrast the impotent man's illness is chronically severe: the Bible points out that it has been ongoing for some 38 years! Jesus heals this man also, who has suffered for the majority of his life.

Putting these two miracles together gives us a very simple, yet very profound, teaching about Jesus' ability to heal. It is a *total* ability; an ability to heal wounds either chronically severe or acutely severe. Translating this to the spiritual plane, as the gospel of John constantly provokes us to do, provides us with much comfort for our own condition. There is no sin we can have committed which causes a wound too deep (i.e. no spiritual sickness too acutely severe) for Christ to heal. Nor is there any condition or lifestyle that we can have perpetrated for so long (i.e. no spiritual sickness too chronically severe) for Christ to be able to heal. There are wounds that sometimes are too severe for the sufferer to generate the necessary humility to seek absolution, but that is strictly a (further) weakness of the patient, and not a limitation of the healer. It is manifestly apparent in these verses that no wound is beyond the healing power of Jesus. These are powerful moments in the gospel of John: we do well to pay them full attention.

2.3 *Encounter at Jacob's Well*
Time…

Read John 4:1-43. Jesus encounters the Samaritan woman at the well near Sychar. Let us clearly define the terms 'Jew,' 'Israelite' and 'Samaritan' and ensure we understand the tension existent between the people bearing these names.

Abraham's grandson Jacob had his name changed to "Israel" by God (Genesis 32:28). Therefore any descendant of Jacob is an Israelite. Israel had twelve sons (Genesis 49), the fourth of whom was named Judah – the Hebrew is 'Yehuda,' meaning 'celebrated.'

Day 2 Exposition: Waters Above

[1] The tribe of Judah became prominent since from him was derived the lineage of King David and Jesus, the Christ. When the kingdom of Israel split in two, ten tribes formed the northern kingdom which retained the name 'Israel' and whose capital city was Samaria. The southern kingdom comprised the two tribes Judah and Benjamin under the name 'Judah' (Judah being by far the larger and more powerful of the two tribes) and the capital city was Jerusalem. The term 'Jew' derives from Judah's name and refers to any descendant of the southern kingdom, i.e. of the tribe of Judah or Benjamin. Thus every Jew is an Israelite, but not every Israelite is a Jew. (Often the terms 'Israelite' and 'Jew' are used synonymously, but this is not strictly correct.)

The term 'Samaritan' has its origin in the northern, ten-tribe kingdom of Israel. Israel was overthrown by the Assyrians in 722 BC. They took control of the capital city Samaria and installed many of their men there. A 'Samaritan' is one who is descended from this city of Samaria and, by reason of the Assyrian invasion and occupation seven centuries before Christ, probably has partly or wholly Assyrian blood. For this reason the Israelites hate the Samaritans, although the mixed bloodlines act as temperance to that. The southern kingdom, Judah, did not fall to the Assyrian invasion however (the kingdom remained for ~150 years until taken by the Babylonians). For this reason the hatred of the Jews for the Samaritans is especially intense since the Samaritans represent the conquerors of the Jews' Israelite brethren and the Jews have little or no mixed lineage with the Assyrians by which such enmity might be diluted. Not only that, but such animosity was greatly exacerbated when the Samaritans sided with the Seleucid Greeks fighting against the Jews in the Maccabean revolution (168-165 BC). The Jewish victory in that battle resulted in the execution of many prominent Samaritans and fueled the continuing revulsion of Jews towards them.

---

[1] Strong J. H., 'Dictionary of the Hebrew Bible' in "Strong's Exhaustive Concordance of the Bible," 1894, 1st Edition reprint 1994, Abingdon Press, Ontario, Canada, p 47

Day 2 Exposition: Waters Above

In this context John introduces the situation where Jesus, an Israelite and a Jew, begins a conversation with a Samaritan woman: a grave violation of the social protocol borne of the racial tension between Jews and Samaritans. John specifies the details of the meeting, in terms of both place and time.

> Jacob's well was there, and Jesus, tired as he was from the journey, sat down by the well. It was about the sixth hour. (4:6)

The meeting was at noon. This presents a striking contrast with the visit of Nicodemus, who approached Jesus by night (3:2). This is instructive in the light of the contrasting social placement between Nicodemus and the woman. The repeated contrast (Table 2_1) is exhortational: in all points the contrast declares the social superiority of Nicodemus over this woman. Yet their relative rank is reversed by one thing: their approach to Jesus. The Samaritan woman approaches Jesus in the light of the noonday sun, whilst Nicodemus, of such higher worldly rank, deemed it prudent to conduct his meeting with Jesus under clandestine cover of darkness.

Character	Gender	Nationality	Social position	Approach to Jesus...
Nicodemus	Male (high status)	Jewish (high status)	Sanhedrin (high status)	at night (3:2)
Woman at Jacob's well	Female (low status)	Samaritan (low status)	5 husbands (low status)	at noon (4:6)

Table 2_1: Characterizing parameters of Nicodemus and the Samaritan woman in the light of their approaches to Jesus in Days 1 and 2 of John's gospel.

How commonly we see in scripture willingness to respond to God's calling arising from those outside of the covenant relationship: people other than God's chosen. Consider Jonah, where the Gentile sailors who do not believe in the true God are

Day 2 Exposition: Waters Above

the first to pray – not only to their own gods (Jonah 1:5) but also to Jonah's God! (c.f. Jonah 1:14 & 2:1). So frequently those outside the covenant promise display greater faith than those within. When Jesus remarked to the crowds: "I say unto you, I have not found so great faith, no, not in Israel" he spoke of a Roman centurion (Luke 7:9), and not of any member of the house of Israel.

What is the general principle underlying all these cases? The Spirit revealed to Paul:

> But God has chosen the foolish things of the world to put to shame the wise, and God has chosen the weak things of the world to put to shame the things which are mighty; and the base things of the world and the things which are despised God has chosen, and the things which are not, to bring to nothing the things that are, that no flesh should glory in His presence. (1 Corinthians 1:27-29, NKJV)

The Samaritan woman at Jacob's well is another such example. One whom the Jews, and perhaps ourselves, would consider 'second-class' in righteousness is deliberately presented approaching the Master 'in the light' as opposed to Nicodemus who approached 'in the dark.' This reinforces to those who consider themselves 'the chosen' that no flesh should glory in His presence. As the interaction between the Samaritan woman and Jesus proceeds we see the Jews' apple cart of righteousness comprehensively upset as one from outside the covenant walls eclipses them with a more sincere and humble faith.

The elevated covenant position so frequently presents the opportunity for pride – humility's nemesis – and thereby frustrates approach towards the Master. This should give ourselves today, who claim to be the children of the living God and spiritual Jews, considerable pause for thought…

…and Place

That the well is named after Jacob is also significant. It echoes the only previous occasion when the scripture presented

Day 2 Exposition: Waters Above

Jacob at a well: Genesis 29:1-8. At first thought the Genesis passage seems an innocuous conversation between shepherds: hardly necessary to record for the edification of later generations! But the culminating statement rings loudly on the spiritual plane. Jacob instructs the shepherds to water the sheep, and they reply:

> "We can't," they replied, "until all the flocks are gathered and the stone has been rolled away from the mouth of the well. Then we will water the sheep." (Genesis 29:8)

An intriguing statement, not so much in the physical sense in which its explanation is obvious, but in terms of its spiritual counterpart as Jesus sits atop Jacob's well some centuries later. There are two stipulations to watering the sheep: firstly that the 'flocks are gathered,' and secondly that the 'stone is rolled away.'

This division between Jews and Samaritans helps us understand the first part of the prophecy: the gathering of the flocks. The Samaritans were hated by the Jews, as we have explained. The rift was so entrenched that a Pharisee would not even use an article of crockery or cutlery which a Samaritan had used. The woman references this behavior in her statement: "For Jews do not associate with Samaritans" (4:9): the Greek word translated 'associate' refers to a common sharing of articles or practices. [2]

How appropriate therefore that when the Good Shepherd comes to water his sheep, he sits down at Jacob's well! The name triggers our memory of the time the patriarch was told the flocks had to be gathered before the sheep could be watered. We presume Jesus reveals himself as Messiah to the Samaritan woman deliberately, in beginning the gathering work he must perform.

---

[2] Strong J. H., *Op. cit.*, 'Dictionary of the Greek Testament,' p 67

Day 2 Exposition: Waters Above

"I have other sheep that are not of this sheep pen. I must bring them also. They too will listen to my voice, and there shall be one flock and one shepherd." (10:16)

The second stipulation for the flocks to be watered was that the stone must be rolled away. We consider this in the light of the gentle refusal given by Jesus to the woman when she asks to receive the "living water" of which Jesus has spoken.

The woman said to him, "Sir, give me this water so that I won't get thirsty and have to keep coming here to draw water." He told her, "Go, call your husband and come back." "I have no husband," she replied. Jesus said to her, "You are right when you say you have no husband. The fact is, you have had five husbands, and the man you now have is not your husband. What you have just said is quite true." (4:15-18)

The woman approaches Jesus for the living water, yet interestingly she is gently repelled, and told to go and bring her husband. We remember from Genesis 29 that the sheep's watering from the well was also impeded by a stone (There are also specific reasons concerning her conduct that frustrate her union with the Lord, which we consider later: Section 2.4). It required the shepherd to take the stone away. On the spiritual plane the physical parallel is simple to translate. The impediment between the living water and ourselves is our sins: it has been that way since Eden. The Shepherd (10:14) takes this impediment away by his crucifixion and resurrection (Hebrews 2:14). The sign of Jesus' resurrection is no more boldly proclaimed than in the empty tomb: the stone rolled away from its mouth (Matthew 28:2). The woman cannot yet receive the living water because the flocks have not yet been gathered (the Samaritans and Gentiles have not yet been included in the fold) and the stone has not yet been rolled away (Christ has not yet exited the open tomb, risen from the dead).

Day 2 Exposition: Waters Above

<u>Waters Above the Divide</u>

> Jesus answered her, "If you knew the gift of God and who it is that asks you for a drink, you would have asked him and he would have given you living water." "Sir," the woman said, "you have nothing to draw with and the well is deep. Where can you get this living water? Are you greater than our father Jacob, who gave us the well and drank from it himself, as did also his sons and his flocks and herds?" Jesus answered, "Everyone who drinks this water will be thirsty again, but whoever drinks the water I give him will never thirst. Indeed, the water I give him will become in him a spring of water welling up to eternal life." (4:10-14)

Consider both the statements and physical choreography of this setting in relation to Day 2 of the creation sequence. Day 2 in Genesis presents two bodies of water and a spatial divide between them: the living waters are above the divide, the earthly waters beneath. This conversation in John 4 also presents both living water and earthly water, and notice the setting: Jesus is sitting at the top of the well! Observe the cunning placement: 'ordinary' earthly water is at the bottom of the well, there is a spatial divide of air in the well shaft, and Jesus (the living water) is sitting at the top of the well (Figure 2_1). The woman asks: "Where is this living water?" Yet we shouldn't need to wait for Jesus to respond because the creation pattern in Genesis has taught us where to see the answer in the geometrical arrangement of the conversation – the living water is drawn above the divide: it's sitting at the top of the well!

Pertinent to this geometry is Jesus' question:

Jesus said to her, "Will you give me a drink?" (4:7)

Jesus attractively contrasts which type of water can be supplied by the one person to the other and thereby emphasizes the presence of the creation structure. The mortal woman, ("he that is of the earth is earthly," 3:31) can supply Jesus with the earthly water from the *bottom* of the well, whereas Jesus ("The one

Day 2 Exposition: Waters Above

who comes from above is above all," *ibid*), *sitting at the top of the well*, can supply the living water from himself. What elegant constructions John's gospel contains!

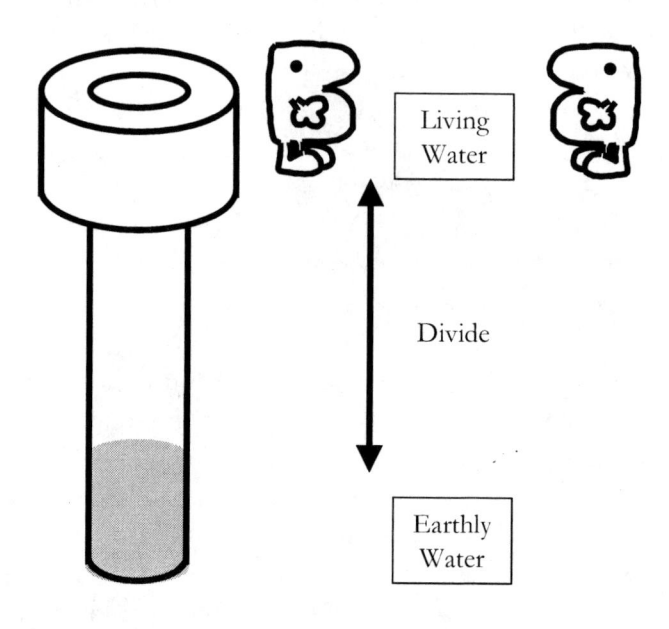

Figure 2_1: Choreography of the meeting between Jesus and the Samaritan woman at Jacob's well, matching the spatial arrangement created by God in Day 2.

There is one more essential point: the profound implication this pattern has on defining the nature of Jesus Christ (Appendix C). Day 2 graphically shows how the Living water was originally drawn from the Earthly (dead) water, and transformed by God to be in the elevated position. What an accurate description of the nature of Christ! Jesus was born of a woman as a mortal human man (Galatians 4:4) yet raised by God into a heavenly state where he could supply life for all men (Ephesians 2:6) and receive the very Name of God himself (Philippians 2:9-10). How beautifully these things are encapsulated in the physical arrangement at Jacob's well!

2.4 'Come' and 'Go'

There are still deeper levels to explore in this exchange which lead to a broader understanding of the disciple's ability to approach Jesus and remain in his company. The woman is explicitly sent away from Jesus.

"Go, call your husband and come back." (4:16)

Jesus does not say this in desire to meet the woman's partner. She is dismissed from the presence of the Lord, at least temporarily, because there is a matter she needs to address before she can return. Jesus is gentle with her, yet the firmness is also unmistakable: as she continues her life in promiscuity she is not, in spiritual terms, able to walk in the Lord's company. There is beauty in the scriptural record in the association of this promiscuous woman being from Samaria. When the Assyrians captured the northern kingdom of Israel, Samaria became their chief city of occupation. The Assyrians installed and worshipped their gods in Samaria and, as is always inevitable, the children of God began to be drawn away there to worship them also. Samaria thus became the center of religious promiscuity. This facet of history is attractively addressed in underlying parallel in the conversation Jesus has with the Samaritan woman who has conducted a life of physical promiscuity.

The broad scriptural trend of those who are told 'Go' by the divine authority is educational, especially when contrasted with those who are invited 'Come.' Table 2_2 shows an exhaustive listing of those who are invited to 'Come' by Jesus, as well as some contrasting examples of those who are told 'Go.'

We can be confident about any common theme we see running through the four cases of the word 'come' because the list is exhaustive. Consider all four cases carefully, (it is advisable to read the full Biblical context): the first calling of the twelve; Peter walking on the water; John being shown the apocalyptic vision; and the invitation to the water of life. In every case Jesus is addressing a brave, sincere and humble disciple, one who knows enough to come to Jesus, and one who knows such

Day 2 Exposition: Waters Above

company will yield him far greater learning yet. The trend reveals the state of heart and mind in which one is invited into the presence of the Master. If we cultivate a state of desire to approach Christ, acknowledging we have a dependency to rely on him and knowing we have so very much to learn from him, we have the opportunity to be invited into his presence. Scripture shows the invitation 'Come' is not distributed from the Lord to anyone exhibiting any different attitude!

By contrast those who are directed 'Go' (Table 2_2) generally harbor some imperfection. The leper and the blind man suffer physical imperfections: they constitute the human equivalents to the offerings of the Mosaic Law that were not acceptable inside the Temple (Deuteronomy 15:21). Under the covenant of Christ, these people escape both their disabilities and their exclusion. The disabilities remain excluded, but the people are released from them. In front of Christ all stand halt, blind and leprous, but, subsequent to his touch, all are healed and can approach the presence of the King. This also applies in the other two cases. The rich young ruler and the Samaritan woman's imperfections are spiritual, (love of money and sexual promiscuity respectively). These defects prevent them from remaining in Messiah's presence, even though their afflictions are invisible to the human eye: very much unlike leprosy and blindness. Yet Jesus responds to those with invisible defects in an identical way to those with visible defects. In all cases the dismissal is temporary: it is inherent in the text, either explicitly or implicitly, that Jesus desires the person who is told 'Go,' to ultimately 'Come' back. But something initially inhibits each of these people from walking in Jesus' company, so Jesus tells them, clearly but gently: go away, address the problem, and come back and share company with me.

But, lest we suspect this command is pointing at everyone *except* ourselves, we recall the directive of Christ towards ourselves:

> "Therefore, if you are offering your gift at the altar and there remember that your brother has something against you, leave

your gift there in front of the altar. First **go** and be reconciled to your brother; then **come** and offer your gift." (Matthew 5:23-24)

Jesus invites: 'Come!'	Jesus directs: 'Go!'
Andrew + another disciple "Come," he replied, "and you will see." (1:39)	**The Leper** "But go, show yourself to the priest and offer the sacrifices that Moses commanded for your cleansing…" (Mark 1:44)
Peter "Come," he said. Then Peter got down out of the boat, walked on the water and came toward Jesus. (Matthew 14:29)	**Samaritan Woman at Well** He told her, "Go, call your husband and come back." (4:16)
John "Come up here, and I will show you what must take place after this." (Revelation 4:1, also Revelation 6:1, 3, 5, 7)	**The Blind Man** "Go," he told him, "wash in the Pool of Siloam." (9:7)
Whoever thirsts for living water The Spirit and the bride say, "Come!" And let him who hears say, "Come!" Whoever is thirsty, let him come; and whoever wishes, let him take the free gift of the water of life. (Revelation 22:17)	**The Rich Young Ruler** "Go, sell everything you have and give to the poor, and you will have treasure in heaven. Then come, follow me." (Mark 10:21)

Table 2_2: A comparison of all those who are invited 'Come' (Greek: 'erchomai') in the NT scriptures, with some who are told 'Go' (Greek: 'hupago'). [3]

It is not a physical altar at which we meet, nor is it a physical blood sacrifice which we present, the 'letter' of the Mosaic Law

---

[3] Strong J. H., *Op. cit.*, 'Main Concordance,' pp 204-206, 396-397

Day 2 Exposition: Waters Above

being done away. Nevertheless we meet before that spiritual altar, the memorial table of the Lord, to offer the sacrifice of our own humble and contrite spirit: which God esteems as the only good thing in all creation which has He has not explicitly made with His own Hands (Isaiah 66:1-2). The command is clear: if we have anything against any brother or sister we are to rectify that matter *before* we take bread and wine. Yet sadly, though the interpretation is unambiguous, the practice is seldom, if ever, realized. But those who are told 'Go' by Jesus (Table 2_2) are so instructed because there is a *very real* impediment between themselves and fellowship with their Lord which they *absolutely must* remove before they can receive the invitation 'Come.' It must be equally obvious to us that, for all we may physically consume bread and wine, we will not share communion with Messiah until we have first healed any breach with any brother or sister with whom we do not share full sibling love. Hopefully this reminder of who is told 'Go' when they approach Jesus, and why, will help provide the necessary impetus to make this command of reconciliation a living reality amongst God's people.

2.5 Resurrection

The natural extension of this limitless healing power of Jesus is seen in the ability to recover a soul, not only up to, but from *beyond* the brink of death: the power of resurrection. Read John 5:16-47. John's gospel leads directly to this subject, which corroborates the presence of the 'raising above' theme in these chapters. The closing words of John 5, of Day 2, deal wholly with the resurrective power of God being fully manifest in His Son: the ultimate healing waters of life.

> "For just as the Father raises the dead and gives them life, even so the Son gives life to whom he is pleased to give it... Do not be amazed at this, for a time is coming when all who are in their graves will hear his voice and come out--those who have done good will rise to live, and those who have done evil will rise to be condemned." (5:21, 28-29)

Day 2 Exposition: Waters Above

The conclusion of the Day's pattern is the Son's power to 'draw up' to life, of all those who are in the graves: wielding the power of 'drawing above' in the fully ultimate sense.

We must consider one final detail from John 5 which fascinates. It is verse 19, given in the context of justifying that Jesus has the power of resurrection.

> "I tell you the truth, the Son can do nothing by himself; he can do only what he sees his Father doing, because whatever the Father does the Son also does." (5:19)

Principally this verse demonstrates the Son has the power to give life because the Father gives life and the Son performs all the works of his Father. Yet consider a broader application of this verse, especially in light of our consideration of John's gospel in terms of the creation sequence. The verse assures us 'whatever the Father does, the Son also does.' The Father created the world, and all things therein, in a period of time evidencing six discrete sections. This verse assures us the Son does whatsoever the Father does! Thus in this small verse we find a microcosm confirmation of the pattern that we are exploring: in some way Jesus will create a whole world, evidenced in six sections. The full justification of this proposal may well not be apparent to us now; but will fully crystallize in the latter portion of this study (Section $\Omega.3$).

2.6 Conclusions from Day 2

Many events in this part of John's gospel use the vehicle of water to deliver their message, which message is of drawing above of something life-giving from that which was not life-giving beneath.

We have also seen the superiority of the component of the spiritual creation over the corresponding component of the natural creation. The encounter at Jacob's well shows many draughts of natural water are required to provide temporary life for a man, yet a single draught of spiritual water from Jesus

Day 2 Exposition: Waters Above

provides eternal life. As with Day 1, where spiritual light excelled natural light, so here too, spiritual water excels natural water.

The institution of a divide between 'things below' and 'things above' is also graphically seen. Accounts of healing in John 4 and 5 illustrate earthly things are dead, yet all have the chance to be drawn above the divide to live with Christ. This seems the central message of this portion of John's gospel. We perceive the divide through illumination: Light, which translates as 'understanding' in the spiritual creation (Sections $\alpha.4$, 1.1-1.4), helps us perceive the divide and that our origin is with those 'things beneath.' But for all the understanding (illumination) this brings, it does not heal the divide itself. We can only be transported to the realm of 'things above' by receipt of the living water from Christ. This is a particularly attractive picture because to be 'drawn above' we actually have to become part of the spiritual creation itself, (because the living waters are drawn up). To be part of a new creation necessarily implies we must be 'recreated,' reborn in the waters of baptism: the life giving waters from Christ.

Day 2 Exhortation: To See the Face of the King

EXHORTATION 2: *2 Samuel 14, Luke 15, John 5*
To See the Face of the King

But the king said, "He must go to his own house; he must not see my face." So Absalom went to his own house and did not see the face of the king. (2 Samuel 14:24)

Why does King David suddenly order this?

Those who read scripture regularly sometimes forget to challenge just how peculiar some statements are. With the myriad blessings that regular attention to God's Word brings comes that tiny disadvantage: familiarity negates the feelings of surprise we should have when something truly surprising is said or done. This statement of David's is one such example, because at first analysis it is completely contrary to the flow of the account. Let's remind ourselves of the broader context.

Frustrated Reunion

King David has, amongst others, two sons: Amnon (his firstborn) and Absalom: of different mothers they are half brother to each other. Absalom also has a beautiful sister whose name is Tamar. Amnon rapes Tamar: a terrible thing! Absalom

Day 2 Exhortation: To See the Face of the King

nurtures his fury over the rape of his sister and, two years later, exacts revenge by murdering Amnon; whence he subsequently flees to his maternal grandfather in Geshur and lives in self-imposed exile for three years.

During those years King David comes to terms with the death of Amnon and no longer mourns him. Furthermore he grows to miss Absalom, and Joab, the commander of Israel's armed forces, detects this. Joab sets up a complicated ruse by which he moves David to act upon his secret longing for Absalom's return. Joab is thus despatched to Geshur to fetch Absalom back to Jerusalem. Here is where our exhortation opened. As Absalom re-enters the city of Jerusalem to greet the father from whom he has been long separated we encounter this most incomprehensible response:

"He must go to his own house; he must not see my face." (2 Samuel 14:24)

The contrary nature of this comment is now fully apparent. Why would David commission his commander-in-chief to fetch Absalom from Geshur and then refuse to greet him, or even let him into his presence?

This ancient record has profound relevance for us. As we approach the throne of grace on a Sunday morning, we seek forgiveness for the wrongs we have done; we seek extension of the golden scepter in bread and wine; we hope to achieve reunion with our Father. We each enact the role of Absalom, returning from exile to seek reunion with his father. Thus: that there has been a total breakdown between the reunion of David and Absalom, without any apparent reason why this reunion has gone so badly wrong, should suddenly seem very relevant to us indeed. Without knowing why this Christ-like father turned away the son who sought reunion, we cannot know whether our Good Father might not suddenly respond to us in the same way, and say: "Return to your own house! You have no place here! You cannot see the face of the King."

Day 2 Exhortation: To See the Face of the King

In fact, how are we to know that this is not the response we will encounter this Sunday morning? We may glibly respond: "But God would never do that to me! He's a loving Father and therefore I would never be turned away from His presence like David turned away Absalom!" Certainly our Father is a God of love, but are we sure that guarantees our inclusion at His table? Should we assume David's behavior towards Absalom was incorrect (i.e. ungodly) and therefore David is to blame for the reunion's demise? Or is there another explanation?

It is fruitful to investigate whether David truly is at fault for this extraordinary and sudden refusal to see his son, or if not, what Absalom has done to prevent the reunion working properly. Please note that we are not investigating who is at fault for the purpose of apportioning blame to either David or Absalom. It is not, nor should it ever be, our intention to be judgmental or condemnatory to those either in that time period or this. The reason we investigate what has happened is to obtain exhortation for ourselves, so that when we, as badly behaved sons, return to the presence of our Father, we can mold our behavior to a greater assurance of obtaining the reunion we desire, and not be cast out of the King's presence.

Protocol for Reunion Between Father and Son

Jesus teaches the model protocol of the reunion between a father and son in the parable of the prodigal son (Luke 15:11-32). The father in the parable represents God, the prodigal son represents one of his children, such as any one of us. The reunion procedure follows four steps:

Step 1: The son repents.
When he came to his senses, he said… "I will set out and go back to my father and say to him: 'Father, I have sinned against heaven and against you. I am no longer worthy to be called your son; make me like one of your hired men.' " (Luke 15:17-19)

Day 2 Exhortation: To See the Face of the King

Step 2: The father approaches sympathetically.
So he got up and went to his father. But while he was still a long way off, his father saw him and was filled with compassion for him; he ran to his son, threw his arms around him and kissed him. (Luke 15:20)

Step 3: The son confesses.
The son said to him, "Father, I have sinned against heaven and against you. I am no longer worthy to be called your son." (Luke 15:21)

Step 4: The father forgives all.
But the father said to his servants, "Quick! Bring the best robe and put it on him. Put a ring on his finger and sandals on his feet. Bring the fattened calf and kill it. Let's have a feast and celebrate. For this son of mine was dead and is alive again; he was lost and is found." (Luke 15:22-24)

Jesus presents this four-step model of reunion in this parable to all disciples who will listen, including us. As always with divine teaching it has a certain beauty, and symmetry: the four steps oscillate in responsibility between the son and father. The son repents, the father approaches, the son confesses and the father forgives. The speech that the son has prepared to give his father (v 18-19) is cut short: the father's forgiveness is so swift in coming that the son cannot finish the very sentences he has designed to say! This is an excellent lesson to each of us, that when our brother comes to us in penitence for a past wrong, we should be equally swift in the forgiveness we are prepared to offer. Nevertheless, although the father's forgiveness is so swift that the son is not permitted to finish the words he began, he certainly does get to confess sinning against heaven and against his father. His father seems to ensure that these words be spoken, but once they are, forgiveness is immediate.

Forgiveness is not only immediate; it is also absolute. This also provides a stern lesson to the manner in which we forgive one another, both in our personal lives and in the church

Day 2 Exhortation: To See the Face of the King

community. Observe the absences from the parable, for they are as instructive as those things present. There is no 'trial-period' of reinstatement, there is no program of 'probation' over which the returned prodigal is required to prove himself before being returned to the status of a fully recognized son within the household. In the human world, (and all too often regrettably in the community in Christ), it is predictable that forgiveness would follow a much less generous line. We might anticipate the father to say something like: "Well, son, it's certainly good to have you back again, and we're all very pleased to see you here safe and well. We're glad that you're willing to make amends for your behavior; but in the light of your little *ahem* 'escapade' I'm not sure that reinstating you to the full authority of sonship in the household right away is a good idea. Perhaps you should just keep a low profile for a while, and then we can think about getting you back to your full status and responsibilities a little bit further down the road."

Not only is this a highly likely and oft heard response in situations of forgiveness in our society, but perhaps we would also be foolishly tempted to applaud such a response. We might think the protocol is: 'measured,' 'prudent,' and 'appropriately cautious;' in terms of rebuilding a relationship between father and son. But this wholly contradicts the Biblical prerogative of instant and total forgiveness! The idea of a probationary term for one who has repented is wholly unscriptural, and the father of the prodigal son, who represents God Himself, implements no such thing. For Him forgiveness is as total as it is swift. The prodigal has declared his actions sinful and declared a desire to change his ways. The father thus provides every opportunity for him to achieve these goals within his household. What evidence this is to the son as to how much he is loved! We cannot overlook the importance of every prodigal receiving encouragement. It is the driving force for them to walk a more loving and obedient path in future.

It is certainly contrary to the human spirit to forgive in this way. But it is equally certain that this is exactly what we must do each and every time our forgiveness is sought. After all, perhaps it helps us to remind ourselves that this is exactly what our Heavenly Father provides for us every time we take bread and wine before Him…

Absalom: The Unrepentant Prodigal

Now let's return to the main task: solving why the reunion between Absalom and David broke down. 2 Samuel 14 suggests at first glance that David is the one at fault. He seems to prevent the reunion, dismissing Absalom from the palace to his own quarters in the city without even letting him see his face. However, our close study of the 'text-book' case for reunion between father and disobedient son (Luke 15) unlocks the mystery. Step 1 for atonement is the repentance of the prodigal: a necessary penitence on the part of the one who has sinned. Thus Luke 15 shows us beyond doubt that it is *Absalom*, and not David, who is at fault, because there is no penitence in his heart. Rather Absalom blusters bold and arrogant claims of innocence, even rectitude.

> "Why have I come from Geshur? It would be better for me if I were still there! Now then, I want to see the king's face, and if I am guilty of anything, let him put me to death." (2 Samuel 14:32)

This reveals why reunion must fail. Absalom's heartfelt spirit declares he has done no wrong, those who welcome him back to Jerusalem must do so on these – his – terms. Thus we learn the attractive contrast between 2 Samuel 14 and Luke 15: the chapters are essentially opposites of each other. Luke 15 tells of the repentant prodigal, whereas 2 Samuel 14 tells of the *unrepentant* prodigal. It is not surprising therefore that the father, 'God-like' in both cases, displays the opposite response to each son's return.

Having accepted that it is Absalom's impenitence that has destroyed the reunion, perhaps we need to ask a qualifying question. Are we confident that David's response was still appropriate? He may well have been correct not to restore his

Day 2 Exhortation: To See the Face of the King

son to his full (princely) status within the palace by reason of Absalom's impenitence, but was dismissing him altogether from his presence justified, or was it an over-reaction?

The scriptural record offers no criticism of David's behavior in expelling Absalom from his presence. This is in itself very telling, for we know that the leaders of God's people are held to a very high standard of accountability in everything they do (c.f. James 3:1). As a result whenever they behave badly they are punished more severely than those in positions of lesser responsibility. The judgments meted against David in the case of Bathsheba and Uriah (2 Samuel 12:7-12); Moses in the case of the struck rock (Numbers 20:12); and the Pharisees in the case of just about everything (e.g. Matthew 23) are powerful testaments to this truth. In each case the judgment is severe, and for the same reason: each of these was the spiritual leader of Israel at the time, and therefore held to high account. 2 Samuel 14 offers no criticism of David's behavior when he is in the extremely responsible position as the leader of God's people; this is already a significant clue that he has acted with wisdom and justice in God's eyes. And this interpretation is validated unambiguously when the Bible states David sinned once in his life, and once only, in the matter of Uriah's wife (1 Kings 15:5).

Dismissed from the Presence of the King

Once we realize David has behaved in a godly manner, we are able to draw more learning from the passage by noticing an attractive parallel with the case of God's judgment on Cain. Firstly notice how well Cain and Absalom match: Both are firstborn sons and both are murderers. Cain murdered his brother Abel; Absalom murdered his half-brother Amnon. More importantly: neither murderer ever showed any remorse for his crime. This observation is of principal importance for it establishes both Cain and Absalom as unrepentant prodigals. Now we see the way God, who is never unjust, deals with Cain: He dismisses him from the presence of the King!

Day 2 Exhortation: To See the Face of the King

> The LORD said, "What have you done? Listen! Your brother's blood cries out to me from the ground. Now you are under a curse and driven from the ground, which opened its mouth to receive your brother's blood from your hand..." Cain said to the LORD, "My punishment is more than I can bear. Today you are driving me from the land, and I will be hidden from your presence..." So Cain went out from the LORD's presence and lived in the land of Nod, east of Eden. (Genesis 4:10-16)

Cain is driven out from the presence of the King. Cain's murder is not unforgivable in the eyes of God, but whilst Cain remains unrepentant for his crime even his very presence cannot be tolerated. We learn the basic tenet: 'An unrepentant prodigal cannot stand in the presence of the King.' God establishes this principle as Cain is banished: East of Eden. This same principle is embedded in the Man after God's own Heart. David makes the first move to assist reunion in sending Joab to fetch his son Absalom from banishment in Geshur, but, as Absalom entered the city, David learns of his son's mindset and will know he cannot remain in the presence of the King. It is probable that Absalom, a man of incurable, indeed fatal, vanity, rode into Jerusalem with full entourage of splendor. This, plus the messengers who would have traveled ahead to inform David of the Prince's arrival, would have supplied all the information David needed about the state of his son's heart and mind. Thus in full knowledge of Absalom's impenitence, David is moved to make the same ruling which God Himself made against Cain: "You must go away from this place to a place where you belong. You cannot remain in my presence. You cannot see the face of the King."

This solves the mystery of Absalom's dismissal from the King's presence. We reiterate: there is no desire to pour scorn on Absalom, or Cain. We consider this wholly for our own exhortation, and to answer our opening question: why did the reunion of Absalom and David break down, and what can we learn about who was at fault to prevent a breakdown between

Day 2 Exhortation: To See the Face of the King

ourselves and our Heavenly Father when we draw into His presence? We have learned that the first step to reunion is a penitent heart on the part of the prodigal: penitence neither Absalom nor Cain felt for the slaying of their brothers. We have also learned God's judgment for unrepentant sinners: dismissal from before the face of the King. To remain in the presence of the King requires true penitence on the part of those who would be His sons. It is an important lesson, for, though simple, it is often a matter that is little in evidence at the forefront of our minds. On a Sunday morning we have pleasure in seeing our brothers and sisters and friends. We have pleasure in singing hymns we enjoy, and savoring the quietness of prayers and readings for reflection and contemplation, and this pleasure is evident. But can we truly find within us a genuinely heavy heart, caused by those parts of our lives that cheapen the high calling with which we are invested? Perhaps even when such feelings are present, they are the most invisible to each other; but we would do well to ensure they are present, for we have seen beyond doubt that those prodigals who return to their Father without a genuine desire to apologize and *change* are not permitted to see the face of the King.

"Father, give me"; "Father, make me"

So with the idea of 'desiring to change' within our minds, look again at the parable of the prodigal son as we develop the exhortation to a deeper level. Jesus' choice of words in recounting the parable provides instruction in reflecting exactly how the change of heart occurs in the young man.

> The younger one said to his father, "Father, give me…" (Luke 15:12)

We stop there, mid-sentence, for already we have enough to grasp his initial attitude. Those three words adeptly summarize the young man's entire state of mind: 'Father, give me.'

Now look at the way he expresses himself after he has come to his senses, when his state of mind has transformed.

Day 2 Exhortation: To See the Face of the King

> I will set out and go back to my father and say to him: "Father, I have sinned against heaven and against you. I am no longer worthy to be called your son; make me…" (Luke 15:18-19)

Again we stop in mid-sentence, and again just three words comprehensively summarize his state of mind. 'Father… make me.' What a contrast! What an extraordinary degree of spiritual growth, to have developed from a mindset of 'Father, give me' to 'Father, make me'!

Here exhortation deepens. We are compelled to point the question at ourselves: How many of my prayers, when the details are stripped away, fundamentally reduce to the phrase 'Father give me?' By contrast, how many of my prayers are best summarized with the phrase 'Father, make me?' How many times when we pray are we doing little more than presenting a shopping list of needs and desires before the Lord, and how many times are we rather asking God's active hand in our own spiritual growth to realize a creature that operates more directly to His Glory?

This thinking is absolutely central to communion bread and wine. With which mindset shall we approach these emblems? "Father, give me this bread?" "Father, give me this wine?" "Father, give me forgiveness of my sins?" (For indeed all are freely given.) But what a tragedy! This constitutes approaching the emblems with the attitude the prodigal son had at the beginning of the parable: hardly an appropriate mindset before the Living God! Can we rather find it within ourselves, during those few quiet moments as we share bread and wine together, to offer that very different prayer, indeed that very much *better* prayer: "Father, with this bread, and with this wine, *make* me that son which I am not; but earnestly desire to be."

A Healing Change

Thus we have identified the important need of the desire to change, which must be cultivated internally and confessed externally. The internal realization is the spirit of penitence that

Day 2 Exhortation: To See the Face of the King

necessarily precedes any reunion between son and Heavenly Father, and the external confession should be heard in the prayers we offer and in the conversations we share with our spiritual family.

One more step is needed to complete our exhortation. It is not just *a* change required when we pray "Father, make me," but specifically a *healing* change is needed. We repair to the gospel of John, to consider the case of the impotent man by the pool of Bethesda, detailed in the opening 15 verses of John 5. The invalid has lain under the arches of Bethesda, where the pool is rumored to have healing qualities at certain times, for a total of 38 years (5:2-5).

Jesus asks the man a question:

When Jesus saw him lying there and learned that he had been in this condition for a long time, he asked him, "Do you want to get well?" "Sir," the invalid replied, "I have no one to help me into the pool when the water is stirred. While I am trying to get in, someone else goes down ahead of me." (5:6-7)

The tone of voice in which Jesus spoke is not recorded for us. Nevertheless we deduce Jesus poses the question here in anger (which does not detract from our knowledge of the deep sympathy and compassion of Jesus' character). The evidence is twofold. Firstly, the words Jesus speaks to the man at the very end of the matter, after he is healed, reveal the man's behavior has been reprehensible. Jesus says to him:

"See, you are well again. Stop sinning or something worse may happen to you." (5:14)

Secondly, we deduce the aggressive nature of Jesus' question from the answer the invalid gives, because the answer reveals exactly what the invalid *thought* he was being asked, including the tone he perceived. Consider Jesus' question in the simplest, most innocent sense: "Do you want to be made well?" Logically the

85

Day 2 Exhortation: To See the Face of the King

only available answers are: "Yes please," "No thank you," or "How can you possibly do that?"

Yet look at what the man says!

> "Sir… I have no one to help me into the pool when the water is stirred. While I am trying to get in, someone else goes down ahead of me." (5:7)

How can this possibly be an answer to the question he has been asked?! Yet this is a vital clue, because by studying the answer he gave we can work backwards to extrapolate the question he felt he was being asked. We need to find a question that fits the given answer. That question is: "Do you want to get well?" expressed as: "How is it that you've lain here for *thirty-eight years*, and in all that time you've totally failed to use the water in the pool to heal yourself?! Are you serious about trying to be healed or not?!" Now the given answer ("Sir, I have no man…") fits perfectly, so we can deduce this is indeed the sense of Jesus' question.

This forms the justification to the final stage of our exhortation: desiring to change is not enough until we understand that the nature of the change is a desire to be healed. This is a very important distinction and we need to realize why. God has a plan for us, which will offer a better existence than we currently experience. But if we advance our understanding no further than this we might be misled into thinking we are healthy in our current existence, and God is merely offering something better in union with Him: a form of 'super-health,' if you will. Rather we must understand (as Absalom never did, sadly) that in our current state we are desperately ill. Thus we must not only desire to change, but desire to be healed, and desire it most earnestly, as all those do who know they are dangerously, life-threateningly, unwell. A desire to be healed cannot be cultivated until one recognizes one is sick. We do not approach bread and wine to 'better ourselves' but rather to 'make ourselves better.' The distinction may be subtle, but that this distinction should be recognized is a matter of desperate importance.

Day 2 Exhortation: To See the Face of the King

Bread and Wine: Lying by the Poolside

Why is the account of the man laying by the poolside relevant to our Sunday morning worship? Because the impotent man has the potential to mirror our condition alongside the healing waters of memorial bread and wine. Jesus is angry with the man because, although the healing waters lie right alongside him and have been accessible for many years, he has made no concerted effort to plunge into them and be healed. It is highly probable this is because his current lifestyle is convenient. Bethesda is a place where the crippled congregate (5:3), and here amongst those who beg for a living is found a stable, if meager, income; living off the charitable alms received from those who pass by. The fundamental change of the waters' healing would actually be rather frightening. He would have no further justification to beg, and would have to begin working for a living. Given that he doubtless has no trade or profession, (he has lain by the poolside for 38 years don't forget), there is a genuine probability his material situation will worsen, rather than improve! Thus he maintains an equilibrium state from the charitable donations he receives: alive, yet permanently crippled, by the poolside.

We must realize that our situation on a Sunday morning can be exactly the same! How do the sacraments of bread and wine to relate to the elements in John 5? Are they the alms that we receive lying by the poolside, or are they the pool itself? We deduce the answer: they can be either the alms or the pool, depending on the attitude with which we approach them! And what are these different attitudes we might adopt? We have met them already! They are 'Father, give me' or 'Father, make me!'

Consider. If we approach bread and wine with the attitude 'Father, give me' then the sacraments will operate for us as the alms by the poolside: for alms are *given*. Bread and wine will then merely fuel our equilibrium state by the poolside: spiritually ever crippled, but surviving on this charity. John's gospel shows us this angers the Master to the point of grabbing us by the shoulders and demanding: "Wilt thou be made whole?"!

We can do so much better. To approach bread and wine with the attitude 'Father, make me' enables them to operate as the

Day 2 Exhortation: To See the Face of the King

pool: for it was within the pool that a healed man was *made*. Regardless of how many years we may have lain by the poolside, as we pass bread and wine quietly from hand to hand, if we can find within ourselves the courage to offer that better prayer, this time we will plunge into the pool and be healed. We will accept the challenge of being made a new man and be strengthened to walk an entirely new path toward our Father when we emerge. For that new path we know, though it be strait, though it be narrow, will lead towards the Kingdom of God's Son.

In summary, what shall we say? We recognize the approach to the mercy-seat of the King requires true penitence, ("Father, I have sinned against heaven and against you"). The alternative is to be dismissed from the King's presence as Cain and Absalom before us! We recognize that the desire to change is not simply that we might improve ourselves, but rather that we may be rid of the debilitating disease of human nature which threatens our lives and offers no glory to our Maker. Above all we see in these elements of bread and wine, and the sharing of them together in thoughtful meditation and fellowship with the prayer 'Father, make me' the way to access that change. And with that change we hope to walk the path towards the presence of the King himself: Jesus Christ in his Kingdom. This is our motivation. We desire to follow the one who blazed the trail: to plunge into the pool, to bring about the healing change, to walk the straitened path and indeed, one day, to see the Face of the King.

DAY 3 *John 6:1-6:71*

EXPOSITION:
Bread of Heaven

Day 3 is the Day of food and nourishment, the provision of all things by which living animals, including man, will be sustained (Genesis 1:29-30). It is the Day of Bread, and our basic premise follows accordingly:

Basic premise:
In this section of John's gospel we expect to find Jesus presented according to the metaphor of bread, the generic term for food, in the manner of one who nourishes and sustains God's children.

How fitting it is we immediately encounter the miracle of the feeding of the 5 000! Jesus is presented as the provider to the hungry mouths who follow him, both in the physical and the spiritual sense.

Day 3 Exposition: Bread of Heaven

3.1 Passover – whose Passover?

Read John 6.

> Then Jesus went up on a mountainside and sat down with his disciples. The Jewish Passover Feast was near. When Jesus looked up and saw a great crowd coming toward him, he said to Philip, "Where shall we buy bread for these people to eat?" (6:3-5)

There is a tiny detail hidden in the text: it is Passover (v 4). This detail is easily overlooked, and seemingly quite erratic: this arouses our curiosity. Passover is a Feast day; one of the fundamental religious anchors of the Jewish year; and the central focus of Passover is the Lamb. John has already taken particular care to introduce Jesus as the Lamb of God, with two direct statements in the opening chapter:

> The next day John seeth Jesus coming unto him, and saith, "Behold the Lamb of God, which taketh away the sin of the world…" Again the next day after John stood, and two of his disciples; And looking upon Jesus as he walked, he saith, "Behold the Lamb of God!" (1:29, 35-36, KJV)

Passover is the time when the children of God should be seeking a Lamb (without blemish) to remove the burden of their sins. John shows the timing of this miracle of feeding coinciding with the Passover, when Israel should be seeking the Lamb.

John's description of the Passover Feast subtly differs from that of the Old Testament. John uses the terminology "the Jewish Passover," not "the Lord's Passover" one finds in the Old Testament (e.g. Exodus 12:7). We need to be clear how consistent the divide is between Old and New Testament descriptions: this is not a singular occurrence. Where reference to 'ownership' of the Passover is made, it is *always* said to belong to God in the Old Testament and it is *always* said to belong to the Jews in the gospel of John: there are no exceptions (see Table 3_1).

Day 3 Exposition: Bread of Heaven

Passover in Moses' time	Passover in Jesus' time
"This is how you are to eat it: with your cloak tucked into your belt, your sandals on your feet and your staff in your hand. Eat it in haste; it is the **LORD's Passover**." (Exodus 12:11)	"When it was almost time for the **Jewish Passover**, Jesus went up to Jerusalem." (2:13)
"The **LORD's Passover** begins at twilight on the fourteenth day of the first month." (Leviticus 23:5)	"The **Jewish Passover** Feast was near." (6:4)
"An alien living among you who wants to celebrate the **LORD's Passover** must do so in accordance with its rules and regulations. You must have the same regulations for the alien and the native-born." (Numbers 9:14)	"When it was almost time for the **Jewish Passover**, many went up from the country to Jerusalem for their ceremonial cleansing before the Passover." (11:55)

Table 3_1: Whose Passover? A comparison of passages from Moses' day and Jesus' day declaring to whom the Passover meal 'belonged.'

The transition of ownership of Passover, from being God's feast to being the Jews' feast is absolute. The significance of the linguistic transition proclaims how the Jews had turned away from God within the celebration of Passover. By the time of Jesus Christ, the celebration of Passover is devoid of any recognition of salvation from the Omnipotent Creator. An important Feast day it remains, but only through the exclusivity of Jewish culture. In terms of a memorial to God, Passover is bereft of spiritual power: as empty as the water jars at Cana.

But where man fails, as ever, God gives more grace. A new Passover Lamb has arrived, announced by the herald (1:29), and witnessed by all. And the multitude have chosen on this particular day, at Passover time (6:4), to congregate around the Lamb, albeit the choice is doubtless not for these reasons. They knew Jesus only as a prophet and a miracle worker, and were following him

Day 3 Exposition: Bread of Heaven

for these reasons, blind to the deeper relationship that they could have with him as the Lamb of God. But they have chosen to assemble around the Lamb at Passover; and we can anticipate they will be well blessed in the path they have (perhaps unwittingly) taken.

3.2 Bread from Heaven, Bread of Heaven

> Jesus said, "Have the people sit down." There was plenty of grass in that place, and the men sat down, about five thousand of them. Jesus then took the loaves, gave thanks, and distributed to those who were seated as much as they wanted. He did the same with the fish. (6:10-11)

A fundamentally miraculous provision from God! What can one say? There is no useful or deductive comment to offer, one is wholly at a loss. Five thousand men, plus women and children, are fed from the five loaves and two small fishes by miraculous provision of the Hand of God. There is nothing we can add to such an incredible act, we can only be still and marvel; and perhaps that is the best response.

The miracle's location is important: a desert place where one cannot find food. This emphasizes the fragility of the human condition: a simple journey into a wilderness place realizes an environment in which we are helpless. Yet this is precisely the environment in which the natural pride we bear, when we wallow in the illusion of self-sufficiency, is finally swept aside! Doubtless this is the reason Jesus has led them to this desert place so that their (and our) total dependency on the Father might be convincingly demonstrated. It echoes the Egyptian Exodus where Israel was provided with bread from heaven in the wilderness, in precisely that way and for precisely that reason.

> He humbled you, causing you to hunger and then feeding you with manna, which neither you nor your fathers had known, to teach you that man does not live on bread alone but on every word that comes from the mouth of the LORD. (Deuteronomy 8:3)

Day 3 Exposition: Bread of Heaven

When patterns are repeated in scripture the latter occurrence commonly supersedes the former. Here in John 6 are two parallels. Jesus actions establish one parallel (in time) between the Old Testament and the New. The supply of bread in the wilderness repeats the events in the Wilderness of Paran in Moses' day. Manna was provided in the wilderness, a small, sweet, bread-like flake formed in the dew on the ground, and a meal of bread and fish has been provided for these Israelites contemporary with God's Son. Yet this is not the most important parallel: the greater parallel is between the natural and the spiritual world. Jesus performs a miracle on the mountainside in the physical sense, and then repeats and supersedes it by performing exactly the same miracle on the spiritual plane. For those who marveled at the physical bread from heaven, they must steel themselves for all-out astonishment at the declarations that follow. Jesus elevates the level of teaching and reveals to them the true bread from heaven: the lesson born from the physical chrysalis of the feeding of the 5 000 into the spiritual beauty of the Lord Jesus Christ himself.

> Jesus said to them, "I tell you the truth, it is not Moses who has given you the bread from heaven, but it is my Father who gives you the true bread from heaven… I am the living bread that came down from heaven. If anyone eats of this bread, he will live forever. This bread is my flesh, which I will give for the life of the world." (6:32, 51)

This is the second miracle, and yet really the same miracle, only elevated to the spiritual plane. The principle of the chronological latter excelling the former (introduced in Exhortation 1) shines through. The spiritual bread from heaven supplied eternal life, whilst the natural bread sustained only for a matter of hours. How rewarding it is, having learned this scriptural principle of death in the firstborn and life in the second, to be able to anticipate its appearance here too:

Day 3 Exposition: Bread of Heaven

> "Your forefathers ate the manna in the desert, yet they died. But here is the bread that comes down from heaven, which a man may eat and not die." (6:49-50)

Finally, we have another important clue to the nature of Jesus Christ from Day 3. He is the bread from heaven, which echoes the provision of manna in Moses' day. Does this mean Jesus physically descended from heaven to Earth? Indeed it does not, such is the beauty of scriptural patterns that the formation of the manna itself attested to this from many years before.

> Then the Lord said to Moses, "I will rain down bread from heaven for you..." That evening quail came and covered the camp, and in the morning there was a layer of dew around the camp. When the dew was gone, thin flakes like frost on the ground appeared on the desert floor. When the Israelites saw it, they said to each other, "What is it?" For they did not know what it was. Moses said to them, "It is the bread the Lord has given you to eat." (Exodus 16:4, 13-15)

The manna is referred to as "bread from heaven," "the bread the Lord has given you." Yet the scripture is equally insistent to point out that this provision from the Lord, the bread from heaven, was formed *on the ground*, crystallizing out of the morning dew. This parallel forms telling insight into the nature of the spiritual bread from heaven and his point of origin! (see Appendix C).

3.3 Times and Seasons

The spiritual bread in John's Creation also excels the bread from natural creation's third Day in the manner of its availability. The Bible emphasizes the well-known natural law that physical fruits are only available at certain times and seasons. We recall the time when Jesus approached the fig tree, apparently looking for figs:

Day 3 Exposition: Bread of Heaven

> Seeing in the distance a fig tree in leaf, he went to find out if it had any fruit. When he reached it, he found nothing but leaves, because it was not the season for figs. (Mark 11:13)

Even the provision of manna, the former bread from heaven, was only available to the children of Israel for a finite period of time: during the morning hours before the sun grew hot. This detail is announced explicitly to Israel and preserved in the Bible for us to learn from.

> Each morning everyone gathered as much [manna] as he needed, and when the sun grew hot, it melted away. (Exodus 16:21)

Always the lesson is the same: there is goodness provided in the natural bread, but it is only available at a certain time, in a certain place, during a certain season. Contrast this with the spiritual bread from heaven:

> Then Jesus declared, "I am the bread of life. He who comes to me will never go hungry, and he who believes in me will never be thirsty… and whoever comes to me I will never drive away." (6:35, 37)

The spiritual bread of John's Day 3 permanently flourishes in life-giving food! This is metaphor, of course, but these abstract principles translate to our daily lives in a tangible way. Sustenance from Christ comes in many forms: in prayer initiated by us, and in direct blessing from the Hand of God. Both of these very real facets of spiritual bread from heaven are unconstrained in time and season. We can *always* approach our Heavenly Father and the Lord Jesus in prayer, to obtain either the education of meditation, the catharsis of confession or the solace of the realization of One who truly hears, and answers. Similarly the myriad blessings that rain down from heaven upon us, many of which doubtless escape our inattentive senses, are distributed at all times and seasons.

We are indeed blessed with every sufficiency.

Day 3 Exposition: Bread of Heaven

3.4 Gathering Fragments

> When they had all had enough to eat, he said to his disciples, "Gather the pieces that are left over. Let nothing be wasted." So they gathered them and filled twelve baskets with the pieces of the five barley loaves left over by those who had eaten. (6:12-13)

Why does Jesus command the apostles to collect together the fragments left over? Presumably not to demonstrate the magnitude of the miracle: that a multitude has eaten their fill is evidence enough! This is again a puzzling detail from John with no immediate logical answer.

A solution is approached when we remember bread is used in scripture as synonymous with the word of God (e.g. Deuteronomy 8:3). The idea of a man being 'fed' or 'sustained' by the word of God is a scriptural picture with which we are familiar, and it underlines God's Word as something nourishing. John's gospel follows that trend precisely: now we have entered Day 3 of John's Creation we find not only physical bread, but also spiritual bread in the format of God's words spoken by Jesus following the meal (6:26-65). And this picture helps us solve the puzzle of Jesus commanding his disciples to pick up every fragment.

Consider the scene. Jesus is distributing physical bread on the mountainside to the multitude. Simultaneously, he is also distributing spiritual bread (i.e. the words of God he is speaking) to the same multitude. As they are eating the physical bread, some crumbs fall to the ground and are not digested. Similarly on the spiritual plane whilst they are 'eating' (i.e. listening to) the words Jesus is speaking, some sentences are not digested, either because the people were distracted at that moment, or because Jesus said something beyond the individual's ability to comprehend. Here then is the powerful part: at the end of the 'meal' Jesus instructs his disciples to walk around the area and pick up every fragment that has not been ingested! What the disciples enact on the physical plane, gathering the crumbs together into baskets, should be best heeded on the spiritual

Day 3 Exposition: Bread of Heaven

plane. None of the words of God that Jesus had spoken to them (and us!) should be allowed to 'fall to the ground' and not be fully digested with the rest of the message!

Earlier scriptures provide pointers towards this teaching, for this is exactly how God describes His Word in the prophets: as sustaining bread that does not, and must not, fall to the ground and be wasted.

> As the rain and the snow come down from heaven, and do not return to it without watering the earth and making it bud and flourish, so that it yields seed for the sower and bread for the eater, so is my word that goes out from my mouth: It will not return to me empty, but will accomplish what I desire and achieve the purpose for which I sent it. (Isaiah 55:10-11)

Even before the prophet Isaiah recorded these words, faithful Samuel had anticipated the principle:

> The LORD was with Samuel as he grew up, and he let none of his words fall to the ground. (1 Samuel 3:19)

Thus here in Day 3 Jesus gives the graphic demonstration that the provision of 'bread' from God should be fully digested, and he achieves this by instructing his disciples to gather the fragments of those things that have been spoken "that nothing be wasted." We have reasoned some of Jesus' teaching was not digested was because it may not have been heard, but there is a more important problem too. There are parts of the spiritual bread that were not attractive to the listener's palette, and which the multitude did not *want* to digest (e.g. 6:60). Thus the people then, (as us now?), merely consumed the portions that were attractive to them to obtain their fill, and discarded the fragments that were not attractive on the ground. How telling then that Jesus should instruct his disciples to walk all around the grounds and collect every crumb that has been eschewed! This is not fastidious litter collection: this is the demonstration of an important spiritual principle! The bread of God is not a meal at which we may pick and choose; and the point of our 'eating' at this table is not simply that we might be filled. Here the whole meal must be digested: every truth appreciated, internalized and implemented. With physical food we have a plateful before us and we eat the bits we like and discard the rest, or perhaps merely eat until we are filled, and leave the rest. This is not appropriate behavior with God's Word: those who begin the meal must eat it all, both the digestible and desirable, and those parts less savory to our palette. The glory of the provision of spiritual bread must lie with the Provider, and not the partaker.

3.5 The Spiritual Physique

The above reasoning directly impacts our view of Bible study. How shall we regard Bible study: A worthy role? A necessary duty? Indeed not: John's spiritual creation demonstrates it best understood as a hearty meal. If Bible study were a duty, some level of praise would be due to the student for his application, or if a worthy role then it would be somewhat optional, to be followed only by those blessed with the 'gift of study.' Rather the Word of God is food, and by understanding this, our resulting attitude is educated. We give thanks to God for his provision of physical food and that is well for so we should (Ephesians 5:20). But how much more then should we give thanks for the gift of spiritual food, and the greater promise of life it brings!

This argument also demonstrates how vital absorbing the Word of God is. Bible reading can no longer be considered an optional extra any more than can eating physical food. If we desist from physical food we become weak and sickly, our physique wastes away, eventually to extinction. In that weakness we are reliant on the help of others, and are quite unable to help another. We are one in need of being carried, and certainly not one who could ever carry another. John shows us our spiritual physique responds likewise. Without constant feeding on God's Word we become spiritually weak: directionless of mind and listless of spirit. Thus we give thanks to God for the wonderful, strengthening meals that he provides in His Word, His bread

Day 3 Exposition: Bread of Heaven

from heaven, and are grateful for the strength this gives to help those who do not dine as healthily as they could.

3.6 Conclusions from Day 3

This portion of John's gospel focuses on sustaining food, the fruits of the Earth. The provision of physical bread in the feeding of the 5 000 is a prime example. But once again John's gospel is not limited to merely repeating the natural creation, but presenting a sequence soaring above it. Thus we are introduced to the spiritual bread from heaven: Jesus Christ, speaking the nourishing words of the Father. From this we also learn to regard our Bible study as the opportunity to build up our spiritual physique on fine and health-giving food and to give thanks before eating for the provision we receive.

John also alerts us that the miracle of the feeding of the 5 000 occurs at Passover (6:4). This reflects his earlier introduction of Jesus as the Lamb of God who takes away the sin of the world (1:29) and reinforces the representation of Jesus in this part of the gospel as one upon whom the world feeds to find salvation.

Once more we see the natural creation excelled by the spiritual. Spiritual bread excels natural bread because natural bread provides only temporary (mortal) life, whereas spiritual bread provides everlasting life (6:49-50, 58). Spiritual bread is also superior because of the constancy of its availability. Natural bread is only available at certain times and seasons, whereas the Bread from Heaven assures us that whenever he is approached (e.g. in prayer) he will never turn us away (6:37).

Finally we learn from the example of the collection of the fragments that no part of God's word is to be ignored. The bread from heaven is not to be eaten merely until one is filled, or until one has consumed such parts as are agreeable to one's palate. Rather it is to be ingested, and digested, in its totality. No fragment of God's instruction should ever fall to the ground and be wasted.

EXHORTATION 3: Beyond the Water

John 6

The feeling of being at home is a powerful one. The feeling is strikingly easy to recognize, although surprisingly difficult to define. When one has had a stressful day, returning to the confines of the place we call "home" can provide a tremendous source of comfort. Problems previously besetting us are dispelled. Nor must displeasure necessarily precede to enjoy the pleasure of home. One can enjoy the most spectacular vacation, traversing the most exotic lands and exhilarating of times and still, upon one's return, delight in the additional pleasure of "coming home." The sensation can be a powerful one: pleasant and reassuring because of the confidence we feel with the familiarity of our surroundings; the powerful sense of association. Everyone has his own set of sights, sounds, or smells that characterizes the magical preserve of 'belonging' we describe as 'feeling at home.' This idea is central to exhortation drawn from John 6. Nevertheless, having introduced it, we shall temporarily store it on a mental shelf and return for it later.

John 6 is (seemingly) focused on feeding and sustenance in the provision of bread, yet we will see as events unfold much

Day 3 Exhortation: Beyond the Water

more lies beneath. As we study the chapter we will consider every facet on three levels simultaneously. On the simplest level we shall observe what is happening physically; but we will also be sensitive to two parallels: the contemporary spiritual equivalent in the lives of the disciples; and the modern spiritual equivalent in our own discipleships.

Beyond the Water

> After these things Jesus went over the sea of Galilee, which is the sea of Tiberias. (6:1)

A seemingly innocuous opening; yet we are familiar enough with John to know that such details warrant particular attention. On the simple, physical plane this demonstrates that anyone who wanted to share bread from heaven with Jesus that day had first to cross a body of water. In the spiritual creation, the principle is equally simple and yet attractively powerful: anyone who wishes to share bread from heaven must first cross a body of water. Both for the disciples then and ourselves now, communion with God's Son takes place on the other bank from where we began our lives: beyond the waters of baptism.

Philip: Overwhelmed at the Task

> When Jesus looked up and saw a great crowd coming toward him, he said to Philip, "Where shall we buy bread for these people to eat?" He asked this only to test him, for he already had in mind what he was going to do. Philip answered him, "Eight months' wages would not buy enough bread for each one to have a bite!" (6:5-7)

The text implies that the answer Philip gives, though doubtless true, was not what Jesus was hoping for. But what was Philip supposed to say? Just how explicitly was Philip expected to have the solution to providing food for this multitude?

This passage is important: it realizes a defining moment in the apprenticeship of the twelve. We do not suppose Jesus expects Philip to have the logistical solution to feed these 5 000 men and families. Rather this is a test of what Philip understands as the bigger picture of his discipleship. In this situation here on the mountainside (physically) and throughout the rest of Philip's life (spiritually) — and our spiritual lives — there will be those who provide, although always from the hand of God, and those for whom provision must be made. We suppose what Jesus is trying to provoke from Philip is a recognition of the divide, and a provocation to recognize which side he should be on. Has Philip learned yet that as one of the twelve he is going to be required to supply the needs of others, rather than to be just another hungry mouth himself? Does he know he must be no longer someone who leans on others, but someone others will lean upon? We suspect it is this recognition for which Jesus gently probes: the twelve should be looking to themselves to play a leadership role in feeding those who are hungry, whilst leaning upon their Heavenly Father as the ultimate provider. (We know ultimately this is to be their role, Jesus commissions them in exactly this way when speaking to Peter: "Feed my sheep" 21:15, 16, 17.) But at this stage it seems Philip has not yet grasped his functional role as a *provider* in discipleship and emulation of his Lord.

Andrew: A Humble Submission of Effort

John sets Andrew in counterpoint to Philip. Andrew says:

"Here is a boy with five small barley loaves and two small fish, but how far will they go among so many?" (6:9)

An excellent response! Andrew is aware of the realism of the situation: his offering is pathetically small — but he makes the offering anyway. How exhortational is Jesus' response to Andrew: he takes the tiny provision that Andrew has found and uses it as the basis of the miracle! (6:11) What excellent teaching this is for how we should labor towards our Father! Truly everything we have to offer our Father is as five loaves and two small fish to feed a multitude: a futile insufficiency to the task at hand. But Andrew's offering is neither mocked nor even dismissed by the Lord for its inadequacy. Rather it is taken by

Day 3 Exhortation: Beyond the Water

Jesus and used as the basis for the miracle of provision from the Hand of God! It is not that God *required* such an offering from which to work, but it is manifestly apparent that God *desires* us to make such offerings in His service. Indeed the miracles He provides (as on this occasion) often utilize those things that we bring to Him, to encourage us in being fruitful towards Him (15:2). There is much exhortation in the contrasting responses of Philip, who balked at the enormity of the problem, and Andrew, who knew enough to bring his humble effort to the Master.

The Miracle: Blessing for Sacrifice

> Jesus then took the loaves, gave thanks, and distributed to those who were seated as much as they wanted. (6:11)

A miracle from God! Observe to whom the miracle is given. One might be tempted to think it is given to everyone, but that is not strictly true. As we pointed out at the beginning, the bread from heaven is only made available to those who had crossed the body of water. In fact, the discrimination is even more limited than this. Jesus has given a command for the people to sit down and he only gives the food to those who are seated. Jesus is feeding all of those who have taken it upon themselves to follow him to a place where they can no longer support themselves, and who, once there, follow the instructions he gives. The bread is given to those who have placed themselves at risk of missing a meal in order that they might follow Jesus. Well do we remember the words:

> "And everyone who has left houses or brothers or sisters or father or mother or children or fields for my sake will receive a hundred times as much and will inherit eternal life." (Matthew 19:29)

On this occasion these people had given up their meal, possibly the only meal of their day, to follow Jesus. For many of them who were poor that may only have been meager fare. For their sacrifice they are rewarded with feasting on as much food as

Day 3 Exhortation: Beyond the Water

they can eat. How many of that multitude, had they returned home to eat, would have been able to eat their fill? Half of them? Ten percent? Less…? And yet because they had made that small sacrifice, to follow Jesus rather than to serve the natural needs of the body, they all ate until they were filled. How true is the promise – indeed the challenge – God gives us to sacrifice to Him in order that He might prove His goodness by showering us with blessings:

> "Bring the whole tithe into the storehouse, that there may be food in my house. Test me in this," says the LORD Almighty, "and see if I will not throw open the floodgates of heaven and pour out so much blessing that you will not have room enough for it." (Malachi 3:10)

A remarkable promise, and made by One who cannot lie. How foolish we are to have any cares at all for the material provisions of our lives! How convincingly do both this promise in Malachi and account in John testify that our trust in God will always be rewarded, and encourage us to cultivate and treasure a relationship wholly reliant upon Him.

<u>Disaster Looms: Divided Company</u>
Alas, after the miracle things (quite literally) come apart.

> Jesus, knowing that they intended to come and make him king by force, withdrew again to a mountain by himself. When evening came, his disciples went down to the lake, where they got into a boat and set off across the lake for Capernaum. (6:15-17)

Separation between Jesus and his disciples: a breach of company. Jesus heads upwards, towards the top of the mountain; the disciples head downwards, towards the sea. John uses simple

Day 3 Exhortation: Beyond the Water

patterns such as these to demonstrate deeper spiritual parallels. [1] Here John invites us to consider the spiritual parallel of Jesus heading upwards whilst the twelve are heading downwards: a spiritual parallel of divorce from the company of the Lord. Spiritually this departure describes a failing on the part of the disciples. Some may bridle at this conclusion, claiming it an unfair indictment of the twelve, all they are doing is going down to the boat! Additionally, other gospel records strongly suggest Jesus caused the separation by deliberately sending the apostles away (Matthew 14:22). Yet the separation of company must still be laid at the feet of the disciples if we understand *why* Jesus dismisses the twelve. All present misunderstood the miracle that they had witnessed. The multitude saw a demonstration of power and mentally leapt at the opportunity to utilize Jesus as a revolutionary leader for their selfish means, to claim a king and overthrow the Roman occupation of Israel (6:15). The gospels suggest Jesus sent his disciples away because they were not spiritually strong enough to resist the mindset of the mob, and thus the divide in company is forced. This miracle has shown that the twelve, notwithstanding the excellent humble advance of Andrew, are not fully ready, quite yet, to abide with their Master.

John parallels the parting company by announcing the arrival of evening: "When evening came, his disciples went down to the lake…" (v 16). John deliberately makes the departure of Jesus (the Light) synonymous with the arrival of physical darkness. John repeats the phrase to ensure obtaining our attention: "By now it was dark, and Jesus had not yet joined them." (v 17). We have already seen John is interested throughout his gospel in this simple but attractive cameo of light and darkness being contingent upon the presence or absence of Jesus – and here we find another small resurfacing of this principle. Without the Lord, we walk in darkness.

---

[1] For example the scene with Jesus and the Samaritan woman at Jacob's well where Jesus, the living water, sits at the top of Jacob's well, earthly water resides at the bottom, and a physical divide sits between (Section 2.3).

Day 3 Exhortation: Beyond the Water

Disaster Strikes: Recrossing the Water

But, an even more important point is what the disciples actually do:

> ...his disciples went down to the lake, where they got into a boat and set off across the lake for Capernaum. (6:16-17)

They set out to row back across the water, to the side from which they first came. The spiritual parallel is ominous. We identified the disciples' crossing the body of water, in order to share the bread from heaven with Jesus, with the act of baptism. Consider how seriously their current actions indict them: they seek to travel back across the water to where they first began. Spiritually this translates as an enacted renunciation of their baptisms! Already we anticipate this chosen action will not bode well for the twelve.

We pause to consider why the disciples chose this course. The answer is trivial on the physical level, but has profound implications on the level of discipleship. They were going to re-cross the water after breaking bread together with Jesus *because they were going home*. They were responding to the pull of "home": that strong sensation with which we introduced this exhortation. They had traveled across the water to be with Jesus, had shared the bread from heaven with him which God had provided. But at no point did they truly consider that that was where they *belonged*. They marveled at the miracle and doubtless were uplifted by the Lord's presence, as we are whenever we feel the presence of the Master. But at the end of the day, being with Jesus simply wasn't where they felt they belonged: it wasn't home. Their home was Galilee, on the original side of the water. So they got into the boat to row back across the water, in response to the natural urge recalling them to their identified comfort zone: home. Yet because the home of the natural man is always contrary to Christ's company, we anticipate this decision will lead to troublesome times.

> A strong wind was blowing and the waters grew rough. (6:18)

Day 3 Exhortation: Beyond the Water

Conditions worsen and the disciples find themselves in trouble. They are 3½ miles into their journey across the Sea of Galilee (6:19). A cursory glance at a map shows the Sea of Galilee to be 7 miles wide and thus their placement, indeed predicament, is confirmed. They are in the center of the sea: both shores are as far away as they can be.

Often in scripture when a man gets into trouble it is because the man places himself in a poorly chosen position before any trouble actually strikes. In many cases being in the "wrong place at the wrong time," sometimes willfully so, necessarily allows the problem to arise. A classic example is David, in his one great crime of adultery with Bathsheba and conspiracy in the murder of her husband. The problems seem a random circumstance, as David espied the beautiful Bathsheba from his palace roof. But the Biblical record takes pains to point out that David, the King, was at home at a time when all kings should have been at the battlefront (2 Samuel 11:1).

The pattern is repeated over and over. So many times when a man falls into hardship and temptation, seemingly a victim of mere happenstance, closer examination of the circumstances reveals the true culprit is a reckless, even willful, misplacement of the individual himself. Naturally we do not identify this concept to better vilify the characters we meet in our scriptural journeys, but only that such a yardstick might be used to better examine our own moments of trial and hardship. It is true that many a time in our lives we may find ourselves on stormy seas. But how did we get to be on those seas in the first place? And where exactly were we rowing at the time? So frequently we use gentle metaphors like "I stumbled," to describe what is all too often a headlong dive from our discipleship's path…

Walking on water: Healing the breach

…they saw Jesus approaching the boat, walking on the water; and they were terrified. But he said to them, "It is I; don't be afraid." Then they were willing to take him into the boat, and immediately the boat reached the shore where they were heading. (6:19-21)

Day 3 Exhortation: *Beyond the Water*

Salvation is on hand, Jesus comes to them. But why are we shown this unique detail of Jesus walking on the water? The miracle convinces no unlearned multitude of the divine origin of the Master, because the only audience is the apostles. What then should we learn? Perhaps we should learn that the breach of company is healed by the Lord, not the disciples. The disciples were responsible for the divide opening up, yet the Lord closes it. Jesus comes to them, not they to him. This principle is in Jesus' teaching as well as his behavior. Consider this verse, plucked from the parable of the prodigal son:

> The older brother became angry and refused to go in. So his father went out and pleaded with him. (Luke 15:28)

Notice the immediacy of the text. The son refuses to go to the Father – therefore the Father comes directly to the son! There is not the slightest pause in which a standoff might develop. Here again the Father, who clearly represents God, initiates the move to heal the divide created by the son's behavior. How compellingly we are challenged to examine our own lives! How many times when we have wandered away from God can we truly claim that it was ourselves who healed the breach? Or how many times is our own return preceded by some seeming turn of fortune in our lives that provides the impetus for us to return to the Lord's company?

This must profoundly impact our behavior as a church. How clearly does this teach us to actively seek out those who have walked away! All too often nothing is done for these lost sheep. Worse yet, inactivity is even justified with expressions such as: "Well he walked away from us, not vice versa. If he wants to come back, he knows exactly where to find us." Sad words to hear, and in total contradiction to the Christ-like example of recovering lost sheep! (Luke 15:3-7) When was the last time we made active effort to contact a 'lost' former-member? Perhaps we never before gave the matter much headroom. Perhaps we will now; and with resolution to act upon it.

Day 3 Exhortation: Beyond the Water

<u>Walking on water: Demonstrating God's Love</u>

Jesus' walking on the water miracle may still seem bizarre. It has passed from the Bible into modern metaphor: to this day man refers to acts of achieving the impossible as 'walking on water.' But why did Jesus do this at all? The miracle serves no apparently useful function!

Here is a possible answer on which to muse. Consider this verse from Romans:

> For I am persuaded, that neither death, nor life, nor angels, nor principalities, nor powers, nor things present, nor things to come, Nor height, nor depth, nor any other creature, shall be able to separate us from the love of God, which is in Christ Jesus our Lord. (Romans 8:38-39)

We suggest the miracle fulfils its central function as a living demonstration of this assurance. Jesus walked, by the love of God for those He had called, across 3½ miles of stormy seas to come into their field of vision, to comfort them and to bring them immediately to shore. Observe the mention of: "nor height, nor depth" from Romans. What height of waves was able to separate those disciples from the love of God in Christ? None! What depth of sea could keep them from Jesus, when he had decided he would come to them? Again, none! Neither height, nor depth, nor any other creature was able to separate those apostles from the love God had for them in His Son that stormy night. And as always the spiritual dimensions of the situation are the most profitable. How black can it feel in our lives that we cannot feel the approach of Christ at the remembrance table of the Lord? What depths of sin can keep the Lord from us when we call? Or what heights of pride…? We are assured, not only by Paul's writings but, as ever, by the demonstrated actions of Jesus that neither height, nor depth, nor any other creature can separate us from the love of God. This miracle, interestingly shown to believing disciples only, gives graphic demonstration of just how Jesus fulfils that role.

Day 3 Exhortation: Beyond the Water

<u>The Concept of Home: 12 Apostles</u>

Having provided bread from heaven physically, Jesus repeats the miracle on the spiritual plane, where he is himself the Bread from Heaven (as Section 3.2).

> "I am the bread of life. Your forefathers ate the manna in the desert, yet they died. But here is the bread that comes down from heaven, which a man may eat and not die." (6:48-50)

In good accordance with a common scriptural pattern, the spiritual display of the miracle, coming latterly, excels the former natural miracle. Within this chapter the physical feeding of the 5 000 chronologically precedes the superlative revelation of Jesus as the bread of life. As we have said (Section 3.2) this principle is also true on the broader scale in the context of the history of God's people. God provided physical bread (manna) from heaven through the hand of Moses, and excelled His provision with the revelation of Jesus Christ as the spiritual bread of life in a later time. Natural bread (manna) provided temporary sustenance in a mortal condition; spiritual bread offers eternal life in an immortal condition. This spiritual bread is the body of Jesus Christ destroyed on the cross, and Christ himself establishes this symbol in this very chapter.

> "I am the living bread that came down from heaven. If anyone eats of this bread, he will live forever. This bread is my flesh, which I will give for the life of the world." (6:51; c.f. Matthew 26:26)

At this declaration the faith of some withers and they follow Jesus no more (6:66). Jesus then asks his disciples:

"You do not want to leave too, do you?" (6:67)

At first glance, the question seems to bear the familiar hallmarks of human self-sympathy: an over-exaggerated pathos derived from the disappointment of some walking away. Yet the

Day 3 Exhortation: Beyond the Water

Lord Jesus Christ is the speaker, so this cannot be the explanation! Rather, Jesus is putting forward a test, as he did to Philip the previous day (6:6). Some may be skeptical: Even as a test, what is the value of Jesus asking whether the twelve will leave him when they have shown no sign of doing so? Because leaving Jesus is precisely what they *did* do after the natural miracle! The previous day ended with his disciples attempting to row across the lake, going away from Jesus (6:16-17), and for the simple reason that they were going *home* – their idea of home was a geographical place (Galilee) where their domestic lodgings were located.

This is what makes John 6 such a deep chapter. It has a premier place in John's gospel because it contains, very subtly, a fundamental transition in the minds of the disciples, about their sense of "home." Simon Peter answers:

> "Lord, to whom shall we go? You have the words of eternal life. We believe and know that you are the Holy One of God." (6:68-69)

Success! Peter leads the way in this revelation concerning *home*. Up to this point in John's gospel the apostles considered that 'home' was Galilee. Peter's answer brokers the transition: his 'home' is no longer a geographical location: it is by the side of his Lord and Master! For the remainder of Jesus' ministry, we will see that 'home' for the apostles is identified as by Jesus' side. The sixth of John is indeed a most remarkable chapter.

The Concept of 'Home': Us

Yet this is little more than interesting speculation unless we apply it in our own lives; that most delicate of domains to regard! We have seen the provision of bread from heaven; we have come beyond the water to share it in communion with each other and with our Lord. We know each Sunday morning a whole multitude of our brothers and sisters share this bread together: truly it is more than 5 000 that this spiritual bread feeds, and has fed over the years. And we, in the same way as the apostles of old, must

111

Day 3 Exhortation: Beyond the Water

also address the fundamental challenge this miracle presents. Once the miracle is passed, where will we go? Where, truly, is *home*? Will we silently thank our Master for his wonderful company, in which we were so privileged to share, and then row back across the very waters whose crossing brought us to him? Is the trip to this particular mountainside still just a 'day out,' some novel experience atypical to our lifestyle? Or has the company of the people in our local church with whom we can best hope to share the Master's company, truly become 'home'?

Perhaps we would say: "But I don't really feel I belong there." Worse still, we might say: "Other people don't make me feel I belong there," – though we should not countenance such evil-spirited deflection of our own shortcomings. We must allow this chapter, the sixth of John, to rebuke us, educate us, and most of all *encourage* us, into making that remarkable transition which the apostles, led by Peter's declaration, did those many years ago. The church assembly, and the presence of those whom the Lord has called as our siblings, truly must be our home.

Furthermore: this thinking is not grown merely to bloom into that most inadequate of flowers: increased attendance at church. It strives for much more! It drives towards true spiritual growth: to cultivate for ourselves a true 'home' within the family of God; to cultivate that strong 'pull towards' of home, with which we introduced this exhortation, amongst our spiritual family. To grow in our hearts a genuine desire to flee the clamorous self-satisfaction of this world and enjoy the peace of being at home. And we desire to cultivate that feeling so that, were we to be questioned by Jesus at the end of each memorial service: "Will you also go away now?" we can reply in all honesty: "No Lord, for here is family. Here is *home*. Where else would I go?"

DAY 4 *John 7:1-13:38*

EXPOSITION:
Light to Rule

Day 4 heralds an important point: the beginning of the second creative sub-cycle of Heaven, Sea and Earth (see Figure α_1). Day 4 develops the basic component of Light, created on Day 1, by producing the lights to rule day and night.

Basic premise:
We expect to find a resurgence of the illuminating element 'Light' in this section of the gospel. We expect to see Jesus' character developed as 'The Light of the World,' (i.e. echoing Day 1) by containing a specific focus of judgment, rulership, authority, kingship.

4.1 The Light to Rule
Read John 7:14-34. The focus of the text is Jesus' authority: the authority by which he teaches and the authority by which he heals.

Day 4 Exposition: Light to Rule

> Jesus answered, "My teaching is not my own. It comes from him who sent me. If anyone chooses to do God's will, he will find out whether my teaching comes from God or whether I speak on my own." (7:16-17)

This marries well our premise for Day 4. Jesus justifies his authority as deriving from both God's will and the Mosaic Law. He also rebukes the Jews for their own behavior as lords over God's children. The illumination (light) he brings shows the Jewish leaders of God's children have abused their authority, thus judgment is caused upon them.

> "Stop judging by mere appearances, and make a right judgment." (7:24)

We also encounter the familiar element of Light, returning from Day 1. The description of Jesus as the light of the world, which we first heard in John 1, is repeated. Read John 8:12-59, and see how John inextricably binds light and judgment together in this section:

> When Jesus spoke again to the people, he said, "I am the **light** of the world. Whoever follows me will never walk in darkness, but will have the **light** of life." The Pharisees challenged him, "Here you are, appearing as your own witness; your testimony is not valid." Jesus answered, "Even if I testify on my own behalf, my testimony is valid, for I know where I came from and where I am going. But you have no idea where I come from or where I am going. You **judge** by human standards; I pass **judgment** on no one. But if I do **judge**, my decisions are right, because I am not alone. I stand with the Father, who sent me." (8:12-16)

4.2 Absolute Authority

John now steps up a gear in presenting the authority of Jesus Christ. Read John 10-11. (We defer discussion of chapter 9 to a later section, as the perfectly encapsulating finale of this theme.)

Day 4 Exposition: Light to Rule

> "Therefore Jesus said again, "I tell you the truth, I am the gate for the sheep. All who ever came before me were thieves and robbers, but the sheep did not listen to them. I am the gate; whoever enters through me will be saved. He will come in and go out, and find pasture. The thief comes only to steal and kill and destroy; I have come that they may have life, and have it to the full. I am the good shepherd. The good shepherd lays down his life for the sheep" (10:7-11)

The authority of Jesus is defined in this double metaphor where he represents both the leader (shepherd) of the sheep, and the access to their pasture. The dual nature of the metaphor itself is perhaps explained by the cultural observation that, in all but winter months, sheep in Israel are pastured overnight in walled enclosures which have neither roof nor door.[1] The walls are high enough to prevent predators jumping over, although a man could certainly climb them – notice how Jesus says: "I tell you the truth, the man who does not enter the sheep pen by the gate, but **climbs in by some other way**, is a thief and a robber" – lending credence to the notion Jesus is referring to such a structure. The central power of the metaphor is that during the night the shepherd sleeps in the doorway: he is both shepherd and gate! No-one can enter or leave the sheepfold without the shepherd having knowledge of it. Such is the authority of the gentle Son of Man, well preserved in this attractive dual metaphor.

> "The reason my Father loves me is that I lay down my life-- only to take it up again. No one takes it from me, but I lay it down of my own accord. I have authority to lay it down and authority to take it up again. This command I received from my Father." (10:17-18)

John shows Jesus has power over his own life and death: a level of authority not matched by any other human in history.

---

[1] Errico R. A., Lamsa G. M., *Op. cit.* p 135

Day 4 Exposition: *Light to Rule*

Furthermore John goes on to demonstrate this unique level of authority is not limited to Jesus' own life, he also wields this ability (both the dynamic power and the authority) in the lives of others. This understanding is crucial, because it reveals why John then proceeds to recount the resurrection of Lazarus at this stage of his gospel: it is the perfect demonstration of this unique authority.

> Jesus said to [Martha] "I am the resurrection and the life. He who believes in me will live, even though he dies; and whoever lives and believes in me will never die." (11:25-26)

We must pay close attention to the implications of these statements because a new component of authority emerges. God is investing *absolute* authority in His Son. This is a new component both in the history of man and in the gospel. It is sometimes, wrongly, said that a ruler of ancient times, for example a Roman Emperor or an Egyptian Pharaoh, had "absolute power"; that they held the "power of life and death" in their hands. This statement is factually incorrect. Certainly they had the authority to put virtually any man to death at any moment their whim dictated, yet this is the ceiling limit of human authority and it is *not* the power of life and death, it is *only* the power of death. Humans cannot dispense life even if they want to, yet absolute authority is the power to dispense either death to a living person or life to a dead person. This is why John connects this teaching to the miracle of Lazarus' resurrection: firmly making the point that Jesus was the only human to hold this power.

Once again the excellence of the spiritual creation over the natural creation shines through. The ultimate level of human authority is the power to distribute death, and the ultimate level of spiritual authority is the power to distribute life.

> Jesus called in a loud voice, "Lazarus, come out!" The dead man came out, his hands and feet wrapped with strips of

linen, and a cloth around his face. Jesus said to them, "Take off the grave clothes and let him go." (11:43-44)

And the man who was dead, under the authority of Jesus Christ, the Ruling Light, walks from the tomb.

4.3 Judgment from the Ruling Light

We understand why the miraculous resurrection of Lazarus dominates the eleventh chapter of John. John is rarely concerned with the healing miracles of Jesus (see Appendix A), yet this particular miracle forms ideal demonstration of Jesus' authority, which is now John's focus. Nor is John finished with this theme. Chapter 12 shows the final, uppermost level of this authority: a Throne. The Son of Man enters Jerusalem for the first time, though not the last, as King. We read of Jesus' triumphal entry into Jerusalem in John 12:12-50.

The next day the great crowd that had come for the Feast heard that Jesus was on his way to Jerusalem. They took palm branches and went out to meet him, shouting, "Hosanna!" "Blessed is he who comes in the name of the Lord!" "Blessed is the King of Israel!" (12:12-13)

The Bible presents for us – in powerfully juxtaposed fashion! – the manner in which life will be realized by Jesus Christ: in his crucifixion. Ultimately the power of life will come through death. It is not just that the King must die; the King must die to become King.

"The hour has come for the Son of Man to be glorified. I tell you the truth, unless a kernel of wheat falls to the ground and dies, it remains only a single seed. But if it dies, it produces many seeds. The man who loves his life will lose it, while the man who hates his life in this world will keep it for eternal life." (12:23-25)

Day 4 Exposition: Light to Rule

Here is the Son of Man's glory. (Remember, Day 1's Exhortation defined glory as a combination of 'giving evidence of greatness' and 'fulfilling one's designed purpose.') Here Jesus perfectly fulfils God's purpose for him and thereby gives full evidence of God's greatness by resigning himself to death; thereby obtaining absolute authority. Light has victory over darkness, and darkness is judged: sin and the power of death are destroyed in the victory of the Son of God on the cross.

It would be easy for the direction of the gospel to extend the idea of Jesus' Kingship forward into the Kingdom of God, the Millennium, the restoration of the Temple and suchlike. Instead the gospel remains firmly grounded in Day 4's creative elements: light and judgment, providing further evidence of the creation pattern's presence. Therefore John's record clothes Jesus' ride into Jerusalem for his final, dreadful Passover in the language of light and judgment.

> "Now is the time for **judgment** on this world; now the prince of this world will be driven out." (12:31)
>
> Then Jesus told them, "You are going to have the **light** just a little while longer. Walk while you have the **light**, before darkness overtakes you. The man who walks in the dark does not know where he is going. Put your trust in the **light** while you have it, so that you may become sons of **light**." (12:35-36)
>
> "I have come into the world as a **light**, so that no one who believes in me should stay in darkness. As for the person who hears my words but does not keep them, I do not **judge** him. For I did not come to **judge** the world, but to save it." (12:46-47)

It is edifying to understand how judgment falls. The world is judged (12:31), but not by Christ (12:47). The illumination of Christ (the Light) causes the actions of the world to be seen; and it is *these actions themselves* that condemn the world. The world is therefore self-condemned by its own actions seen in the revealing light. John carefully explain this both in the general case and in the specific case of the traitor Iscariot, whose unfortunate story we shall explore in greater depth in the exhortation.

"What you are about to do, do quickly," Jesus told him... As soon as Judas had taken the bread, he went out. And it was night. (13:27, 30)

4.4 To See or Not to See?

The principal account of Day 4's light and judgment theme is the restoration of sight to the man born blind (9:1-41). In Day 1 Jesus was introduced as the Light, and Israel as the darkness, characterized by a series of 12 questions that indicated their complete lack of understanding (Section 1.3). We see a resurgence of both those characteristics, Jesus as the light and Israel as the ignorant darkness, in this very chapter.

Read John 9. Firstly notice the (re-)introduction to Jesus:

Light...
"While I am in the world, I am the light of the world." (9:5)

...and Judgment
Jesus said, "For judgment I have come into this world, so that the blind will see and those who see will become blind." (9:39)

Likewise our reintroduction to the Jews, who are presented as blind (i.e. in the dark); again characterized by a series of questions! (Table 4_1) How exciting to behold the consistency of the patterns that the Bible lays before our eyes!

In both Day 1 and Day 4 the final question is almost comical, revealing the totality of the Jews' incomprehension. Yet this is humorless comedy, betraying the enormity of how far astray God's people had drifted. They couldn't even recognize the very things they should have been longing to behold.

Day 4 Exposition: Light to Rule

Jews in Day 1 (1:1-3:21)	Jews in Day 4 (9:1-41)
"Who are you?" (1:21)	"Isn't this the same man who used to sit and beg?" (9:8)
"What then?" (1:21)	"How then were your eyes opened?" (9:10)
"Are you Elijah?" (1:21)	"Where is this man?" (9:12)
"Are you the Prophet?" (1:21)	"How can a sinner do such miraculous signs?" (9:16)
"Who are you, that we may give an answer to those who sent us?" (1:22)	"What have you to say about him?" (9:17)
"What do you say about yourself?" (1:22)	"Is this your son?" (9:19)
"Why then do you baptize if you are not the Christ, nor Elijah, nor the Prophet?" (1:25)	"Is this the one you say was born blind?" (9:19)
"What sign do you show to us, since you do these things?" (2:18)	"How is it that now he can see?" (9:19)
"It has taken forty-six years to build this temple, and you will raise it up in three days?" (2:20)	"What did he do to you?" (9:26)
"How can a man be born when he is old?" (3:4)	"How did he open your eyes?" (9:26)
"Can he enter a second time into his mother's womb and be born?" (3:4)	"What?" (9:40)
"How can these things be?" (3:9)	"Are we blind too?" (9:40)

Table 4_1: Unable to grasp the Light. The list of questions (NKJV) asked by the Jews in the discrete sections of Day 1 (1:1-3:21) and in Day 4, the case of the man born blind (9:1-41).

Yet can we berate the Pharisees for their lack of perception? Rebuke is well deserved, but are we in a position to deliver it, as we read John's gospel from two thousand years downstream? Before we risk such an enterprise, perhaps we should call to mind the events of the last days preceding the return of the

Day 4 Exposition: Light to Rule

Bridegroom. These 'signs of the end' (Matthew 24) should be equally long-awaited by us. Are we fully confident that we know exactly what we should be looking for, and what we shall see…? Or do we too still have broad ranging questions…?

Mindset of Rejection

Rejection 1	Of the man's identity	"No, he only looks like him." (9:9)
Disproof 1		But he himself insisted, "I am the man." (9:9)
Rejection 2	Of his being born blind	The Jews still did not believe that he had been blind and had received his sight. (9:18)
Disproof 2		"We know he is our son," the parents answered, "and we know he was born blind." (9:20)
Rejection 3	Of Jesus' authority as a healer	"Give glory to God," they said. "We know this man [Jesus] is a sinner." (9:24)
Disproof 3		"We know that God does not listen to sinners. He listens to the godly man who does his will. Nobody has ever heard of opening the eyes of a man born blind. If this man were not from God, he could do nothing." (9:31-33)
Rejection 4	Of the man himself	They answered and said to him, "You were completely born in sins, and are you teaching us?" And they cast him out. (9:34)

Table 4_2: Catalogue of rejection. Four consecutive, insistent rejections from the Pharisees of the evidence of Jesus' miracle restoring the sight of the man born blind.

Day 4 Exposition: Light to Rule

In a similar way to the Wedding at Cana (Day 1), events here in John 9 (Day 4) are concerned with how the miracle was received: who understood what they saw and who did not. Not only did the Pharisees not understand what they saw, they refused point blank to accept the evidence of the miracle and this was their downfall. They are condemned by the mindset they had already adopted *prior* to investigating the facts of the miracle. Scripture reveals that in their hearts they had chosen to reject the miracle at any cost, regardless of what they witnessed. Table 4_2 reveals this in their dialogue, for even after each rejection is disproved they create a new rejection of the evidence before their eyes.

The final quote is especially damning. "You were completely born in sins" very likely refers to the man's being born blind since the Pharisees, as the disciples, were persuaded of the erroneous notion that this was indicative of sin. Yet this accusation itself condemns the Pharisees, since the very fact of being born blind, which they use as evidence of sin, is itself a fact they previously had denied ever happened! (compare 9:18 and 9:34). Such are the self-ensnaring webs of the deceitful: the Pharisees confound themselves utterly with their own words.

This is the mentality with which Jesus contended: the closed minds of those who would not see, and therefore could not see. John parallels them alongside a man who had been physically blind all his life. John unfolds the compelling lesson that Jesus can, and will, heal physical blindness – even if it has been present all of our life – but no cure can be found for willful (spiritual) blindness. For those who have eyes and will not see, they must remain in darkness (Isaiah 6:9-10). Those who are blind by birth are blind by the hand of time and chance, which time and chance lend themselves for the evidencing of God's will:

> "Rabbi, who sinned, this man or his parents, that he was born blind?" Jesus answered, "Neither this man nor his parents sinned, but that the works of God should be revealed in him." (9:2-3)

Day 4 Exposition: Light to Rule

But those who are blind by choice are those who have seen the light and chosen to hide in the darkness, where they believe their evil deeds will not be seen. Once again, the actions of the individual orchestrate his own judgment:

> Jesus said to [the Pharisees], "If you were blind, you would have no sin; but now you say, 'We see.' Therefore your sin remains." (9:41)

<u>Double Vision: Spiritual and Natural</u>

Again we need to be sensitive to the presence of both spiritual and natural elements in Jesus' work. Jesus addresses the blind man:

> "Go," he told him, "wash in the Pool of Siloam." (9:7)

The blind man is dismissed: "Go" (see Table 2_2); echoing the law that no blind sacrifice was acceptable upon the altar of the Living God (Deuteronomy 15:21, Malachi 1:8). But notice the power of God's mercy invested in Jesus Christ: Jesus rejects the blindness, *without* rejecting the man who bears it. A blind man is sent away from the Lord: but a sighted man returns.

> So the man went and washed, and came home seeing. (9:7)

Yet here is an interesting point: can the man who returns from the Pool of Siloam *really* see? After his return he is asked where Jesus is:

> "Where is this man?" they asked him. "I don't know," he said. (9:12)

On the physical plane this seems trivial. The man has never been in Jesus' presence with the power of sight and therefore doesn't even know what Jesus looks like. Yet at the risk of overextending interpretation, we suggest that this verse (9:12) is recorded for its spiritual testimony. The man's eyes have been

123

Day 4 Exposition: *Light to Rule*

opened, for sure, but Jesus is still not in sight. This observation is underscored, for emphasis, by the later exchange:

> Jesus… said, "Do you believe in the Son of Man?" "Who is he, sir?" the man asked. "Tell me so that I may believe in him." (9:35-36)

John's record stresses the man cannot "see" Jesus. Jesus therefore reveals himself to him:

> Jesus said, "You have now seen him; in fact, he is the one speaking with you." Then the man said, "Lord, I believe," and he worshipped him. (9:37-38)

Once again John gives us a demonstration of both the physical and spiritual levels on which Jesus effects his miracles. The man's physical blindness has been taken away in the Pool of Siloam; in a way this formed a baptism for his eyes. But even after his eyes have been 'immersed,' it does not provide him with the perception to spiritually see (believe) in the Son of Man. Revelation of Jesus still had to follow the baptism of his eyes, and the transition is made by his willingness and faith to see that which is beyond his natural vision.

On the broader scale, the words of the blind man are a precursor of what the Israelite crowds say later in Day 4. John uses the condition of the blind man as a foreshadowing of the spiritual blindness affecting all Israel who, John shows us, are also unable to see the Son of Man.

> Jesus said, "This voice was for your benefit, not mine. Now is the time for judgment on this world; now the prince of this world will be driven out. But I, when I am lifted up from the earth, will draw all men to myself"… The crowd spoke up, "We have heard from the Law that the Christ will remain forever, so how can you say, The Son of Man must be lifted up? Who is this Son of Man?" (12:30-34)

Day 4 Exposition: Light to Rule

Israel, unlike the man born blind, not only failed to see the Son of Man, but also failed to see their own blindness. Thus Jesus does not heal them: they remain in darkness. As always the spiritual excels the natural, for whilst the natural eye-opening provides the blind man sight with which to conduct his natural life, his spiritual eye-opening provides him with a sight that will *provide* eternal life.

4.5 Conclusions from Day 4

In this part of John's gospel judgment and culpability are shown as necessary consequences of illumination. One who stands in the light is responsible for those actions he performs because he can see what he is doing. Even a return to the darkness is itself an enlightened decision. And such a decision: to knowingly depart from the Light of the world back into the darkness, is utterly fatal, as John graphically illustrates (13:30).

The inescapable logic of John's thought train, presenting Jesus in Day 4 as the ruling light, is wonderful. He covers the absolute nature of the power Jesus owns: to prescribe – though he does not deliver – death to the living (9:41) and prescribe and deliver life to the dead (11:43-44). John extends to the natural conclusion of absolute authority: Kingship, so John details here in Day 4 the first, though not the last, triumphal arrival of the King in Jerusalem (12:12-13).

Once again we see the superlative nature of the spiritual creation over the natural. In the natural world the height of judgment, the highest level of authority attainable, is the power to sentence a living man to death. But in the spiritual creation in John's gospel, we see the higher level – the authority to 'sentence' a dead man to life! This gives an excellent introduction to the concept of mercy: for only by mercy can a man, who has no *right* to life, be granted life. Mercy itself constitutes another superlative facet of spiritual rulership above natural rulership. In the animal kingdoms of the natural world all business is conducted entirely devoid of mercy. Animals behave logically for survival; and they can also evidence elements of loyalty, loving care and even altruism that extend beyond logic. But there is no mercy within

Day 4 Exposition: Light to Rule

the natural creation, nor can there be. Mercy is an element deriving solely from an understanding of the Almighty, and is only seen in those who reflect some portion of His mind.

We also learn that those who are brought into the Light, and become aware of the spiritual implications of the lives that they lead, are not made perfect by this illumination. Being brought into the Light is a beginning and not an end. The blind man returned from the Pool with the capacity of sight, yet he was still unable to recognize Jesus when he saw him, until an additional revelation was made. Thus spiritual growth must continue beyond the baptismal event. No resting place is found for the true disciple on the land beyond the water. Rising from the baptismal pool gives no guarantee of perceiving the company of Jesus Christ and any assumption that it does is made in error. The point of illumination enables the search for the Lord in hope that he will reveal himself. Those who have come to the land 'beyond the water' do not necessarily have Jesus yet in sight; a journey still needs to be embarked upon, an eye-opening walk of discovery still lies ahead.

EXHORTATION 4: The Mark of Blood

John 13

One of the great writers of our time was the English author Sir Arthur Conan Doyle, the creator of the world-famous detective: Sherlock Holmes. Through the mind and imagination of Conan Doyle, Holmes was enabled to make a variety of intelligent deductions and philosophical observations. To assist matters, he was always ably counter-pointed by the incomparably devoted Dr Watson, eternally at hand to shower admiration and astonishment on Holmes' latest deduction and thereby augment his greatness.

One of Holmes' observations has particular pertinence to scriptural study. Holmes promulgated the notion that things *absent* from a (crime) scene are equally important to things present, for the determination of what happened there. All would pay great attention to the bloodstains on the floor in a murder scene, or to the article of clothing found outside in the shrubbery. Holmes was equally absorbed by the umbrella stand being devoid of umbrellas; that there were no footprints on the lawn; or no smell of perfume in the adjoining room. In a notable example of

Day 4 Exhortation: The Mark of Blood

this tenet Holmes identifies the thief of a prize racehorse as the trainer himself by reason of the absence of barking from the stable dog upon the intrusion – the dog being at ease in the presence of its master. The investigating inspector, suspecting that Holmes has become aware of a relevant clue, converses with him thusly:

> "Is there any point to which you would wish to draw my attention?"
> "To the curious incident of the dog in the night-time."
> "The dog did nothing in the night-time."
> "That was the curious incident," remarked Sherlock Holmes. [1]

This principle profoundly impacts study of God's Word. How many times do we remember to pay attention to those things that do *not* appear? Those who read the Bible regularly are familiar with the characters and events of the text, yet it is these people who are most susceptible to this blindness. One may have read the events of the gospels (for example) so frequently that one fully anticipates the explanation of a parable of Christ, or the outcome of a particular exchange with the Pharisees, without ever pausing to observe how utterly extraordinary such events or comments sometimes are. Perhaps the one and only *disadvantage* of reading the Bible frequently is this anaesthesia to its sometimes bizarre omissions. Yet within these omissions, as we shall see, are hidden priceless treasures of understanding from the life and teaching of the Lord.

Omission at the Last Supper

Perhaps no more surprising omission in scripture occurs than in the 13th chapter of John. Read John 13. This relates the Last Supper shared between the Lord Jesus Christ and his twelve

---

[1] Sir Conan Doyle A., "Silver Blaze," 1894, from "The Penguin Complete Sherlock Holmes," 1981, Penguin Books, Harmondsworth, UK, p 347

Day 4 Exhortation: The Mark of Blood

apostles. It incorporates Judas Iscariot's betrayal of Christ and, of more lasting consequence, the institution of the new covenant of salvation in the body and blood of Christ.

Do we see what is missing? *There is no mention of bread or wine!* Pause for a few moments to reflect on what an incredible omission this is. Neither the breaking of bread nor the drinking of wine – the very institution of the covenant of the communion of the body of Christ – is included within John's gospel record! The words 'bread' and 'wine' do not even appear in the text here (the word 'bread' appears in v 27, but in a context not directly related to the sacraments).

Christian communities are centered on the memorial elements of bread and wine, and some define them, seemingly appropriately, as the focal point of fellowship. The omission of the sacraments from John's gospel challenges this centrality and demands our attention. It is probably fair to say that John is the most spiritual of the four gospels: the gospel least concerned with the direct matters of the day (see Appendix A). He is most concerned with the weightiest matters of Christ's ministry: Jesus' spiritual impact on the relationship between God and His people and his role in their salvation. At first consideration this would seem to make things worse. If the one gospel record from which explicit mention of bread and wine disappears is the most spiritual; then that seriously indicts those who hold the position of identifying the bread and wine as central to discipleship! The emblematic absence suggests the physical sharing of bread and wine merely a tradition, which the most spiritually-minded would not take as a serious necessity but rather view as one of the practices done away in the spiritual creation. Those who discount the importance of remembering Christ's death in bread and wine seem ratified by John's gospel. John seems to support the oft-heard claims: "Physical practices such as baptism and communion are not necessarily part of a spiritual life!" and "All God wants is for us to be kind to one another and be 'good people' " and other such nebulous epithets. Such claims would seem – on the surface – to be supported by John's omission of bread and wine from the account of the Last Supper.

Day 4 Exhortation: The Mark of Blood

Consider a second example case. Imagine you are a Sunday school teacher. Imagine you have charge over an older or more advanced group, to which you have set the assignment: "In your own words, write an account of the Last Supper." Suppose one student submits an account of the Last Supper that fails to include any mention of bread or wine. Would you award that student a relatively high grade, or a relatively low grade? Without thinking, and without reading John's gospel, one might be tempted to award a relatively low grade. One might offer the critique: "Thank you for your effort, but I think you missed the whole point of the Last Supper: it was the institution of the new covenant in Christ in shared bread and wine!" But now, having read John's account, we are aware this conclusion is not available, for John's own divinely inspired writing leaves out the same facts. How then are we ever to understand this most curious omission?

The Passover Model

Our answer must stem from scripture, and John's opening verse of the account yields a clue:

It was just before the Passover Feast. (13:1)

The association between Passover and the crucifixion is well known. The sacrifice of the Lamb of God taking away the sin of the world is indeed a powerful celebration, and fulfillment, of the Passover institution. John's deliberate mention of Passover at the opening of his report of the Last Supper lends more weight to the association. He deliberately inserts the word 'Passover' into our thoughts before relating the events of the Last Supper, to act as a clue to what follows, a key by which the mysterious balance of his account might be unlocked.

Thus we will pause to remind ourselves of the sequence of events forming the Passover observation. We will pay special attention to the precise point salvation was granted from the impending Angel of Death. Read Exodus 12. We create a brief paraphrased summary of the protocol, which is recorded twice,

Day 4 Exhortation: The Mark of Blood

(as so often is the style of the Hebraic writers), once in verses 1-13 and again summarized in verses 21-23.

1. Take a lamb. (v 3, 21)
2. The lamb must be a year-old male without defect. (v 5)
3. Kill it on the evening of the 14th day of the month. (v 6, 21)
4. Make a mark of blood on the doorframe of your house. (v 7, 22)
5. Eat the roasted lamb in haste: it is the LORD's Passover. (v 11)
6. Remain in the house all night: do not go out into the street. (v 22)
7. When the Angel sees the mark of blood, He will Pass Over. (v 13, 23)

This last point defines the moment of salvation. Salvation comes when God sees the mark of blood on the house. Eating the Passover meal, which we re-enact in memory of the crucifixion with the bread and wine, is present in the essential list for salvation (pt 5), *but it is not the point at which salvation occurs!* Salvation comes later (pt 7), when the Angel sees the mark of blood made on the house where the meal was eaten. The Passover meal was itself vital; for without partaking of the meal no one could escape the Destroying Angel. Yet salvation from destruction came from a point beyond the meal: the Mark of Blood on the house.

Passover at the Last Supper

John has used the word 'Passover' in the opening sentence as a prompt to remember that in Exodus 12 salvation comes at a point *beyond* sharing the meal together. Now the beautiful subtlety of John's record is seen. He focuses wholly on events *beyond* the meal! The meal passes from the text as early as verse 2. [2] John's

---

[2] The King James asserts that supper has concluded by this point: "And supper being ended..." (13:2). Most other translations imply that supper was still ongoing, nevertheless from verse 2 onwards the focus of all versions is on events other than the meal itself.

Day 4 Exhortation: The Mark of Blood

record highlights the actions which sharing the meal together provokes them to go on and do.

Clearly we can relate the sharing of the memorial emblems with the Passover meal, since both represent, either physically or spiritually, the broken body and shed blood of the blemishless (blameless) Lamb. This already establishes the vital point that the death of the Lamb can never be dismissed: it was impossible to be saved without the sharing of the Passover meal. Thus we have partly answered our earlier problem: disregarding the sacraments can only bring disaster for one who would see salvation. But – and here is the key to answer our question as to why the bread and wine are missing from John 13 – the point of salvation did not come from eating the Passover meal, it came from God seeing the marks of blood, from the lamb, made on the house where the meal was shared. Translating this physical concept into the spiritual world of the New Testament we learn this: the point of salvation at the Last Supper comes from the actions which sharing the bread and wine together provoke the participants to go on and do. These actions constitute the 'marks of blood,' which catalyze our salvation granted from God's grace. Within the model of Passover therefore, it is completely understandable that John concentrates on the "marks of blood": the actions each of them makes from the meal they have shared.

Jesus' Mark of Blood: The Absence of Condemnation

John highlights the "marks of blood" from two characters in particular: Judas Iscariot and Jesus Christ. For our exhortation we shall consider carefully what sharing the communion meal provoked each of them to do. We begin by looking at Jesus' comment to Judas.

> As soon as Judas took the bread, Satan entered into him. "What you are about to do, do quickly," Jesus told him, but no one at the meal understood why Jesus said this to him… As soon as Judas had taken the bread, he went out. And it was night. (13:27-28, 30)

Day 4 Exhortation: The Mark of Blood

We began this exhortation by noting things *absent* from the scriptural text can be just as instructive as things apparent. In these words of Jesus to Judas is contained another dramatic absence: indeed so many absences. Where is Jesus' anger? Where is his hatred? Where is his condemnation, or self-justification? Pause to consider how amazing these absences are given the circumstances to hand. Jesus sits at table with a man he knows is going to attempt to murder him! Further, he knows the attempt will be successful! How would we react if we had an opportunity to talk face to face with a man we knew was plotting our death? What would we say to such a man? What streams of condemnatory invective would be outpoured! What torrents of hatred, fear, and self-righteous fury would we hurl across the table!

We are much exhorted by the words of Jesus: "That thou doest, do quickly." (KJV) Just one short sentence: devoid of anger, devoid of hatred, devoid of self-justification and devoid of condemnation of the intended murderer. Exhortational absences all! Truly Jesus passes judgment on no man (8:15), yet man does not escape judgment. All men are condemned by their own actions, just as the son of perdition is here. And we should be clear: this method of judgment – directly from the actions of the guilty – is not new: it has been this way from the beginning. The precedental murderer, Cain, is not condemned by God; he is condemned by the blood on the ground:

> The LORD said, "What have you done? Listen! Your brother's blood cries out to me from the ground." (Genesis 4:10)

Council for the prosecution, in both Cain's case and ours, comes from our own hand: it is solely ours to direct, fuel and execute. The Lord Jesus does not and will not speak against us: indeed he has already acted, and continues to act, as our best possible defense. The same is true here in John 13, as the record clearly bears out.

Day 4 Exhortation: The Mark of Blood

Judas' Mark of Blood: Departure "Out Into the Night"

Verse 30 details the actions to which Judas has been provoked. We are given two details:

a) "...he [Judas] went out..."

The Last Supper evening is Passover night (which precedes the feast day: the Jewish night always preceding the day). The command God gave to the children of Israel to save their lives at Passover was: "Not one of you shall go out the door of his house until morning" (Exodus 12:22). Judas departs from the house into the streets, and thereby secures his own destruction.[3]

b) "...and it was night."

The reader is already aware the Last Supper is taking place in the evening, the description of physical darkness is unnecessary. John, as always, is drawing a spiritual parallel to the physical conditions (the contrast between light and darkness is a major issue throughout the gospel of John, as we have seen). Jesus says:

"I am the light of the world. Whoever follows me will never walk in darkness, but will have the light of life." (8:12)

---

[3] As an aside, one might counter this point is invalid because Jesus and all the other disciples also leave the house that night, to go to the Garden of Gethsemane. This seemingly indicts them all of transgressing Passover: including the Lord himself! Yet this conclusion is erroneous: it misses the parallel between the physical world in Exodus 12 and the spiritual world in John 13. What is established on the physical plane in Egypt is fulfilled in the spiritual plane in the covenant of Christ. In Egypt there was a physical lamb without blemish; in John there is a spiritually blameless Lamb. In Egypt there was a physical body and blood meal; at the Last Supper there is the spiritual body and blood of the Lamb: bread and wine. In Old Testament days there was a physical house in which fellowship is shared; here in the New Testament we have a spiritual house of fellowship, defined as the company of the Lord Jesus, (Hebrews 3:4-6). This is the house Judas forsakes on Passover night. He has forsaken the fellowship of the Lord Jesus Christ, with malice aforethought, and walks out into the streets, where the Angel of Passover awaits him.

Day 4 Exhortation: The Mark of Blood

Against this backdrop Judas departs from his Master. The reason we study Judas at all is to gain exhortation for ourselves. As we said with Absalom (Exhortation 2) it is not our place, nor should it be our desire, to heap condemnation upon Judas, one whom Jesus also desired to save. Evil characters appear throughout the Bible for our education and edification. But they do not appear for us to condemn them from the comfort of our armchairs, all the while mentally fixing a gulf between ourselves and the character who has sinned. We are to despise and desist from their actions – and genuinely fear the consequences such actions inevitably engender. But we are not to disconnect from them: rather the reverse is true. Only by constant reminder of the striking similarities between our behavior and all the unsightly contents of the human heart the Bible shows us are we enabled to approach the Master in humility to obtain that new heart of which David spoke (Psalm 51). Furthermore it is completely insufficient for us to acknowledge only those 'popular' faults that society condones: stubbornness, a short-temper, recklessness and the like. We must also necessarily confess possession of those types of behavior from which we would be tempted to recoil and deny: Cain's jealousy and murderous hatred; Amnon's twisted sexual lust; Absalom's vanity and insatiable greed for power; the Pharisees' unyielding pride and blindness; and even Judas Iscariot's cowardly and murderous betrayal of the one who loved him. A heinous catalogue, and yet one with which every human heart who would find salvation must concede intimate association. In the light of these thoughts we are qualified to consider Judas Iscariot at the Last Supper. He has basked in the Light of the world, yet being convinced of, and convicted by, his own mind, he departs into the darkness. And for Judas, sadly, how dark that darkness is to prove.

Jesus' Mark of Blood: Washing the Disciple's Feet

As we read of Judas' departure from the upper room, perhaps we should allow him to disappear from this text also. We turn our attention to the actions of the Lord Jesus Christ, to learn what 'marks of blood' sharing communion provoked him to perform.

Day 4 Exhortation: The Mark of Blood

> Jesus knew that the Father had put all things under his power, and that he had come from God and was returning to God; so he got up from the meal, took off his outer clothing, and wrapped a towel around his waist. After that, he poured water into a basin and began to wash his disciples' feet, drying them with the towel that was wrapped around him. (13:3-5)

What is the significance of this particular "Mark of Blood?" Ostensibly it demonstrates both his love for his disciples and teaches them that he who would be greatest must be servant of all. This is a profound spiritual truth, which, as ever, is the complete antithesis of the thinking of human society. In society the greatest is recognized as he that serves *least*, and for whom the most service is performed by others. Jesus shows that the reverse is true in his community: the greatest will be recognized as the one performing the most service for his fellows, and who is tended the least.

We should be aware of the depth of this truth. At the simpler level, we might be tempted to think this is saying that one becomes the greatest by performing service *temporarily*, e.g. in this age, after which one is exalted to the level of 'greatness' later, in Christ's kingdom. This seems to be implied from Matthew's account:

> "The greatest among you will be your servant. For whoever exalts himself will be humbled, and whoever humbles himself will be exalted." (Matthew 23:11-12)

Yet at the deeper level, our understanding can do better. Mark's gospel explains that one does not humble oneself in service for the purpose of being made greater in the future, but rather the state of humility *is* greater: that one becomes the greatest *during* the acts of service to one's brethren, and should seek no augmentation beyond that point. Nor is this contradictory to Matthew's teaching: it explains the service is itself the exaltation we should seek.

Day 4 Exhortation: The Mark of Blood

Jesus called them together and said, "You know that those who are regarded as rulers of the Gentiles lord it over them, and their high officials exercise authority over them. Not so with you. Instead, whoever wants to become great among you must be your servant, and whoever wants to be first must be slave of all. For even the Son of Man did not come to be served, but to serve, and to give his life as a ransom for many." (Mark 10:42-45)

This then truly is the state of rulership defined by the example of the life of Jesus Christ in this mark of blood made with the communion meal. He serves his cherished spiritual family.

<u>Jesus' Mark of Blood: Laid Aside His Clothing</u>

Additionally, a puzzling detail: Jesus first laid aside his clothing in order to wash their feet. Why did he do this? Was it merely to avoid getting his clothing wet? Presumably such a trivial detail would not have found its way into the gospel record. What then was the purpose of his disrobing? These thoughts occur.

Firstly, in the human world, both in the contemporary culture of Jesus and today, clothes form status symbols of one's position in society. In every culture, Western or Eastern, military or civilian, adult or youthful, social standing amongst one's peers is partly determined as a function of the style, format or expense of dress one wears. In military organizations rank and seniority are wholly determined by the insignia borne on each individual's clothing. The civilian world is similar, if not so rigidly demarcated. An important businessman is recognized by his expensive suit and tie, likewise a teenager is often better socially placed by adornments of the favored clothing brand names of the day. An unclothed man, either in that day or this, has no position in society: he is beneath everyone as an object of embarrassment, ridicule and contempt. As Jesus removes his clothes, and lays them deliberately to one side, he is consciously divesting himself of all status symbols the world recognizes. The act is reminiscent

Day 4 Exhortation: The Mark of Blood

of his disassociation with the material world and his simple, yet total, humility.

Secondly, it may well be that Jesus is enacting the living parable of the 'Divine Soldier' spoken of in Isaiah's prophecy (Isaiah 59): the Redeemer who will comes to Zion 'like a pent-up flood that the Lord drives along.' This prophecy is laced with striking pictorial images: he wears a helmet of salvation and a breastplate of righteousness. Paul faithfully recapitulates these elements in his explanation of discipleship to the churches at Ephesus and Thessalonica (Ephesians 6:13-18; 1 Thessalonians 5:8-9). What is instructive, in the context of Jesus' acts at the last supper, is the garments:

> he put on the garments of vengeance and wrapped himself in zeal as in a cloak. (Isaiah 59:17)

The garments were garments of vengeance, the cloak was a cloak of zeal. These are certainly garments that Jesus had every right to wear, and indeed it was with zeal and righteous vengeance that he clothed himself as he drove the moneylenders out of the temple courts (Matthew 21:12-13). And perhaps it is entirely in keeping with this theme that Jesus lays aside his garments in the upper room. He is explaining to his disciples that the time of zeal and vengeance is not now. The Son of Almighty God, who has twelve legions of angels and more at his instant bidding (Matthew 26:53), is laying down his right of zeal and vengeance, (the garments) so that the perfect will of the Father might be realized.

And there is still more to this simple act. Humans are creatures easily stimulated by visual images, quite possibly Jesus exploits this faculty at the Last Supper. The disciples see Jesus devoid of his clothing at the Last Supper, and they will also see him this way on the cross, which Jesus knows. Jesus may therefore be deliberately showing them a cameo precursor to the crucifixion and for a very good reason. On this occasion the disciples realize he has removed his clothing *of his own free will*, in order to wash them, his loved ones, and make them clean. The clever part is that when the disciples see Christ stripped of his clothing on the cross, this memory should be called to mind; with the association that Christ had removed his clothing *of his own free will*. Perhaps Jesus is trying to teach them that when they see him hanging naked on the cross they should not be misled into thinking Judas Iscariot, or the Sanhedrin, or the Roman soldiers, have brought this about. No-one could overpower the Son of God! This was the man who had the Spirit of the Living God without measure and twelve legions of angels and more at his immediate disposal! (3:34, Matthew 26:53) At the Last Supper Christ lays his clothing aside that he might wash their feet and make them clean. The following day stands as the superseding reiteration. Christ will lay all aside, not just his clothing, but even his very life, and in the same way: of his own free will. The reason is also the same in both cases: to wash the ones he loved and make them clean. This is the full extent of Jesus' love towards us (13:1, NIV). How privileged we are both to read the record of it in scripture and live the very real benefits of it together as a family in Christ! This is our example, and our provocation, to achieve true spiritual greatness: through humility and service to our brothers and sisters.

Jesus' Mark of Blood: A Command to Love

Judas' departure is likely to have engendered a dramatic change in Jesus' mood that evening. Jesus has been sharing the evening with a man he knows is plotting to betray and kill him and eleven others who have no concept either of this evil plan, or of the greater good the inevitable outworking will realize. This knowledge weighs heavily upon the mind of the Lord, troubling his spirit (13:21). Thus when Judas leaves the upper room (13:30), we predict the atmosphere, at least from Jesus' perspective, changes considerably. His troubled spirit is probably eased a little. Perhaps, with the betrayer gone, he is able to draw a little closer to the faithful ones who have forsaken everything to gain the prize of his company, even though they do not yet realize the magnitude of what they hold or witness. At this point Jesus chooses to share these words with them:

Day 4 Exhortation: The Mark of Blood

"A new command I give you: Love one another. As I have loved you, so you must love one another. By this all men will know that you are my disciples, if you love one another." (13:34-35)

A command to love: a command based on the motivations and intents of the heart beyond even the actions to which one is called. As is so often the case, Jesus demonstrates his acts of service first, in washing their feet, and then imparts the command to his disciples to do likewise. He does not command service he has not first performed himself. Notice the importance such loving acts form: a definition of those who are truly Christ's followers! How instructive that is to us today! The definition of who is, and who is not, a true follower of Christ has formed the central issue of discussions, debates, divisions, arguments, murders and wars for centuries (as if it were ever the human prerogative to determine who was acceptable before God and who was not!) Yet the definition of Christ's true followers, spoken in an upper room many years before to an audience of just eleven souls, is plainly recorded in every Bible: those who show the love of Christ to each other.

The Mark of Blood: Conclusions

This definition answers the problematic question with which we began, as to why the bread and wine are absent from John's record of the Last Supper. John's gospel does not in any way contradict the accounts of Matthew, Mark and Luke, who focus on the bread and wine as the components of salvation in the new covenant. Rather, as ever, John invites us a step closer in our understanding. He invites our realization of salvation arising *beyond* the meal of bread and wine, from the acts of love we are provoked to perform through sharing that meal together. John uses the model of Passover to achieve this, with bread and wine communion reflecting the Passover meal, and the acts of love within our household reflecting the marks of blood made on our house for God to see.

Day 4 Exhortation: The Mark of Blood

These final two verses (13:34-35) also define beyond doubt what those 'marks' should be. Acts of kindness towards our fellow disciples: a phone call to one we haven't seen in a little while, a card to those who celebrate, a visit to those in mental or physical discomfort, help in Bible study to reinforce the faith of another. Superior to these are the gift of our prayers, our company and our time – for these are the most valuable things we have to give – towards those whom we love, whom Christ has taught us how to love. What provokes us to perform these acts? As with the Passover model, the blood used to make the marks on the house must come from the Passover lamb shared in the meal.

John's gospel's teaching also emphasizes the relevance of the bread and wine to the week *following* it, not just the week that went before. How easily we fall into the trap of regarding bread and wine as solely 'backward-looking' elements, washing away the sins of the week that has passed! The communion meal certainly does wash away those sins, (when taken with an appropriately penitent heart), and this is essential to recognize. But John's account of the Last Supper extends our appreciation to observe the 'forward-looking' aspects of the memorials by focusing on the events beyond the meal, the actions initiated by communion. Powerfully we are reminded that sharing bread and wine together on Sunday is an intense provocation to acts of love in the week that *follows*, even more than it cleans us from our sins of the week past.

Thus as we turn to bread and wine John encourages us to design loving actions for the coming week (from our experience of the love of Christ in giving his life for us), as well as generating the appropriate spirit of gratitude in remembrance of the past week's sins that have been forgiven. These future acts constitute the Marks of Blood we make on our house for God to see, which God *will* see. And in our endeavors to perform them, may God bless us all.

DAY 5
John 14:1-19:42

EXPOSITION:
Waters Beneath

"Hereafter I will not talk much with you: for the prince of this world cometh, and hath nothing in me... Arise, let us go hence." (14:30-31, KJV)

Day 5. This is the day that relates to the populace beneath the 'waters above' in the natural creation: the contrasting counterpart to Day 2.

Basic premise:
In the natural creation Day 5 focused on the area below Day 2's "waters above" and their population, including "tanniyn": the leviathan. In Day 2 John's gospel reflected the drawing up from the dead human state towards the life giving waters above. By contrast in Day 5 we anticipate seeing the dead elements of the waters that were left beneath, and all that populate them.

Day 5 Exposition: Waters Beneath

5.1 *The Serpent Stirs: Division*

A gruesome portion of the gospel is this! A cursory appraisal confirms it contains the more malign aspects of Jesus' ministry. He speaks explicitly of having to "lay down his life" (15:13); and we also encounter frequent use of the word 'hatred,' in the world's rejection of their Messiah. Two thirds of the occurrences of the word 'hatred' in John are here in this section we have defined as Day 5. No longer are the world portrayed as leaderless sheep, (although they still are); rather here in Day 5 the darker, though equally appropriate, picture is used of the world as enlightened and vitriolic rejecters of the gentle Son of Man. Jesus warns his disciples they will face persecution (15:20), even to the extreme of a time "when anyone who kills you will think he is offering a service to God" (16:2). The contents of this section of John's gospel are more negative than any preceding or following.

One of the principal elements of these chapters in John is the growing separation between Jesus and his disciples. They are unable to "go where he is going" in both the physical sense, to the cross, or the spiritual sense in being able to truly grasp what he is telling them. Read John 14, and see the evidence from the discourse.

> Thomas: "Lord, we don't know where you are going, so how can we know the way?" (v 5)
> Philip: "Lord, show us the Father and that will be enough for us." (v 8)
> Judas: "But, Lord, why do you intend to show yourself to us and not to the world?" (v 22)

The lack of understanding is broad. Take for example the case of Philip:

> Philip said to him, "Lord, show us the Father, and it is sufficient for us." Jesus said to him, "Have I been with you so long, and yet you have not known me, Philip?" (14:8-9, NKJV)

Day 5 Exposition: Waters Beneath

The question seems rhetorical and tinged with sadness. Philip has heard the earlier declaration of Jesus:

"I and my Father are one." (10:30)

More importantly he has seen the very actions of his Master that render this statement undeniable, yet he fails to connect the components spiritually, or even intellectually, to learn the truth. And Philip is not the sole offender: none of the disciples comprehended either the role of sacrifice, or the role of the King that their Master was to play until after he was risen from the tomb (c.f. 2:19-22, 12:16).

5.2 Lifted Up, Brought Low

John contrasts the confusion that Jesus' words causes here in Day 5 with the uplifting effect of his words in Day 2.

Day 2: And because of his words many more became believers. (4:41)
Day 5: Some of his disciples said to one another, "What does he mean…?" They kept asking, "What does he mean…? We don't understand what he is saying." (16:17-18)

Sadly, the beleaguered expressions of the disciples bear more relation to the darkness of the Pharisees (e.g. Table 4_1) than to the light of Christ. Their bewilderment testifies to the divide opening between Jesus and his followers. This divide is understandable, as is its emphasis at this stage in the gospel. Jesus is the source of life, as we have seen in Day 4, he does not belong with the 'things beneath.' As Day 5 focuses on the things beneath, we expect a rift therefore between the subject matter and the standpoint of the Lord. Nevertheless Jesus will temporarily be brought to the lowest point, of death, and he refers to this as his moment of being 'lifted up,' (as the crucified physically were), perhaps with intentional irony to communicate the juxtaposition of his death and his glory.

Day 5 Exposition: Waters Beneath

We have already seen the spiritual and intellectual separation between Jesus and his disciples, but Jesus also speaks of the necessary physical separation as he departs; first to the grave and then to his Father. Nevertheless such is the nature of the Lord Jesus that these comments contain no self-sympathy; rather they express the fullness of his Father's love in the actions he will shortly perform. Although he is being drawn above, his concern is only for those he leaves below:

> "Do not let your hearts be troubled. Trust in God; trust also in me... I will not leave you as orphans; I will come to you... Peace I leave with you; my peace I give you. I do not give to you as the world gives. Do not let your hearts be troubled and do not be afraid." (14:1, 18, 27)

Chapter 14's conclusion sees Jesus leave the upper room and cross the city of Jerusalem with his disciples. John 15-17 records the conversation and prayers as they traverse the city from the supper room to the Eastern city gate by the Temple. Throughout this walk we see both the widening expanse between Christ and his disciples and his comfort and love for those who cannot "follow him now."

> "My command is this: Love each other as I have loved you. Greater love has no one than this, that he lay down his life for his friends." (15:12-13)
>
> "I came from the Father and entered the world; now I am leaving the world and going back to the Father... I have told you these things, so that in me you may have peace. In this world you will have trouble. But take heart! I have overcome the world." (16:28, 33)
>
> "I will remain in the world no longer, but they are still in the world, and I am coming to you. Holy Father, protect them by the power of your name--the name you gave me--so that they may be one as we are one." (17:11)

Day 5 Exposition: Waters Beneath

Jesus is preparing his disciples for the time he will no longer be with them. His pioneering work is done, he is to depart. Herein is a small detail attractively comparative with Day 2 in John's spiritual creation. Day 2 records the completion of the preparatory work of John the Baptist, Day 5 records the perfection of the mortal Christ. Both John and Jesus speak of the result of their work using the same idea: the completeness of joy. These are the only times this phrase is used in John, and they are shown in Table 5_1.

The verses shown in Table 5_1 are parallel: in each case someone is coming to the fruition of their walk on God's path. The fruition of John's preaching is the appearance of Christ; the fruition of Christ's mortal ministry is his own crucifixion. This both ratifies a link between Days 2 and 5 and shows their opposite nature. The fullness of John's joy in Day 2 is the appearing *presence* of Jesus, the one who will rule all nations; whilst the fullness of Jesus' joy brings his temporary destruction and *removal* from the world of the living, leaving a Rulerless world behind.

Day 2: Waters Above	Day 5: Waters Beneath
John the Baptist completes his work: The Messiah appears	Jesus completes his work: The Messiah disappears
"The bride belongs to the bridegroom. The friend who attends the bridegroom waits and listens for him, and is full of joy when he hears the bridegroom's voice. **That joy is mine, and it is now complete.**" (3:29)	"I have told you this so that my joy may be in you and that **your joy may be complete.**" (15:11) "I am coming to you now, but I say these things while I am still in the world, so that they may have the **full measure of my joy** within them." (17:13)

Table 5_1: Comparison of the words of John the Baptist and Jesus on completion of their particular roles in the Father's plan.

Day 5 Exposition: Waters Beneath

<u>Those Drawn Above; Those Cast Beneath</u>

Chapter 18 sees Jesus leave Jerusalem, and cross the Kidron Valley to enter the Garden of Gethsemane on the lower western slopes of the Mount of Olives. Yet the tranquil picture of Christ with his faithful is shattered. The waters beneath contain leviathan. Judas Iscariot, into whom Satan has entered, arrives in the olive grove with an armed brigade and has Jesus arrested. One fascinating detail – exclusive to John's gospel – accompanies the arrest:

> When Jesus said, "I am he," they drew back and fell to the ground. (18:6)

This is a most puzzling verse at first appreciation, yet it fits beautifully into the creation pattern we are considering. Day 2 emphasizes the characters that are seeking those things above; and in that section we see that the presence of Jesus causes men to be physically uplifted: e.g. the drawing above of the nobleman's son (4:47-53); the raising up of the impotent man at Bethesda (5:8-9); and the resurrection of all (5:28-29). Day 5, by contrast, emphasizes the worldly characters of those who are 'at home' below. Thus here the presence of Jesus causes such men to fall down to the Earth (18:6). The Word of God is indeed a two-edged sword.

5.3 The Serpent Strengthens: Desertion and Denial

Illustration of the serpent's strengthening power comes in the denial of that one impassioned disciple whose earlier faithful declarations so well glorified his Lord: we speak of Simon Peter. Once able to walk on water, Peter sinks no further beneath the waves than this. In one of the saddest parts of scripture the simple cowardice that so besets us all creeps to the fore as Peter denies any association with, or even knowledge of, his Lord, Master, Savior and friend.

> "You are not one of his disciples, are you?" the girl at the door asked Peter. He replied, "I am not." It was cold, and the

servants and officials stood around a fire they had made to keep warm. Peter also was standing with them, warming himself... One of the high priest's servants, a relative of the man whose ear Peter had cut off, challenged him, "Didn't I see you with him in the olive grove?" Again Peter denied it, and at that moment a rooster began to crow. (John18:17-18, 26-27)

The crow of the rooster: a signature moment. The animal's cry marks Peter's stark realization of the totality of human nature's failure and, ironically, his own descent to the realm of beasts as he fails to reflect the image of the One who made him (c.f. Psalm 49:20). He has denied Jesus, the very man of whom hours earlier he swore he would never be ashamed. Without doubt this is the darkest moment in Peter's spiritual life; and how typical of John's gospel that the spiritual world is shown standing opposed to the natural, for in the natural world the rooster marks the dawn, the promise of the return of light in a new day, and not the darkest hour. Yet perhaps this moment does indeed form a spiritual dawn for Peter, born from the waters of total humiliation (a thought on which we shall expand in the exhortation). But for now we follow the narrative. Leviathan's ugly head has reared from the text to claim his victims: Judas Iscariot has lost faith and Peter, brave Peter, has lost heart.

And worse is to come.

5.4 *Worship of the Beast*

The worse that comes is the trial, the scourging and the death of Jesus by crucifixion. Read John 19. A chilling prelude is the "gifts" Jesus is brought prior to crucifixion. Jesus was brought gifts at his birth and this chapter reveals he is brought gifts at the end of his life also (Table 5_2).

In each case there are three gifts; and in each case the symbolism seems to be the same: one gift for a King (gold/crown) one for the high Priest (incense/purple robe) and one for a sacrifice (myrrh/cross). But the spirit in which they are offered contrasts sharply. Whereas the gifts presented at Jesus'

Day 5 Exposition: Waters Beneath

birth are offered in a humble spirit of praise to worship the newborn King, those presented by the soldiers in John 19 are "given" in ridicule and hatred.

Gift at Birth From Wise Men	Gift at Death from Soldiers	Likely Symbol Of Gift
Gold	Crown of Thorns	Jesus as King
Frankincense	Purple Robe	Jesus as High Priest
Myrrh	Cross	Jesus as Sacrifice

Table 5_2: Gifts for the Messiah: Those presented in praising celebration at his birth (Matthew 2), and those presented in mocking derision at his death (19:1-18).

Consider: gold is a welcome entreaty to a King (e.g. 1 Kings 10:14), incense is the necessary and often exclusive tool of the priest (Exodus 30:37), and myrrh, when mixed with wine, acts as an analgesic for the dying (observe that Jesus is offered some upon the cross, Mark 15:23). These presents offered at Messiah's birth by Eastern nobles are offered in a humble spirit of praise to worship the newborn King. The soldier's offerings could not be more different. The thorny crown will cut the head of the wearer as it is pressed into place. The robe is given to mock his high status, for whilst he wears it he is beaten in the face. The cross not only symbolizes his death, but in crueler spirit also directly realizes it. John is the only gospel writer to record that Jesus carried his cross (19:17). The synoptic records suggest it was carried by the Cyrenian Simon (Matthew 27:32, Mark 15:21, Luke 23:26). Doubtless both are true, but John emphasizes that the cross was 'given' to Jesus.

The theme of Day 5 is maintained in these gifts. The gifts are given in a worldly spirit of antichrist: a spirit of hatred and rejection of the one from above. The spirit of man towards Jesus Christ has utterly changed, from reverence to revulsion. Man has seen the miracles, has been healed by the spirit, has eaten his fill of the bread from heaven, and now turns with violence on the

Day 5 Exposition: Waters Beneath

gentle Son of Man and kills the very one from whom all these good things were distributed. What a chilling insight this proves into the nature of every human soul! But what has gone wrong? How can the Savior who was once so loved now be so reviled, particularly after all the love that he has shown? Day 1 of John's Creation illuminates the matter, (as was always its purpose):

> "This is the verdict: Light has come into the world, but men loved darkness instead of light because their deeds were evil." (3:19)

Ultimately, "truth will out": true colors will always be seen. The heart of man loves darkness and not light. Thus the world is united – Jew and Roman stand together – united in the hatred of Jesus Christ. This is an ugly truth, and some might find the phrasing offensive, but its truth must be acknowledged, for that same spirit lurks within the heart of every human soul. The father of mankind is not The Father, but the devil; so much is revealed at Praetorium where the King of peace was brought before them.

> It was the day of Preparation of Passover Week, about the sixth hour. "Here is your king," Pilate said to the Jews. But they shouted, "Take him away! Take him away! Crucify him!" "Shall I crucify your king?" Pilate asked. "We have no king but Caesar," the chief priests answered. (19:14-15)

Their King is Caesar: by their own declaration. Their King is Rome: for that is Caesar's realm. Their King is the Beast: and they fall to worship him. This last statement is not made for the impact of anaphoric rhetoric, rather it explicitly, pre-emptively, fulfils prophecy concerning leviathan. Prophecy declares the Beast/Serpent as the one who wars against the Seed of the Woman: the man-child and the characteristic by which he will be identified is that all the earth will worship him.

> A great and wondrous sign appeared in heaven: a woman clothed with the sun... Then another sign appeared in

Day 5 Exposition: Waters Beneath

heaven: an enormous red dragon... The dragon stood in front of the woman who was about to give birth, so that he might devour her child the moment it was born. She gave birth to a son, a male child, who will rule all the nations with an iron scepter... And there was war in heaven... The great dragon was hurled down--that ancient serpent called the devil, or Satan, who leads the whole world astray. (Revelation 12:1-9)

Men worshipped the dragon because he had given authority to the beast, and they also worshipped the beast and asked, "Who is like the beast? Who can make war against him?"... He was given power to make war against the saints and to conquer them. And he was given authority over every tribe people, language and nation. All inhabitants of the earth will worship the beast... (Revelation 13:4-8)

Exposition of Revelation is not our concern here, (nor do we even ascribe the primary fulfillment of these apocalyptic words to the crucifixion), but we cannot ignore the primary, chilling observation that "all the inhabitants of the earth" consciously ally themselves in war against Christ. Jew and Gentile, soldier and civilian, proletarian and Pharisee unite to cry: "Away with him! Crucify him!" and thus they worship the beast. They do this for the simple, irresistible reason that it is their nature. Ultimately their father was not The Father, and thus they could never know the Son, any more than the Ethiopian could change his skin, or the leopard his spots. This judgment is revealed from spiritual creation's Day 4:

"You belong to your father, the devil, and you want to carry out your father's desire. He was a murderer from the beginning, not holding to the truth, for there is no truth in him." (8:44)

Their father was the devil, the murderer from the beginning. Thus they, as sons of Cain, unite to free their brother, Barabbas; and reject the Prince of Peace, fulfilling the genetic inheritance of their father in committing a murder of their own. And with that rejection the Seed of the Woman, the man-child, is led away to be crucified.

5.5 The Serpent Strikes: Death

Let us take the time to understand the nature of crucifixion as an execution measure. This is not so we might revel in the macabre, but rather that we should have a better understanding of the actions of Jesus Christ in demonstrating his love for us, God's love, in his death in the ugly and ignominious manner of the cross.

> Then Pilate took Jesus and had him flogged. (19:1)

This small verse, easily overlooked, refers to the Roman practice of beating a condemned prisoner with a flagellum: a multi-thread whip of leather thongs with pieces of lead, or sometimes bone, attached. The lead balls penetrated the skin and tore at the subcutaneous tissue beneath, causing considerable blood loss. The beating continued until the prisoner collapsed (some prisoners died of the flogging before reaching the cross) and it is sensible to consider this flogging as a genuine contribution to the fatality of the event. [1] The two verses immediately following, which speak of the crown of thorns and the facial beating, also imply that Jesus was tortured more than the average prisoner.

> Carrying his own cross, he went out to the place of the Skull (which in Aramaic is called Golgotha). (19:17)

The prisoner was then compelled to carry the patibulum, (the cross bar of the crucifix), to the place of execution: the stipes, the vertical pole, was already mounted at the execution site. This is an

---

[1] Bucher R. P., "Crucifixion in the Ancient World," http://www.ultranet.com/~tlclcms/crucify.htm, accessed Sept 2001

Day 5 Exposition: Waters Beneath

especially hard task because a single beam is more difficult to carry than a crucifix. A cross has a convenient junction against which a shoulder can be braced (many artists depict Jesus' efforts in this way, quite probably erroneously).

> Here they crucified him, and with him two others--one on each side and Jesus in the middle. (19:18)

Upon arrival the prisoner was nailed to the patibulum he had carried, with the nail driven between the ulna and the radius at the wrist, and the patibulum attached to the stipes, forming the cross.

A small sign, the titulus, stated the victim's crime and was carried in the procession to the execution site where it was nailed to the top of the cross. Since Pilate can find no crime of which to convict Jesus, the titulus proclaims: JESUS OF NAZARETH, THE KING OF THE JEWS (19:19). Ironically the titulus performs its function well: it declares in three languages a most heinous crime: the innocent King of the Jews has been taken by wicked hands and crucified. In this case the one beneath the titulus is the crime's victim, not its perpetrator; nevertheless the crime that the occupied crucifix declares is very real indeed.

The social stigma associated with execution by crucifixion is also relevant and instructive. Execution by 'hanging on a tree' was accursed under the Mosaic Law (Deuteronomy 21:22-23). Therefore Christ is one of the shamefully accursed – for our sakes – as the scriptural writers clarify:

> Christ redeemed us from the curse of the law by becoming a curse for us, for it is written: "Cursed is everyone who is hung on a tree." (Galatians 3:13, quoting Deuteronomy 21:23)

> Jesus the author and finisher of our faith; who for the joy that was set before him endured the cross, despising the shame, and is set down at the right hand of the throne of God. (Hebrews 12:2)

Day 5 Exposition: Waters Beneath

Asphyxiation was the commonest single cause of death by crucifixion: the difficulty of breathing from a crucified position is well documented if not commonly appreciated. Exhalation is inhibited by the high, fixed position of the arms from which the body hangs; and with the blood loss from the beating and the nails' punctures the prisoner slowly suffocates under the weight of his own body. Some crosses were constructed with a small shelf from which the feet could push upwards to help the victim exhale. Far from being a kindness this prolonged the fatal result and therefore the suffering. By contrast at other times the soldiers broke both of the victim's legs to prevent them from pushing upwards to exhale and thus greatly speed death (although this is also impossible to argue as a kindness).

> When he had received the drink, Jesus said, "It is finished." With that, he bowed his head and gave up his spirit. (19:30)

The Aramaic text of John quotes Jesus as saying: "It is fulfilled" (19:30, Lamsa translation). This may have more meaning, especially in the light of the other gospels (e.g. Mark 15:34) revealing that Jesus shouted the opening line of Psalm 22: "My God, My God, why have you forsaken me?" – not because Jesus suspected God had forsaken him, as the psalmist also concludes, but as both a preaching mechanism to and indictment of the Jews around him, who knew their psalms, to make them see that they were fulfilling this prophetic psalm in their every action right before their own eyes! The phrase "It is fulfilled" makes perfect sense as Jesus' final reference to the psalm (and indeed other scriptures, such as Isaiah 53,) which were being fulfilled for everyone to see (if only they *could* see).

At last then: death. Real death for the Lord Jesus Christ: an extinction of all sentient existence upon Calvary's cross. The serpent has bruised the heel of the man-child. Ironically it is in this, the serpent's strongest day that he himself is mortally wounded, even destroyed. Yet for now we stand at the foot of the cross and regard the Empty Throne, for Jesus has been

Day 5 Exposition: Waters Beneath

removed from the world, and the serpent stands in the fullest extent of his might.

> Because the Jews did not want the bodies left on the crosses during the Sabbath, they asked Pilate to have the legs broken and the bodies taken down. (19:31)

We have commented before on the spiritual emptiness of the Jewish feasts (Section 3.1), but this stipulation forms a particularly crass attempt to demonstrate piety. God's people, the Jews, have crucified the innocent Messiah and now they wish to demonstrate their purity and righteousness by insisting the corpse they themselves ordered killed (the Passover Lamb indeed) be removed from the cross so that the holiness of the Passover Sabbath (*their* Passover: see Table 3_1) should not be befouled. This, surely, is mankind's lowest hour and yet, precisely for that reason, the revelation of the extent of God's grace.

5.6 Son of Man: Brokenhearted

> But when they came to Jesus and found that he was already dead, they did not break his legs. Instead, one of the soldiers pierced Jesus' side with a spear, bringing a sudden flow of blood and water. (19:33-34)

This detail is interesting, because a corpse under normal circumstances does not bleed. Those trained in the medical sciences (this author not included) conclude that the Lord had suffered a heart rupture some hours previous to the crucifixion: the idea being that the blood seeps through the rupture into the outer sac around the heart (pericardium) where it separates and which the soldier's spear pierced. Additional symptoms of heart rupture include blood seeping through the sweat glands, a condition known as chromidrosis, to which Luke may be referring (Luke 22:44). [2] Medical sources further indicate that

---

[2] This phrase "his sweat was like drops of blood" in Luke is often taken to mean the beads of sweat were large in size, which seems a poor interpretation since the size of sweat droplets and blood droplets are always very similar. We postulate here that Luke is referring to the *color* of the sweat which, normally

Day 5 Exposition: *Waters Beneath*

heart rupture can be induced by severe emotional trauma,[3] which is interesting because the Lord clearly did suffer severe emotional trauma in the garden:

> "My soul is overwhelmed with sorrow to the point of death" (Mark 14:34)

Jesus was suffering badly, for these comments cannot be considered as the melodramatic posturing they might have been from anybody else. Nor should the effects of this suffering be considered limited to the emotional and psychological: the most severe cases of emotional and psychological trauma invariably have consequences on the physical body. We can believe that at this point in Gethsemane the emotional suffering of Christ was sufficient that his heart was physically ruptured.

The medical details are unimportant in themselves. But understanding the causes of the Lord's death are important in other ways, especially if, as it seems, he died quite literally of a broken heart. This is relevant to understand the nature of the Son of Man, because it suggests the cause of his death was not purely physical, but partly *emotional*, bizarre though that may sound. We can speak of the one who 'bore our sins' so glibly. Yet thoughtful meditation on the texts we are so privileged to explore suggests shouldering the sins of all humanity, and truly comprehending the divorce those sins cause from the Father, could break the very heart of a righteous man.

Compare these insightful words of David, the man after God's own heart, with the reality of Gethsemane:

> "You know how I am scorned, disgraced and shamed; all my enemies are before you. **Scorn has broken my heart** and has

---

colorless and dissimilar to blood, in this case was red (as blood) due to the condition of chromidrosis.
[3] Helgason C. A., Wolf P. A., http://www.americanheart.org/Scientific/statements/1997/079706.html, American Heart Association scientific statement, accessed Sept 2001

left me helpless; I looked for sympathy, but there was none, for comforters, but I found none." (Psalm 69:19-20)

And being in an agony [Jesus] prayed more earnestly: and his sweat was as it were great drops of blood falling down to the ground. (Luke 22:44)

Then he returned to his disciples and found them sleeping. "Simon," he said to Peter, "are you asleep? Could you not keep watch for one hour?" (Mark 14:37)

How interesting that David speaks explicitly of a broken heart! Those who leap to assume this statement merely prophetic metaphor may do so too quickly. Truly in Gethsemane Christ endures the (literally) heart-breaking agony of bearing the sins of man, being divorced from fellowship with the Loving Father and finding no-one to sympathize with him, comfort him, or even understand what was happening. Exactly what this 'agony' entailed, in terms of the thoughts that were going through the mind of Jesus, perhaps we can never fully understand. We repair to metaphor, dramatic in expression though feeble in understanding, and speak of 'fighting the beast' and 'bearing our sins,' not to enhance this text through striking pictorial associations, but simply because we fail to be able to offer any better understanding. Maybe we will never really know what the weight of that pain really means, but it will hopefully humble and thus doubtless benefit, each of us to ingest this to our inner core.

5.7 Son of God: Victorious

A signature characteristic of the fifth day of the creation sequence in Genesis is that, unlike the other two days of the latter cycle, there is no ruler. The sun, moon and stars of Day 4 are set to rule over times and seasons (Genesis 1:17-18). Likewise in Day 6 Adam is given dominion over all creatures of Day 6 – and of Day 5 (Genesis 1:28). Day 5 alone stands bereft of a leader, at least before Day 6 arrives. How well this section of John's gospel reflects that scenario! The disciples are deprived of their leader, he hangs dead on the cross; and they are (seemingly) confined to

Day 5 Exposition: Waters Beneath

a fate of wandering the Earth as directionless as the birds of the air and the fish of the sea.

Yet despite the grimness of this bleak day, the darkest of days, the greatest victory of all resides within it. Such is the nature of scriptural truths that this greatest victory is inseparable from the heaviest moment of despair: the death of the Messiah. God's Son has allowed himself to be lowered himself into the waters of death. He dies; and yet, within his death, life for all men can be found.

Once again John compellingly testifies the spiritual creation is superlative over the natural. Adam's death by virtue of his sin, instigated by the serpent's guile, resulted in nothing other than the loss of human life. But Christ's death, here in Day 5 of the spiritual creation, contains the hope of life for every man, and crushes the head of the serpent. In his death he destroyed the devil (Hebrews 2:14) and in the provision of his blood, he provided a road, a road to atonement, for all men to grasp salvation (Romans 5:8-10). He who dies a natural death, as Adam, is dead; and his thoughts are extinguished (Ecclesiastes 9:5-6). But he who dies a spiritual death, in Christ, begins a pathway to life eternal in that death (Romans 6:1-11).

5.8 Conclusions from Day 5

John highlights the separation (expanse) between 'things above' and 'things below' in the growing distance between Christ and his disciples. They cannot cope with the accelerated pace of Jesus' spiritual teaching, nor comprehend he is really about to die. This separation culminates in the desertion of Jesus by all of the twelve. Explicit failures are seen in the betrayal by Peter, and, far worse for it is never recanted, the betrayal by Judas Iscariot.

Centrally Day 5 contains the crucifixion of Jesus Christ, the Seed of the Woman promised in Eden, via his agony in the Garden and actual death at Calvary. Leviathan, the Prince of this World secures his temporary victory over the Prince of Peace; the latter hangs dead – and cursed – upon the cross. Yet the fulfillment of Eden's covenant is completed in full, the Seed

Day 5 Exposition: Waters Beneath

bruises the head of the serpent, as the power of death is itself destroyed.

Finally, we see again the excellence of the spiritual creation over the natural. Death in the natural creation is merely death. But in the spiritual creation we find life eternal – explicitly in death! This life is drawn from the blood flowing from the Seed of the Woman on the cross. This blood forms the wine first asked for in Cana, and the essence of the new covenant between God and His people. Jesus succeeds in becoming the doorway to the House of the Living God, where that life might be found, and found abundantly.

Day 5 Exhortation: Stripped of All

EXHORTATION 5: *Psalm 51, John 18*
Stripped of All

A proverb, attributed to Confucius, reads:

"By three methods we may learn wisdom: by reflection, which is the noblest; by imitation, which is the easiest; and by experience, which is the bitterest."

These are not divinely inspired words and may simply be wrong: indeed the second method is wrong, for one cannot learn wisdom by imitation. One may mimic faithfully every action of a wise man but, because wisdom primarily grows from the motivations and understanding of the heart and mind of man than from his external actions, true wisdom is never gained from simply imitating those actions. Nevertheless the former and latter methods are observations supportable by scripture and therefore we take confidence in their accuracy. There is indeed genuine nobility in man learning wisdom from gentle meditation, although sadly it is a practice almost universally ignored. Worse than this, modern Christian society often derides the practice under the derogatory label of 'armchair theology.' A man who sits alone with an open Bible and attempts to deduce truth by reading with silent meditation and prayer is considered somehow not living a valid Christianity; and not until he is tearing madly across the countryside attempting to gain converts at every corner is he perceived as faithfully following God's will. Make no mistake: this thinking is in error. That the beliefs we hold should provoke us into action is beyond question: James demonstrates the veracity 'faith without works is dead' in eloquent and compelling fashion (James 1:22-2:26). And preaching the word for the salvation of others being a principal duty is also without contradiction. But scripture patiently explains the works themselves are of no value except they stem from a true and well-discerned faith. Establishing that faith in truth, and with discernment, is a task (and a privilege) requiring dedicated commitment in thought and prayer. We know faith without works is dead. But works without faith being equally dead is perhaps less commonly appreciated, yet still equally valid from scripture. Jesus says, when speaking of the time of his return:

> "Not everyone who says to me, 'Lord, Lord,' will enter the kingdom of heaven, but only he who does the will of my Father who is in heaven. Many will say to me on that day, 'Lord, Lord, did we not prophesy in your name, and in your name drive out demons and perform many miracles?' Then I will tell them plainly, 'I never knew you. Away from me, you evildoers!' " (Matthew 7:21-23)

Jesus does not dispute that the 'miracles' (or 'wonderful works,' KJV) have been performed – and performed in his name. Despite this, these people have not known Jesus, so he turns them away from the Wedding Supper of the Lamb. Furthermore Jesus labels the very actions (miracles) they have performed 'evil'! (or 'iniquity,' KJV) 'Wonderful' works alone will not please the Master, but only those which emerge from a true and sincere faith (Hebrews 11:6). There is a danger to extol the works of faith, especially the high profile ones, above the value of the faith

Day 5 Exhortation: *Stripped of All*

itself. Scripture insists that both faith and works are essential and priceless components of the Life of Christ to which we are called.

Wisdom from Reflection: Psalm 119

In Psalm 119 we find one of the few examples of one who has learned wisdom from reflection. The author of this psalm is not certainly known, nevertheless a similar attitude is found in the psalms of David (e.g. Psalm 63:6). The psalmist powerfully testifies how he feels the Hand of God supporting him in his life and – and this may be the surprising part – how he came to perceive that Hand by studying the written works of the Law.

> MEM
> "Oh, how I love your law! It is my meditation all the day.
> You, through your commandments, make me wiser than my enemies; for they are ever with me.
> I have more understanding than all my teachers, for your testimonies are my meditation.
> I understand more than the ancients, because I keep your precepts.
> I have restrained my feet from every evil way, that I may keep your word.
> I have not departed from your judgments, for you yourself have taught me.
> How sweet are your words to my taste, sweeter than honey to my mouth!
> Through your precepts I get understanding; therefore I hate every false way.
>
> NUN
> Your word is a lamp to my feet and a light to my path..."
> (Psalm 119:97-105)

Here is a rare example of a man who has taken the trouble to learn wisdom by reflection: a noble man indeed! Even the psalm's expression of thanks to God has been constructed with painstaking care. Psalm 119 is an acrostic poem: every verse in

Day 5 Exhortation: Stripped of All

each successive block begins with successive letters of the Hebrew alphabet. The quote above shows the eight verses beginning with the 13th letter: Mem and the first verse from the subsequent letter: Nun. Yet each verse says exactly the same thing: the author finds benefit, be it strength, comfort or wisdom, in absorbing the written teachings of God. This single thought is repeated 176 times in the 176 verses of the psalm. This is the level of dedication in expressing to God gratitude for the provision of His Law, the same Law against which modern Christians commonly grumble for being dry, uninteresting and devoid of spiritual value! Rather here is the insight of one who has learned wisdom by his careful appreciation of and dedication to the written principles of God in the Mosaic Law and by him we are well exhorted. Although the ritual observations of the Mosaic Law are fulfilled in the sacrifice of Christ for the modern believer the Law remains of tremendous value. One always gains insight into the mind and character of any author by reading their books and thus in this case one can study the Mosaic Law to learn a little more of the character of the Almighty: a definitively beneficial result (c.f. 17:3).

<u>Wisdom from Suffering: David's Adultery</u>

For the majority of humanity, however, there is only the ignoble and familiar trait of gaining wisdom through the necessary precursor of suffering. We do not desire it should be this way – and we should realize God's will desires this no more than our own. But the constricting pride in which we smother ourselves, and by which we prevent ourselves from achieving the spiritual growth our Father desires, necessarily precipitates suffering as our only road to wisdom. Each successive generation of humanity fails to learn from this mistake of the former, and is thus condemned to repeat it. Well did the prophet intone:

> "Can the Ethiopian change his skin or the leopard its spots? Neither can you do good who are accustomed to doing evil." (Jeremiah 13:23)

Day 5 Exhortation: *Stripped of All*

Humiliation is an unpleasant experience, but one that seems essential in bringing man to approach his Father. Let's remind ourselves of a couple of scriptural examples concerning the transformation of attitude brought about by humiliation.

We begin with David, in his sole moment of ungodliness: his adultery with Bathsheba and conspiracy to murder her husband Uriah. When Nathan the prophet recounts events to him, disguised in metaphor so that he cannot recognize the participants, David's righteous anger is poured out upon the perpetrator.

> David burned with anger against the man and said to Nathan, "As surely as the LORD lives, the man who did this deserves to die! He must pay for that lamb four times over, because he did such a thing and had no pity." (2 Samuel 12:5-6) [1]

Nathan then reveals both the true crime, and the true criminal:

> Then Nathan said to David, "You are the man! This is what the LORD, the God of Israel, says: I anointed you king over Israel, and I delivered you from the hand of Saul. I gave your master's house to you, and your master's wives into your arms. I gave you the house of Israel and Judah. And if all this had been too little, I would have given you even more. Why did you despise the word of the LORD by doing what is evil in his eyes? You struck down Uriah the Hittite with the sword and took his wife to be your own. You killed him with the sword of the Ammonites. Now, therefore, the sword will

---

[1] As an interesting aside we note David's careless words: "He must pay for the lamb four times over." They are starkly brought to realization: exactly four of his sons die as a result of the punishment God exacts from David's sin. Well do we note the words of the Lord Jesus: "I tell you that men will have to give account on the day of judgment for every careless word they have spoken" (Matthew 12:36). Let us never forget these words are true, and the day of judgment to which they refer is not necessarily Judgment Day itself, but maybe some Monday, Tuesday or Thursday in our regular week.

never depart from your house, because you despised me and took the wife of Uriah the Hittite to be your own." (2 Samuel 12:7-10)

David's burning anger is immediately quenched by humility – this is the transformation we mentioned. His nobility returns: he makes no effort to gainsay his guilt, or shift it onto someone else. He simply declares, "I have sinned against the LORD" (2 Samuel 12:13).

Psalm 51: 'You are proved right when you speak'
Central to our thoughts is the outcome of this crushed and humiliated state. Only this way: no longer as king but a man horrified in self-recognition as a greedy, pitiless adulterer and murderer; does David compose the words we know as Psalm 51. Read Psalm 51, and observe the spirit resident there. This spirit will be our guiding light towards the spirit we need before the table of remembrance.

"Have mercy on me, O God, according to your unfailing love; according to your great compassion blot out my transgressions. Wash away all my iniquity and cleanse me from my sin. For I know my transgressions, and my sin is always before me. Against you, you only, have I sinned and done what is evil in your sight, so that you are proved right when you speak and justified when you judge." (Psalm 51:1-4)

David's concurrence with God's judgment is incredible considering God has condemned the child born of the adultery – David's own son – to death! David recognizes the origin of that destruction: sin kills. God is not the killer, rather He is the source of life for all! Therefore David sees *he* is solely responsible for his son's death, because of the evil he has committed. What an extraordinary man to have deduced, and embraced, those incomparably unyielding facts!

Day 5 Exhortation: *Stripped of All*

His spirituality also reveals to him God alone is wronged by his sin. David knows his largest crime, against God, was to enable the surrounding nations to cheapen (blaspheme) God's name (2 Samuel 12:14), and this crime so far exceeds his crimes against men as to render the latter, even murder and adultery, of none account. This is neither arrogance nor insensitivity in David, seemingly dismissing his crimes against his fellow man, rather David demonstrates excellent insight into the perspective between crimes against God and against man. (A similar concept is demonstrated by Jesus in the parable of relative debts in Matthew 18:23-35).

Psalm 51: 'Make me hear joy and gladness'
"Surely I was sinful at birth, sinful from the time my mother conceived me. Surely you desire truth in the inner parts; you teach me wisdom in the inmost place. Cleanse me with hyssop, and I will be clean; wash me, and I will be whiter than snow. Let me hear joy and gladness; let the bones you have crushed rejoice." (Psalm 51:5-8)

This may seem erroneous, for how can one be sinful in the womb, before one has had opportunity to act?! David's insight into the nature of sin is instructive. In the deeper understanding of sin, the root of sin is not action *per se*: to use a mathematical analogy, it is a vector. Sin describes the direction in which one is heading, rather than the point at which one stands. We can then understand specific sinful acts as milestones along the vector (direction) of sin, but sin itself is the direction far more than the action. Therefore when David says he was a sinner from the time he was in the womb he is recognizing the direction, the *only* direction, in which the mortal life can be conducted.

"Let the bones you have crushed rejoice." What an amazing phrase! David is not denying the intense pain of his punishment: he describes it as feeling his bones have been crushed: an intensely painful experience, as any who have suffered compound fractures will know. But our exhortation is not in the sternness of the judgment David suffered; it lies in the absence of bitterness in

Day 5 Exhortation: Stripped of All

David's soul. His life is now devoid of pleasure. But far from wallowing in his pain, or making embittered counter-claims, he rather implores God to help him learn how to hear the voice of joy once more! A truly incredible man! This is a man who watched his baby son die over a seven-day period, knowing full well that the disaster was being effected deliberately from the Hand of God, and pleading all the while for a mercy that was never granted. If this man can turn back to God, devoid of bitterness, and pray from his state of humiliated and broken despair: "Make me to hear joy and gladness" how can we ever permit any bitterness in our lives from the lot we are cast? Truly our only option, regardless of whatever burdens we bear, is to take bread and wine in the knowledge that we are loved, and we are daily inundated by the evidence. With that knowledge, indeed that *certainty*, we are assured the things God has planned for those who love him are infinitely better than those who are loved could have planned for themselves.

That is one reason why we pray 'Thy will be done,' after all.

Psalm 51: 'To teach sinners your ways'

"Hide your face from my sins and blot out all my iniquity. Create in me a pure heart, O God, and renew a steadfast spirit within me. Do not cast me from your presence or take your Holy Spirit from me. Restore to me the joy of your salvation and grant me a willing spirit, to sustain me. Then I will teach transgressors your ways, and sinners will turn back to you." (Psalm 51:9-13)

David does not believe he has 'the right to be happy' (a common contemporary malaise) by holding God accountable for the pain he otherwise feels. He recognizes the source of his unhappiness as his sins, which he asks God to take away, knowing joy and peace are approached by the knowledge of sins forgiven. Best of all, notice David's intent to preach and convert. This psalm is an unusual context for a comment on preaching intentions: but such is the godliness of David's heart. Even amidst his darkest hour, David is not self-focused! He is

Day 5 Exhortation: *Stripped of All*

humiliated, but not self-sympathetic, he is broken, but not bitter, he is brought down, but does not forget to look up. Furthermore, his lack of self-sympathy prompts him to desire forgiveness to spread the word of grace to others, so they might receive it too. This is a vital principle for us to bring to the Lord's table: even our self-reparation should be designed with the Christ-like purpose of benefiting those who remain in darkness. We must ensure in the silent moments of taking bread and wine that the calm of reunion with our Father prompts us to broadcast the grace we feel at His table. This we learn from David's wonderful example.

Psalm 51: 'You do not delight in sacrifice'
"Save me from bloodguilt, O God, the God who saves me, and my tongue will sing of your righteousness. O Lord, open my lips, and my mouth will declare your praise. You do not delight in sacrifice, or I would bring it; you do not take pleasure in burnt offerings. The sacrifices of God are a broken spirit; a broken and contrite heart, O God, you will not despise." (Psalm 51:14-17)

David reminisces upon Samuel's rebuke to his predecessor, Saul (1 Samuel 15:30), that God respects the heart of a contrite man as repentance, not rote observation of the Law. Why then the Law? The sacrifices were designed to assist the heart of man towards contrition. They were not practices that could be performed to achieve reunion with the Father *in place of* contrition, although sadly that was what developed in Israel. This didactic principle holds to this day. We cannot take memorial bread and wine to obtain reunion with the Father *instead of* being sorry for the shame our conduct brings to Jesus' name. Nor does sharing of bread and wine save us, because that would mean we could take the emblems with any attitude we chose. Rather the sacrifice of Jesus Christ has the power to save us by the bread and wine emblematically provoking that broken and contrite spirit the Father respects.

Day 5 Exhortation: Stripped of All

Psalm 51: 'Whole burnt offerings to delight you'
"In your good pleasure make Zion prosper; build up the walls of Jerusalem. Then there will be righteous sacrifices, whole burnt offerings to delight you; then bulls will be offered on your altar." (Psalm 51:18-19)

Finally, notice the excellent conclusion of the psalm: the *ultimate* purpose of David's prayer for rehabilitation is that Zion should once more host sacrifices to God's glory. David seeks self-restoration from his broken and humiliated state, but not for his own benefit! He seeks self-restoration so that he might better glorify his Maker! It is nothing short of incredible that David's goal in his current condition is the greater glory of God. He is recently bereaved of a baby son, caught in the depths of self-loathing for recognition of his part in adultery, murder and, worst of all, causing the name of God to be cheapened throughout the earth. Yet this man, stripped of all, still holds his ultimate goal in self repair as Zion's reconstruction to augment the Name of his Creator! But, incredible or not, this is the truth standing in scripture to this day for our edification. We do well to pay it most heartfelt attention.

Guilt: The Declaration of Innocence
With that in mind, let us develop the idea further, moving into the darkness of the events of John's Creation's Day 5 surrounding the crucifixion. For counterpoint to David, we meet a man who will not humble himself, but has the audacity in the face of God's Son to attempt to demonstrate piety and innocence. We refer to Pontius Pilate.

When Pilate saw that he was getting nowhere, but that instead an uproar was starting, he took water and washed his hands in front of the crowd. "I am innocent of this man's blood," he said. "It is your responsibility!" (Matthew 27:24)

Pilate understood Jesus was an innocent man and did not desire to see him crucified. Because of this many sympathize with

Day 5 Exhortation: *Stripped of All*

Pontius Pilate, even wrongly considering him a good man. Pilate is *not* a good man, for faith, without the works to realize it, is dead (James 2). Whatever Pilate believed about the innocence of Christ, his conviction was insufficient to act upon it and he chose rather to wash his hands before the mob to demonstrate his innocence. Unfortunately for Pilate, and all of like mindset, innocence is not established by self-declaration. Indeed the reverse is more likely true. Those who stand before God and declare themselves innocent do little more than demonstrate their own complete lack of humility – and that to their own destruction.

The Bible presents an attractive contradiction between the physical and spiritual world concerning the act of washing. In the physical world things are cleaned by washing in water and they are made dirty, to the point of a health risk, by washing in blood. Yet the Biblical picture of the spiritual plane is reversed. Washing in blood, specifically the blood of the Lamb, is the only way in which one can become clean. The elder in Revelation explains to John:

> And he said, "These [the saints] are they who have come out of the great tribulation; they have washed their robes and made them white in the blood of the Lamb." (Revelation 7:14)

This deliberately inverts physical reality. And its counterpart also exists, right here on the crucifixion day. Pilate washes his hands in water and then extends them before the crowd, and before God, so their purity might be seen. But this marks the very moment in which he turned his back on Jesus Christ and delivered him to the Jews to kill, becoming as guilty of the death of Christ as any of those crying "Crucify him!" His hands were washed with water, yet from precisely that moment on, they dripped with the blood of the murdered and betrayed Christ.

By extension, notice the similarity this provides between Pontius Pilate and the precedental murderer: Cain.

Day 5 Exhortation: Stripped of All

Cain: "I don't know [where Abel is]," he replied. "Am I my brother's keeper?" (Genesis 4:9)

Pilate: "I am innocent of this man's blood," he said. "It is your responsibility!" (Matthew 27:24)

Both men voice their own innocence. Yet both are wrong, for even as they speak their hands drip with the spilled blood of the righteous.

<u>Innocence: The Declaration of Guilt</u>

Nevertheless we do not advance these thoughts on Cain and Pilate in order to condemn them, but rather to better examine ourselves. We have had an easy time up to now, because we have directed the spotlight of our investigations solely at other people. To rotate that spotlight and point it at ourselves is not the most inviting of tasks, yet it is an essential component of finding communion with our Father, our Lord, and our spiritual siblings. We might suppose our communion is established by baptism and subsequent membership of the church. Along this path disaster lies. We look for baptismal candidates to give a good 'confession of their faith,' – and this is seemly. But sadly in Western cultures this confession is all too easily over-intellectualized, the would-be Christian is called only to present a coherent, well-reasoned understanding of the relationship between God, His Son and His people through history from an emotionally remote standpoint. This is both a pity and an error because this type of confession does not reflect scriptural prerogatives and teachings as much as merely our culture; in which it is awkward to acknowledge, observe, or even discuss any emotively oriented feeling. Our Father has shown us that emotional confessions include the greatest confessions of all! For example, could any man disparage the heartfelt and beautifully self-contradictory cry of the man whose son had been cured of the dumb spirit?

And straightway the father of the child cried out, and said with tears, "Lord, I believe; help thou mine unbelief." (Mark 9:24, KJV)

Day 5 Exhortation: Stripped of All

Surely from this man was made a disciple stronger and more sincere than many who would claim the label of Christian; then or now! Yet his confession was based wholly on a yearning cry of purest sincerity! Some might argue for him to be a true disciple there would have to be other details concerning his understanding and knowledge of Jesus that are not included in the record we behold. Yet that would seem to be the point: such details are *not* necessary for us to witness for us to have seen a thoroughly genuine and powerful confession of faith! The spirit we must look for in one who would be a brother or sister of Christ, and ultimately that means ourselves, must contain more than the seasoned learning of the principles and characters of the scriptural pages. From those same pages must be instilled in our hearts the spirit of the truly broken and humiliated one who cries 'Abba,' 'Father,' towards our God – and make that cry not only in times of dire distress, but at any time, and every time.

Do not the very elements of bread and wine graphically indicate that in their very nature? Consider: one cannot obtain bread unless the seed of corn dies, one cannot obtain wine unless the grapes are crushed. The principal duty of bread and wine is to draw our minds towards the crucifixion of Jesus Christ and, wholly concordantly, the very processes producing them encapsulate the sense of the crushed, and the dead. What appropriate pointers these are to humble the minds of those sharing memorial communion together, seeing the destruction we have wrought! Surely we must feel this humiliated state, and live the consequences arising therefrom; else all our learning has been in vain.

The Fisherman's Denial

We culminate this pattern in John's gospel, with Peter: that remarkable, brave disciple, who in the disastrous events preceding the crucifixion denies knowledge of his Lord and Master. Before we turn to the account directly, let us offer some general observations concerning Peter. Peter's shortcomings and failings, quite unlike yours and mine, are recorded in the pages of the scriptural record: emblazoned across the realms of space and

Day 5 Exhortation: Stripped of All

time, published in hundreds of languages over scores of generations for the general edification of all. This has led to much wrong being spoken about Peter. The modern Christian often speaks in patronizing terms. Frequently when one hears the remark: "there's a little Peter in all of us," what is generally referred to is recklessness and stupidity. We do well to remember Peter will sit on one of the twelve thrones of Israel and he will do so because that is the foreknown will of the Omniscient God Himself! (Matthew 19:28) Peter certainly did deny Christ, and the whole world knows about it. But what is worth remembering is that you, dear reader, have denied Christ too, and so have I. Yet these are secret things, unknown to any but the Father, possibly even denials encapsulated in episodes long forgotten by ourselves. Peter's denial, and other regrettable outbursts, are a matter of international and intercultural record, whilst ours are virtually unknown, but this does nothing to compromise the equality of the crimes. Once that is firmly in mind, and *only* when that is firmly in mind, are we qualified to regard the details of Peter's stumble and fall.

> "You are not one of his disciples, are you?" the girl at the door asked Peter. He replied, "I am not." It was cold, and the servants and officials stood around a fire they had made to keep warm. Peter also was standing with them, warming himself… As Simon Peter stood warming himself, he was asked, "You are not one of his disciples, are you?" He denied it, saying, "I am not." One of the high priest's servants, a relative of the man whose ear Peter had cut off, challenged him, "Didn't I see you with him in the olive grove?" Again Peter denied it, and at that moment a rooster began to crow. (18:17-18, 25-27)

It was a cold night and Peter warmed himself at the fireside of the court officials. This seems irrelevant, but we have learned enough from John's gospel to have our attention piqued by apparently innocuous information. The night was cold. God had chosen to match the lack of mercy and justice of the night with the lack of thermal comfort from the natural elements; in all senses therefore it was a cold night indeed. And in the cold Peter finds some comfort by standing at the fireside of the servants and officials of those wrongfully prosecuting his Master. This is a subtle, yet compelling, picture of transferred allegiance, although we do not suggest Peter consciously meant it that way. But Peter's refuge is poorly chosen (c.f. Psalm 1:1) and, much like the man who shelters in a warm cave on a cold desert night, he finds snakes lurk within. Those snakes gathered at the fireside turn on him and, in precisely the same manner of the precedental serpent, precipitate his downfall. Buckling under the pressures of a terrifying evening and the simple cowardice that comes with feeling alone, Peter denies Jesus Christ, his Lord and Savior.

The Disciple: Stripped of All

We learn from Luke an interesting detail that adds dimension to our consideration of the humbled Peter.

> The Lord turned and looked straight at Peter. Then Peter remembered the word the Lord had spoken to him: "Before the rooster crows today, you will disown me three times." (Luke 22:61)

What a chilling encounter! This is a different type of crushing than we considered before. This is not the crushing brought about by the finality of judgment, as with David's baby son. This crushing (which in some senses is greater) is brought about by an act of kindness – a *stay* of judgment – on the one who realizes he deserves the destructive blow. We wrestle in our own lives against our myriad problems, thorns in the flesh and fleshly thorns and then, out of the blue, can come an intervention so merciful and undeserved as to be unmistakably the Hand of the Almighty. Yet with the magnitude of such a blessing can come the hammer-blow of humiliation at all the frustration and bitterness with which we wrestled throughout the trial itself. Truly God is good, and there are times when those on Earth, in all humility and

Day 5 Exhortation: Stripped of All

thankfulness, really can do nothing better than keep silence before Him (Habakkuk 2:20).

> And [Peter] went outside and wept bitterly. (Luke 22:62)

Surely this is complete humiliation for Peter, and true humility.

Note also a detail from his final, fateful denial:

> ...at that moment a rooster began to crow. (18:27)

Once again, a little detail accompanies: the cock crowed at that moment. The primary reference here is to connect with the prophecy of Peter's denial, (13:38), but perhaps we can appreciate a deeper interpretation too. Cockcrow has a strong association with morning: the start of a new day. So this is unusual, for it to have sounded in the darkness. We have seen Peter's denial in the (cold) dark night, but now, spiritually speaking, morning has come. And what a painful morning! – in the bitter realization of what he has done. Yet for so many the only path to spiritual progress lies through the cathartic, sometimes deadly, waters of total humiliation. Thus although Peter is at the point of total loss (indeed perhaps *because* he is at this point), he has reached the morning. The cock has crowed, and for Peter a full day's work lies ahead to rebuild his broken spirit in the shape in which he can truly glorify his Master.

We must appreciate the concluding lesson from Peter's humiliation, which we glimpsed from Psalm 51. The end product of true humility is restorative action, selflessly, for the glory of God. True humility does not lead to inactivity. Peter stirred himself from his weeping (as Judas was never to) to become a tireless evangelist and minister, whose construction and maintenance of the early Church are detailed throughout the Acts of the Apostles, and culminate in his description as a 'pillar' of the early church (Galatians 2:9). Peter's weeping was indeed cathartic, but it did not result in the paralysis of self-sympathy.

Day 5 Exhortation: Stripped of All

True humility provokes constructive action along the pathway of God's will, and for His glory.

Likewise here is our standpoint at the threshold of communion. We will pass bread and wine from hand to hand, and share sweet communion together as a family before, and with, our Father. For that communion to function we must find, and *be*, that broken-spirited one, which we see so graphically in David and Peter. We must be able, as Peter was, to both see and be seen by the face of the Christ, a face saddened by our desertion, and we must confront, and ingest, the horror that regarding such a visage will bring. We must see in the memorials of his crucifixion (the broken bread and crushed vine), the one whom we have denied, whose body we have broken, and whose life we have crushed. Yet when those few quiet moments with bread and wine have passed, we must not lie dormant in the murky waters of that humiliation. We must also hear the cockerel's crow, and lift ourselves back up, for it is dawning to a New Day, and there is so very much to be done.

DAY 6 $\quad$ *John 20:1-21:25*

EXPOSITION:
The New Man, The Premier

Day 6: the second cycle of Heaven, Sea and Earth draws to its final component as we arrive back at the Earth arena. Natural creation's Day 6 sees the Earth populated. The principal feature is the man Adam: a new man created in the image of God, created to govern, tend and care for all the Earth. From this we formulate our expectations for Day 6 of John's Creation.

Basic premise
We expect to find Jesus presented as the authoritative figure within a new creation, in a similar role to the position of Adam in Eden. We also expect an echo of Day 3, because Days 3 and 6 are partners in the 'Earth' arena of creation (Figure α_1).

Read John 20-21. The first thing we encounter is the empty tomb (20:1): a bold declaration of man having been raised (created) to walk the Earth in a new form. This realizes a strong echo of the Adamic creation, which supports our creation

Day 6 Exposition: *The New Man, The Premier*

pattern. We will see this thought ratified through a more detailed assessment of John 20-21. Jesus' description as the premier man above all men comes strongly to the fore. Some might argue that Jesus' authority as the premier man is present in the entirety of the gospel and thus this is an easy charge to demonstrate. Actually, our charge here is not simple at all! Our charge in Day 6 is stringent, for we must show much more than just the notion that Jesus is the leader amongst men. We are required to show that the level of Jesus' supremacy in this section of John's gospel even outweighs the level demonstrated in all other portions of the gospel! Nevertheless, despite this degree of difficulty, the gospel record does indeed bear out the assertion that Jesus' supremacy is described at a uniquely high level in the last two chapters of John.

6.1 Names Above Names

We observe Jesus' authority being elevated in this portion of the gospel by monitoring two particular titles he owns: "Rabbi" (a transliteration of a Greek word meaning "Teacher" [1]) and "Son of God." Both titles are attributed to Jesus throughout Days 1-4 of John's Creation (see Table 6_1). Interestingly, both titles disappear in Day 5: indicative of how Jesus is 'brought low' on the fifth day. Yet both titles subsequently reappear in Day 6: and do so in a superior format!

"Rabbi" is applied to Jesus throughout Days 1-4 and disappears in Day 5, replaced with mocking insults from the soldiers. In Day 6, the Day of the New Man, the title reappears as "Rabboni": Teacher amongst Teachers, (as Mark 10:51).

> Jesus said to her, "Mary." She turned toward him and cried out in Aramaic, "Rabboni!" (which means Teacher). (20:16)

---

[1] Strong J. H., *Op. cit.*, 'Main Concordance,' pp 824-825

Day 6 Exposition: The New Man, The Premier

Likewise the title "Son of God." Attributed to Jesus throughout Days 1-4, stripped from him in Day 5, as all is stripped from him including his life; the title likewise reappears in Day 6 in augmented form.

Thomas said to him, "My Lord and my God!" (20:28) [2]

John's Creation	Mention of Jesus with title: "Rabbi"	Mention of Jesus with title: "Son of God"
Day 1 (1:1-3:21)	Rabbi (1:38)	Son of God (1:34)
Day 2 (3:22-5:47)	Rabbi (4:31)	Son of God (5:25)
Day 3 (6:1-6:71)	Rabbi (6:25)	Son of God (6:27)
Day 4 (7:1-13:38)	Rabbi (11:8)	Son of God (10:36)
Day 5 (14:1-19:42)	*does not appear*	*does not appear*
Day 6 (20:1-21:15)	Elevated to "Rabboni" (20:16)	Elevated to "God" (20:28)

Table 6_1: Names above Names. An indication of how two important titles of Jesus are elevated to superior format in Day 6 of John's Creation, after disappearing in Day 5.

---

[2] A wonderful declaration, which needlessly troubles many. Thomas' reference to Jesus as "God" is fully appropriate: the declaration goes uncorrected by the Lord, and Jesus *does* take the trouble to correct references to him that are inappropriate (Matthew 19:16-17, see also Matthew 12:24-28). The scripture is well-balanced because the same chapter indicates there is no case for Jesus being the actual person of God (20:17), yet he is one who is worthy of the name. Scripture clarifies God has been pleased to give His Son Jesus the very Name of God for his humble obedience in sacrifice (Philippians 2:6-11). A fuller consideration of the nature of Jesus Christ as revealed by John is given in Appendix C.

Day 6 Exposition: The New Man, The Premier

In this section of John's gospel, the Day of Man's premiership, John reveals the new names of Jesus: firstly Rabboni, and secondly the Name that is above every Name: the Name of God himself. How well this fits Day 6's theme: a new and even greater authority for Jesus in his role as the spiritual equivalent of Adam, the first man – both chronologically and authoritatively – of the spiritual creation.

6.2 The Keyholder

In the natural creation man is created to have authority over all other creatures and with that authority comes responsibility. Adam's responsibility is to tend the Garden that the Lord created in Eden (Genesis 2:15). Day 6 of John's Creation is similar: the New Man is shown in his premier role of "Keyholder": the gatekeeper to God's Kingdom.

We should familiarize ourselves with the scriptural concept of the keyholder. The keyholder role had always been invested in the religious leaders of the day and is nothing new in John. Jesus refers to this keyholder role in his discourse with the Pharisees, who were the incumbent religious leaders, commenting especially on how appallingly they abused the privilege.

> "Woe to you experts in the law, because you have taken away the key to knowledge. You yourselves have not entered, and you have hindered those who were entering." (Luke 11:52)

The preceding verses in Luke clarify that the principal way in which the Pharisees and scribes had hindered God's children was in the rejection, and in some cases murder, of the prophets God had sent. As a result, their own actions passed judgment on themselves.

> "Therefore this generation will be held responsible for the blood of all the prophets that has been shed since the beginning of the world, from the blood of Abel to the blood of Zechariah, who was killed between the altar and the

Day 6 Exposition: The New Man, The Premier

sanctuary. Yes, I tell you, this generation will be held responsible for it all." (Luke 11:50-51)

Fortunately, however, God has provided another Keyholder.

"I will place on his shoulder the key to the house of David; what he opens no one can shut, and what he shuts no one can open." (Isaiah 22:22)

The immediate context shows these words are primarily written about Eliakim son of Hilkiah. Yet the scripture also directly applies the same investiture to Christ:

To the angel of the church in Philadelphia write: These are the words of him who is holy and true, who holds the key of David. What he opens no one can shut, and what he shuts no one can open. (Revelation 3:7)

Isaiah elaborates that Jesus will inherit the throne of David and all the authority along with it (Isaiah 9:7). Jesus also recognizes that role in the words he speaks to John:

"I am the Living One; I was dead, and behold I am alive for ever and ever! And I hold the keys of death and Hades." (Revelation 1:18)

Here in Day 6 Jesus passes on this same authority to his apostles.

And with that [Jesus] breathed on [the apostles] and said, "Receive the Holy Spirit. If you forgive anyone his sins, they are forgiven; if you do not forgive them, they are not forgiven." (20:22-23)

These words share the same spirit as those spoken to Simon Peter, following his confession of Jesus as the Christ. Jesus says to Peter:

Day 6 Exposition: The New Man, The Premier

> "I will give you the keys of the kingdom of heaven; whatever you bind on earth will be bound in heaven, and whatever you loose on earth will be loosed in heaven." (Matthew 16:19)

The image of Peter standing 'at the Gates of Heaven' as the keyholder has passed into popular Western culture and, from there, has been adopted by large portions of Christianity. However Peter standing physically at the Gates of God's community, perched on a cloud forever on the periphery of Heaven, is a gross and comical overstretch of this verse. Furthermore the context demonstrates the role was bestowed on Peter because of the confession he made: "You are the Christ, the Son of the living God." Knowing the consistency of our Father we learn this same status is bestowed on all those who make that confession: a supposition corroborated by the group investiture of authority we witness here (20:22-23).

The idea of Christ as keyholder helps explain a couple of otherwise bizarre details here in Day 6: specifically how John repeatedly demonstrates locked doors as no impediment for Jesus.

> On the evening of that first day of the week, when the disciples were together, **with the doors locked** for fear of the Jews, Jesus came and stood among them and said, "Peace be with you!" (20:19)
>
> A week later his disciples were in the house again, and Thomas was with them. **Though the doors were locked**, Jesus came and stood among them and said, "Peace be with you!" (20:26)

A locked door failing to impede the Son of God is no surprise by this stage in the gospel: we understood as early as Day 1 Jesus received an unlimited supply of God's Spirit (3:34) and an abundance of miracles throughout the gospel demonstrate that point. Thus we attribute the inclusion of this detail about Jesus passing through locked doors, and its emphasis through repetition, not so much as a demonstration of Jesus physical

Day 6 Exposition: The New Man, The Premier

powers *per se*, but as a carefully crafted allusion to the keyholder role. Jesus is shown as the supreme keyholder, the man for whom all doors stand open.

> Early on the first day of the week, while it was still dark, Mary Magdalene went to the tomb and saw that the stone had been removed from the entrance. (20:1)

This concept of open doors in John is a perfect segue to the event of the empty tomb. This is not just any open door, but one we recognize from Day 2: the stone removed from the mouth of Jacob's well. We remember the quote when Jacob talks with the shepherds:

> "Water the sheep and take them back to pasture." "We can't," [the shepherds] replied, "until all the flocks are gathered and the stone has been rolled away from the mouth of the well. Then we will water the sheep." (Genesis 29:7-8)

We considered the implications of this quote previously: the precursors to receiving the living water at Jacob's well were rolling the stone away and gathering the flocks together (Section 2.3). Now in Day 6 the keyholder, the New Man, has caused the stone to be rolled clear: the door stands open.

Two implications arise. Firstly, this implies the return of the Shepherd to gather his flocks is the very next item in this agenda! This is an exciting thought, fuelling our enthusiasm towards the return of the one so longed for! However, the task of gathering the sheep commands our attention. Though it can doubtless only be perfected by the Shepherd, the job is greatly facilitated by whatever gathering the sheep can already achieve themselves: and Jesus' teaching imparts both aspects. The Shepherd gathers the sheep but the sheep are also supposed to follow the Master's voice and gather to him (10:3-4, 16). These scriptures pose the question: Are Christ's sheep as gathered as they can be, in demonstration of willing participation in the Shepherd's bidding? Similarly, do the sheep recognize that any fragmentation in their

Day 6 Exposition: The New Man, The Premier

gathering necessarily impedes the work of the one who comes to gather? We who would name ourselves Christ's sheep, and claim to be cognizant of our Shepherd's bidding, are doubtless obliged to respond to such challenges…

Secondly, the work of the keyholder in rolling away the stone implies certain things about the nature of the open doorway. This is not any doorway, this is the doorway by which salvation is accessed – the doorway to the House of God, the door of the sheepfold. John illustrates this in his gospel by defining both the doorway, and the effects of crossing the threshold:

> "I am the door. If anyone enters by me, he will be saved, and will go in and out and find pasture." (10:9)
> "Finally the other disciple, who had reached the tomb first, also went inside. He saw and believed." (20:8)

The personal nature of the testimony in this latter quote is particularly striking. To see 'belief' falling simultaneously with the action of crossing the threshold of the tomb is graphically powerful in itself, the more so since it concerns the personal witness of the gospel author! [3] John faithfully reports Jesus' words that whosoever goes in by the door will find salvation (10:9). How fascinating to see that played out in his own life! The stark realization that Jesus truly is the Son of God come to save the world strikes him as he enters the door of the empty tomb! These are dramatic moments in the gospel, and we do well to pay them full attention. The door stands open, and those who cross the threshold step into the territory of Day 6: The New Man, where they are utterly, irreversibly, transformed.

---

[3] John is that "other disciple," as he makes clear at the end of the gospel, (21:20-24)

Day 6 Exposition: The New Man, The Premier

6.3 The Three Appearances of the Lord of Heaven, Sea and Earth

Jesus' appearances to his disciples after his resurrection take up the majority of the text (two-thirds) in these closing chapters: a clear indication of their importance. He appears on three separate occasions (20:19-23; 20:26-29; and 21:1-22). We might be led to conclude that there were four appearances in all because he appears to Mary too (20:14-18), but John explicitly does not include this and insistently records the frequency as *threefold* (21:14). Our attention is deliberately drawn to the threefold repetition.

Creative Zone	Days	Genesis Creation (natural)	John's Creation (spiritual)	Appearances of Jesus post resurrection
Heaven	Day 1	Light	Illumination	1a Disciples saw the Lord
Heaven	Day 4	Ruling Lights	Responsibility from Illumination	1b Given power to forgive/retain sins (20:20, 23)
Waters	Day 2	Waters above	Life from Death	2 Showed one alive who was dead
Waters	Day 5	"Tanniyn" in Waters beneath	Death of living	2b Showed death marks in living body (20:27)
Earth	Day 3	Plants for food	Bread from Heaven	3a Served them bread and fish
Earth	Day 6	A Man to Rule	The New Shepherd	3b Gave instruction to disciples (21:12-25)

Table 6_2: The three successive appearances of Jesus after his resurrection compared with the natural and spiritual components that appear in the three constituencies of creation over the six days.

185

Day 6 Exposition: The New Man, The Premier

What is significant about there being *three* appearances? The threefold structure in creation is significant: the six creative days are arranged as two discrete cycles in three geographical areas (see Figure α_1). Days 1 and 4 were performed in Heaven; Days 2 and 5 in Waters; and Days 3 and 6 on Earth. We further realize, since God's power is unlimited, all creation could have been achieved instantaneously, and therefore the organization over six days is deliberate, and for a reason. How does this help us understand why Jesus deliberately makes three appearances to his disciples? Again the creation model lends an answer. The details of each appearance are below (Table 6_2), and are tabulated in comparative format with the three arenas of creation.

> Appearance 1:
> The disciples were overjoyed when they saw the Lord... "If you forgive anyone his sins, they are forgiven; if you do not forgive them, they are not forgiven." (20:20, 23)
>
> Appearance 2:
> Then [Jesus] said to Thomas, "Put your finger here; see my hands. Reach out your hand and put it into my side. Stop doubting and believe." (20:27)
>
> Appearance 3:
> Jesus saith unto them, "Come and dine"... Jesus then cometh, and taketh bread, and giveth them, and fish likewise. (21:12-13, KJV)

Fascinatingly, we see a microcosm of the three regions of John's spiritual creation in the three appearances, although the comparisons are very subtle. The first appearance mentions sight and the investment of authority to the disciples to judge sins. This matches the spiritual equivalents of Days 1 and 4 of creation: light and lights designed to rule. The second appearance attractively counterpoints the evidence of the raised corpse (life out of death) with the marks of death on the living Messiah's body. This matches the spiritual creation elements of Days 2 and

5, the former reflecting life drawn out of death and the latter reflecting the reverse. Particularly attractive is how these death-marks are used to draw Thomas from an unbelieving (dead) state into a believing (living) state. Lastly Jesus appears to feed his disciples bread and fish: a replica of Day 3's feeding of the 5 000 on the mountainside.

But having discerned the comparison, how are we edified by it? The pattern perfectly underscores the message of Day 6: a New Man has come in whom unprecedented authority is instilled. In the natural creation that new man was Adam and his authority was to subdue the natural populations of sea, sky and land (Genesis 1:27-28). In the spiritual creation comes the superior parallel: God has made the risen Christ Lord of Heaven and Sea and Earth, and of all their respective populations! John portrays this through the careful construction of these three appearances with Jesus in command of the three regions of the spiritual creation. The gospel writer paints these images in a manner typical of spiritual teaching: subtly and requiring careful observation, but sufficiently powerfully as to be compelling when the pattern is perceived. No wonder this was "that disciple whom Jesus loved." And for those of us who are excited by glimpsing the divine view through fascinating patterns delicately crafted in the scriptural text, it becomes very easy for us to love him too. John's gospel is, as we have said, a most remarkable revelation.

6.4 Beginning and End

The final picture. The disciples have fished all night [4] without success yet, at the arrival of the Lord, immediately a meal of bounty is secured. John portrays Jesus dining with his disciples on bread and fish by the seaside, with the meal Jesus has provided (21:6, 9). Once again the manner of divine provision is shown in the massive draught of fish: abundance! Numerologists toy

---

[4] Fishing is commonly done at night on the Sea of Galilee for climatic reasons. The fish retreat to the deeps at the center of the lake during the day and rise closer to the surface during the night, especially near the warm springs close to Capernaum's shores. Ray S. K., "St. John's Gospel: A Bible Study Guide and Commentary," 2002, Ignatius, San Francisco, CA, p 385

Day 6 Exposition: The New Man, The Premier

endlessly with the number of fish caught (153): perhaps we do best to observe the scriptural emphasis that the number demonstrates the haul was so huge that the net should have broken (21:11), though it did not. The draught of fish is reminiscent of two previous scenes: the Wedding at Cana, which realized a provision of ~1000 bottles of wine, and the feeding of the 5 000, where the provision of bread and fish fed all to satisfaction and left 12 baskets of excess. Edification does not naturally arise from the numbers themselves and interpretations centered on their precise numeric values seem strained. What remains undeniable is that the numbers convincingly communicate the *character* of the divine provision: one thousand bottles of wine, twelve baskets filled of crumbs from five loaves and two small fish, 153 fish in a single net's draught – a massive abundance! Important insight is thereby lent into the nature of the Father's provision for our needs: truly we are blessed with every sufficiency, and beyond.

Nevertheless we still ask: Why does John choose this as his closing image? Why should the picture of Jesus sharing a meal together with his faithful and beloved ones be the best way to close a witness of his life and ministry? A gospel writer's final scene will be a lasting picture in the reader's mind and is therefore clearly an important one. [5] The picture certainly evokes the pleasurable aesthetics of a peaceful, harmonious union. But with John's gospel we have come to suspect deeper patterns at every turn and the one imprinted here is as profound as any. We propose the beginning and ending of John form, on the smaller scale, a representation of the beginning and ending of the disciple's walk with the Lord.

---

[5] The gospel of Matthew, and Mark from which it was written, both conclude with Jesus' commission to his apostles to preach the gospel to all nations (Matthew 28:16-20, Mark 16:15-20). Luke finishes with the ascension of Jesus (Luke 24:50-51), and also attractively sets his closing image in the temple (Luke 24:52-53), matching the setting three of his opening images (Luke 1:5-80; 2:21-40; 2:41-52). This makes John's closing image, a meal of bread and fish by the seaside, all the more bizarre at first appreciation.

Day 6 Exposition: The New Man, The Premier

To support this idea, consider this statement from the Psalms:

"Taste and see that the LORD is good; blessed is the man who takes refuge in him." (Psalm 34:8)

This statement, an invitation to experience God for the first time, is necessarily made to someone who does not know God and has not established a relationship with him. The two verbs used: 'taste' and 'see' suggest this. 'Taste' suggests the promise of a meal at some later time, as when a chef tastes the food he is preparing. The taste is not the meal itself, merely a pre-cursor, yet by tasting one is enabled to 'see' whether or not what is coming is good.

Contrast this verse in Psalms with the scene at the end of a faithful discipleship. For the one who has run the race and endured to the end, trusting on the constant presence of a loving and merciful Father, the scripture promises an invitation to a very special meal.

"Let us rejoice and be glad and give him glory! For the wedding of the Lamb has come, and his bride has made herself ready…" Then the angel said to me, "Write: 'Blessed are those who are invited to the wedding supper of the Lamb!' " And he added, "These are the true words of God." (Revelation 19:7, 9)

This promise is necessarily made to a faithful disciple who has waited patiently for the Bridegroom's return (Matthew 25:1-13), one who has completed his course (2 Timothy 4:7-8). The disciple who has taken that first taste of which the Psalmist spoke and has seen that God is good, who has held true to the end of days, will sit at the wedding supper of the Lamb. At the beginning the disciple "tasted and saw" and at the end he "dined."

Comparing this pattern with the gospel of John, focusing on the beginning and end of the communion between Jesus and his disciples, we see the attractive comparison. The first direct

Day 6 Exposition: The New Man, The Premier

statement that Jesus makes to his disciples (as we noted before) is:

"Come... and you will see." (1:39)

Here in Day 6 we sample the very end of the disciple's journey, where we have walked with the apostles (at least by proxy) through their various trials, failures and successes. At the end of this journey, the end of John's beautiful testimony, Jesus' final statement to his disciples is:

"Come and dine." (21:12, KJV)

At the beginning, he invites them to see; at the end, he invites them to dine. This is the structure with which John frames his account of the communion between the Son of God and eleven very special and privileged sons of men. How well it reflects the broader picture we considered above: at the opening we are called to see (Psalm 34:8), and at the close, the faithful are invited to dine (Revelation 19:7-9). How enjoyable these carefully prepared pictures are to behold in their subtle simplicity!

6.5 Conclusions from Day 6

John's gospel accentuates that Jesus' authority in this part of his gospel is superior even to the authority he has held before. This is not idle conjecture; we have seen it based in solid fact: his titles of 'Rabbi' (Teacher) and 'Son of God,' used independently in the first four Days of John's Creation, are elevated in Day 6 to 'Rabboni' in the former case, and in the latter case to the Name of God Himself. To reinforce these references John paints the subtle picture of the three appearances of the risen Christ according to the regions of Heaven, Sea and Earth, to show Jesus Christ's supremacy in all of those regions, over the whole creation.

The connection with the creation model is strong here. The prime element of natural creation's Day 6 is Adam, a man raised in new form and given authority over all constituents of Heaven,

Sea and Earth (Genesis 1:26). We could find no better match than the closing chapters of John's gospel where we meet Jesus, raised from the dead in new, incorruptible form (1 Corinthians 15:20), and instilled with authority over all things.

Unavoidably, we see again the component of the spiritual creation standing in excellence to its natural counterpart. Again the reason is the same: the spiritual creation exhibits life where the natural has death. The new, premier man in natural creation's Day 6 is Adam, the bringer of death, and in spiritual creation's Day 6 it is Jesus Christ, the Son of the Living God. Suffice these words of Paul to establish the comparison between these two in terms of death and life:

> For since death came through a man, the resurrection of the dead comes also through a man. For as in Adam all die, so in Christ all will be made alive. (1 Corinthians 15:21-22)

Finally, we see the risen Christ as the Keyholder to the Kingdom of God. This is hinted in his ability to pass through the locked doors at the disciples' gatherings, and more clearly demonstrated by the open doorway he provides as the stone is rolled away from the mouth of the tomb. This latter picture is the fulfillment of the scene at Jacob's well (Sections 2.3-2.4). For the flocks to receive living water from the well the stone was required to be rolled away from the mouth of the well and the flocks were to be gathered. We now see the stone removed; the restrictive hold of death broken, and a doorway opened by which those who enter might believe and find life (20:8; 10:9). With excitement we conclude that the next step can only be the gathering of the flocks to the Shepherd!

6.6 Enfin

Thus we conclude our consideration of the gospel of John. We have presented the contents of the gospel and considered them in detail for our education and edification. A major theme of this work has been to group these records, without altering the order of the accounts, into six periods to reveal the spiritual

Day 6 Exposition: The New Man, The Premier

creation sequence in John. This forms the basis of the proposal we have termed: 'John's Creation.'

In our final chapters we consider the 'big picture' perspective. We form our conclusions as to whether the material of the gospel supports a recapitulation of the creation pattern. We present suggestions for why the perception of the 'spiritual creation' is valuable when viewing the life and ministry of the Lord Jesus. We also present ways in which the spiritual creation has relevance in the broader perspective of reading God's Word and living our lives as Christ's disciples before the Almighty.

But for now we have reached the very end of the gospel, and find these words, as remarkable as any that preceded them: that the marvel of the Lord's acts in the final days with his chosen few confounds the capacity of human effort to record them.

> And there are also many other things that Jesus did, which if they were written one by one, I suppose that even the world itself could not contain the books that would be written. Amen. (21:25)

'Amen' the gospel writer writes. And Amen indeed.

EXHORTATION 6: *John 21, Psalm 82*
Gods

> Simon Peter said to them [James & John plus others], "I am going fishing." They said to him, "We are going with you also." (21:3-4)

Another seemingly innocuous piece of text! What education, or edification, are we supposed to gain from Peter saying he is going fishing, and James and John going with him?

<u>Three Year Whirlwind</u>

We need to remember the bigger picture of these men's lives for the relevance of this incident to become apparent. Consider Peter's case. About three years ago (although it probably feels more like a hundred to Peter), he was a fisherman. Then he meets this most extraordinary man: Jesus of Nazareth. From that point on his entire world has turned upside down. He has seen things that confound both his eyes and brain. He has seen the blind made to see, the crippled to walk, a multitude fed from a tiny amount of food. He has seen the religious leaders of the day, of whom he was doubtless formerly in awe of their righteousness

Day 6 Exhortation: Gods

and scriptural knowledge, overturned – and exposed as fools, hypocrites and charlatans. He has witnessed this extraordinary man Jesus on a mountainside speaking with Moses and Elijah: two famous patriarchs long dead! He has seen multitudes follow Jesus all over the country and he has given up his fisherman's trade and his home in Galilee so that he might follow him too. He has seen this incredible man arrested, tortured and killed. He witnessed first hand the horrors of betrayal and execution of the Master he loved. Hardest of all, Peter has lived through his own desertion of the Lord and borne the subsequent consequences of self-loathing and humiliation. Since then, his memory even insists he has seen the empty tomb where the corpse lay, and met Jesus – in living form! – risen from the dead. In these three years Peter's physical understanding of the world, along with all his intellectual, emotional and spiritual being has been utterly detonated. Everything his mind conceived as real has been blown to tiny fragments and lies scattered all around him; and all by the holocaust presence of Jesus Christ in his life.

Return to the Comfort Zone: Fishermen

This is how we meet Peter in John 21. We can't accurately discern the dominant emotions whirling around Peter's mind, but we can be confident he is extremely confused and equally exhausted: physically, emotionally and spiritually debilitated. The part of his mind he thinks of as logical is trying to rationalize the irrational, solve the insoluble and fathom the unfathomable in all he has witnessed. Perhaps for just one part of his mind there is the feeling the whole three years is beginning to seem like a fantastic but impossible dream. From amidst the clouds of all of this incredible impossibility, out of the fallout Jesus has caused in his life, one old reality is re-crystallizing: once upon a time he was a fisherman. He *is* a fisherman. He will be a fisherman again. And, to that end, he is going to go fishing.

This interpretation renders this seemingly innocuous opening to John 21 both important and ominous. Peter – and James and John with him – are threatening to abandon their high calling and return to the lifestyle they had before. We do not suggest that the

Day 6 Exhortation: Gods

events and teaching of the last three years have completely escaped them, but it is entirely possible they at least want to place some distance between themselves and the events that have occurred, to digest what they have seen and heard without being tangled up in it directly. Using human thinking: what better way to do that than to return to a familiar setting? Returning to their fishermen's lives in Galilee allows them to approach their mutual thoughts and experiences at their own pace and in their own time. Unfortunately, however wise this may seem according to human thinking, turning away from the new direction to which Jesus has oriented them, for whatever reason, is the very worst thing they can do.

As a useful side-note let us remember that the model of John's Creation has shown us that Day 6, in which these words appear, is a development of Day 3: they are partners in the Earth portion of creation (Figure α_1). We recall in Day 3, after the disciples had crossed beyond the water to share the miracle of bread from heaven with their Master (6:1-11, Day 3 Exhortation) they assayed to go back across the water: the spiritual equivalent of renouncing their baptisms (6:16-17). They got into the boat and spent a profitless night laboring against the storm to row back across the Galilean sea. The picture is strikingly similar here in Day 6: once again the disciples have come to an intermission, once again Jesus is no longer with them, alone they must respond to the miracles they have witnessed. And once again, so sadly, it seems their response is to feel all too strongly the pull of their natural lives, prior to the transformation Christ has effected for them, and they collapse back to their former circumstances as if on a spring.

<u>Jesus' Rebuke: Fishers of Men</u>

Inevitably and wonderfully, however, whenever a loved disciple teeters on the brink of failure, God intercedes with more grace. The Lord Jesus appears on the shore, though they do not recognize him at first.

Day 6 Exhortation: Gods

He called out to them, "Friends, haven't you any fish?" "No," they answered. (21:5)

How much more impact this verse has with the interpretation we have offered! This is no longer just a trivial comment made at random to some fisherman, but one that strikes at the very heart of their actions! The three principal apostles: Peter, James and John – called to be fishers of men – have returned to their former lives in the absence of Jesus. Jesus' comment sternly reveals how fruitless that direction has proven: fruitless even in terms of their natural lives as fishermen. By contrast, in the presence of Christ, all things are profitable, even in their natural lives, and a massive draught of fish is taken when they act on faith in Jesus' instruction (21:6).

As an interesting aside, we do not suppose Jesus created fish in the sea that were not there before. Rather the presence of Jesus causes an effect on the fish already present to draw them where they are needed. This has important consequences for our preaching lives. The knowledge that the fish are all around us in the sea of nations is for sure, but how graphically John's gospel reveals the presence of Christ as the winning catalyst to secure them into an unbreakable net.

Nevertheless the main point is that the disciples have drifted away from their high calling and returned to the mundanity of everyday life. Jesus appears, just as he did before in Day 3 (6:16-21), to redirect them towards their higher calling, not fishermen, but fishers of men (Mark 1:17).

Psalm 82: The Disciple's Commission

Yet there is more, for their calling can be defined in higher terms than fishing for men, which higher definition forms both heart and title of this exhortation. Consider this psalm of Asaph (Psalm 82), with both its commission for those who would be righteous and its condemnation of Israel's incumbent rulers. The psalm's commissions and condemnations are paralleled below with those Jesus gave to his apostles (both then and now) and the Pharisees respectively.

Day 6 Exhortation: Gods

1 Commission to rule with impartial judgment
God stands in the congregation of the mighty; He judges among the gods. "How long will you judge unjustly, and show partiality to the wicked?" (Psalm 82:1-2)
"Do not judge according to appearance, but judge with righteous judgment." (7:24)

2 Salvation of the weak
Defend the poor and fatherless; Do justice to the afflicted and needy. Deliver the poor and needy; free them from the hand of the wicked. (Psalm 82:3-4)
Religion that God our Father accepts as pure and faultless is this: to look after orphans and widows in their distress and to keep oneself from being polluted by the world. (James 1:27)
"Give to the one who asks you, and do not turn away from the one who wants to borrow from you." (Matthew 5:42)

3 Condemnation of the blind rulers' failure to answer their commission
They do not know, nor do they understand; they walk about in darkness; all the foundations of the earth are unstable. I said, "You are gods, and all of you are children of the Most High. But you shall die like men, and fall like one of the princes." (Psalm 82:5-7)
"Woe to you, blind guides! You say, if anyone swears by the temple, it means nothing; but if anyone swears by the gold of the temple, he is bound by his oath. You blind fools! Which is greater: the gold, or the temple that makes the gold sacred?" (Matthew 23:16-17)
"Watch out for the teachers of the law. They like to walk around in flowing robes and be greeted in the marketplaces, and have the most important seats in the synagogues and the places of honor at banquets. They devour widows' houses and for a show make lengthy prayers. Such men will be punished most severely." (Mark 12:38-40)

Day 6 Exhortation: Gods

In the context of these comparisons, consider now the final part of the psalm:

4 Call to judge and inherit all the Earth
"Arise, O God, judge the earth; for you shall inherit all nations." (Psalm 82:8)

Commission: "Arise O God, Judge the Earth!"

The translators have capitalized the word 'God' in Psalm 82:8 (in most if not all major translations), assuming that this final bidding is an invocation to the Almighty. This is likely an error: the Hebrew word is 'Elohim:' which appears four times in this short psalm: twice in verse 1, and also in verses 6 and 8. Twice the word is used to refer to men, the translators indicate this by using the word 'gods' entirely in lower case. This is established by the context, not by the Hebrew. With careful consideration of the psalm we conclude that the last verse of the psalm is also directed towards men and not God. The verse is addressed to those who *will* inherit all nations, clearly not the Almighty since He already owns all nations already, indeed everything on Earth is His possession (Isaiah 66:1-2, Acts 17:24-25). Inheritance of all nations is promised to faithful men (Matthew 5:5), whom Asaph explains earlier in the psalm (v 6) wear the title of 'gods.' Thus Elohim (god) in the closing verse of Psalm 82 is actually a continuing reference to the commissioned disciple, in common with the general theme.

This is the commission Jesus gives to his disciples: they are to be gods! This is a commission to be taken extremely seriously! It cannot be a matter of pride to be considered a god, or named a god, rather it is a matter of extreme responsibility. Jesus commissions his disciples to be responsible for the whole world and everything therein! The disciple no longer has the right to walk away from any situation, for a god is ruler of all and father of all, and every father has a responsibility to care for his children. We deduce this as the reason Jesus appears to his loved ones in this final chapter of John, because in the very natural apprehension and disbelief of being called to act as gods and fathers to spiritual Israel they had balked. They slipped back into their occupational comfort zone in Galilee: Peter: "I am going fishing..." James and John: "We will come with you." But Jesus prompts them, particularly Peter, back to the role to which they were called, and the reason they were called to it:

> So when they had eaten breakfast, Jesus said to Simon Peter, "Simon, son of Jonah, do you love Me more than these?" He said to Him, "Yes, Lord; You know that I love You." He said to him, "Feed My lambs." He said to him again a second time, "Simon, son of Jonah, do you love Me?" He said to Him, "Yes, Lord; You know that I love You." He said to him, "Tend My sheep." He said to him the third time, "Simon, son of Jonah, do you love Me?" Peter was grieved because He said to him the third time, "Do you love Me?" And he said to Him, "Lord, You know all things; You know that I love You." Jesus said to him, "Feed My sheep." (21:15-17, NKJV)

The love of Christ is not something to be ignored, and correct response cannot be fulfilled in passive appreciation. Many interpret the threefold affirmation of Peter's love for his Lord as orchestrated reparation for his threefold denial (18:17-27). This seems a good understanding of the passage, particularly given the supporting detail of the charcoal fire present at Peter's threefold reaffirmation (21:9), which is only mentioned one other time in all scripture: the night of Peter's threefold denial (18:18).

Scholars of the Aramaic text of John's gospel point out that on each occasion the word for "sheep" differs: "male lambs... sheep... ewes," adding the insight that these flocks are kept separately during the summer months. [1] This suggests the interpretation that Jesus is commending to Peter the care of *all* of his sheep – a chillingly insightful command given Peter's later predilection to favor the Jews and leave the Gentile 'flocks' untended (Galatians 2:11-16). Perhaps this shortcoming of

---
[1] Errico R. A., Lamsa G. M., *Op. cit.*, p 235

Day 6 Exhortation: Gods

Peter's love is even illustrated in the language of the present conversation. Peter uses the Greek 'phileo' for "love" throughout, yet Jesus uses the Greek 'agape' for "love" in his first two questions and 'phileo' only on the third. [2] One is left to wonder whether Peter cannot yet grasp the depth of the love required from him ('agape,' not 'phileo') yet the grace of the Father, seen in His fullness in the Son, covers the shortcoming of the new disciple.

But more importantly, as we have stressed, the bigger picture is here in John 21 is the disciples being recalled to their duty that, even now after crucifixion and resurrection of the Lord, the potential fracture of their delicate and fragile new faith is threatening to leave undone.

Jesus asks Peter: "Do you truly love me more than these?" At surface reading Jesus seems to be asking whether Peter loves Jesus more than the other disciples love Jesus. This is doubtless not the case, for rivalry between the disciples striving to outdo each other for the rewards of God is exactly what Jesus has taken pains to extinguish (e.g. Luke 22:24-27, John 13:12-17). We propose what Jesus is referring to is whether Peter loves Jesus more than the entirety of the natural world all around Peter, and his place in it. Jesus is asking: "Do you love me more than 'these', Peter?" By 'these' he refers to the evidence of all Peter has: the boat, his life as a fisherman, the record catch of 153 fish lying all about them: all Peter has as a fisherman. [3] Peter has labored all night to gain these fish, which in the end he received from the Hand of God anyway. Jesus is asking whether Peter considers his life as a fisherman truly is more important than his calling as a disciple (and therefore a god). Jesus is asking whether Peter truly loves him more than his home in Galilee, his friends, his whole familiar way of life, which he once resigned, and to which it looks dangerously like he may now return. For Peter will be called to give up all these things, even his own life, in order to follow his

---

[2] Strong J. H., *Op. cit.*, 'Main Concordance,' p 638
[3] The Aramaic text of John corroborates this notion by using the word '*halein*' not '*talmeedeh halein*' indicating that 'these' refers to objects; not people. Errico R. A., Lamsa G. M., *Op. cit.*, p 234

Lord through the turbulent and violent decades of the early Christian Church.[4] Yet all this hangs in the balance here in this final chapter of John's gospel. Truly we stand at a dramatic point in the development of the disciples' spiritual lives: this final chapter is not the tranquil seaside communion we might have first supposed. Jesus arrives just in time to save the collapse of their infant discipleship: he irrevocably redirects Peter and the rest of the disciples back to the path on which they had taken their first faltering steps, the path towards destined salvation for themselves and others.

But why is it of any concern of ours to consider these things? Because this commission from Jesus extends to us also, indeed to any who would forsake all to be a disciple of Christ. This leads to a startling conclusion: just as the disciples have been called to be gods, so have we! That is the ultimate description of our calling, and no wonder it is termed a 'high calling!' (Philippians 3:14, Hebrews 3:1). We are called to be gods – gods! There is no place to revel in the pride of the description: far too much real work awaits.

To Be a God: A Loving Father/Servant of All

We are called to be gods (Psalm 82:5). What is a god? What does a god do? Scripture brings the understanding, through an oft-used metaphor, that God is a loving Father to His children, and paints us as infants before the infinite wisdom of the Almighty Father. What are the signature characteristics of a loving father we therefore need to adopt? The father attends his infant child's every need. Not only that, but he makes the provisions without ever expecting return, recognizing there can be no possibility of equality, for the infant is *wholly* dependent on the provision of the father and thus the provisions are made

---

[4] Historical records suggest Peter too was martyred some time between 25 and 40 years after this conversation with Jesus. According to tradition he was crucified in inverted position, as depicted in Renaissance art, for example, by Filarete's 1435 bronze castings of the Basilica di San Pietro doors and Michelangelo's Palazzi Pontifici fresco, both in the Vatican.

Day 6 Exhortation: Gods

continually and unquestioningly. The father even takes into account, without complaint, the child's inability to recognize the provision made for him and thereby express the gratitude he should.

Here then is our example: not only in how our Heavenly Father operates towards us; but as the directive we have to operate towards all men as gods ourselves. We are called to understand the greatest example of a ruler, (which *can* be seen in the natural world as well as in the spiritual, if we know where to look), is a loving father's interaction with an infant child: in perpetual service of inexhaustible love, asking nothing in return. This is the spiritual ruler, and this is our calling, from God, which dictates our role towards the sons of men.

Specific Examples: Feeding the Poor

Consider encountering a beggar on the street, soliciting money from passers-by. Here are some common responses to the scenario.

- "These beggars actually collect a great deal of money, I'm not giving any more to this one."
- "There's a welfare system to which I contribute: let the man access my money from the proper channels."
- "Secular wisdom suggests that it actually hurts these people more than it helps them to give them charity."
- "He's only going to waste it on alcohol, or something harmful. So actually I'm doing him a *favor* by giving him nothing."
- "If I gave him money I would encourage more people to beg, thus I'm doing the *whole of society a favor* by giving him nothing."

Perhaps the most common practice alongside all these 'gems' of the wisdom of this world is the practice of merely averting one's eyes, pretending one never saw the beggar in the first place, internally reasoning: "That hand wasn't really reaching towards me. It was pointed at someone close to me, but it didn't include

Day 6 Exhortation: Gods

me within its scope." Such behavior is utterly unworthy of a god and is therefore outside the range of acceptable behavior for anyone who desires discipleship of Christ. Christ's instructions are indisputably clear: "Give to him that asks of you," and Christ further *explicitly identifies* that this applies even in the case of blatant exploitation (Matthew 5:39-48).

For those who would do even better, the example of Christ leads us to this action not by command, but by our own desire. For if we have truly assumed the role of gods, then we recognize that all the sons of men are our children: not just the attractive, witty, wealthy, interesting ones whose company we enjoy; but all men, including the street beggar: he is our son. Could we walk past our own son, ludicrously pretending not to see him as he signals for aid? The message from scripture is didactically clear: the measure we use on others is exactly the same measure we will ourselves receive (Luke 6:38). The Bible teaches those who style their lives by deliberately placing themselves outside the beggar's outstretched hand will, by the same token, place themselves outside the reach of Jesus' outstretched hand when he comes to gather the faithful for his kingdom. Truly there will be weeping and gnashing of teeth (Matthew 25:30). We might counter: "God will take care of them. He'll make provision," as we pass by on the other side. Indeed He will, but we must ask ourselves: What if *I was* the provision that was sent?! What have I done with the role I was given?!

We should be mindful that many in former times were called to give their *lives* in order to embrace the disciple's role. Perhaps we suppose risking slight financial or even physical detriment for the gospel should only belong to days of yore, or countries far away from our own, and is far too ugly a matter to bring into our comfortable, modern-day Christian lives. The lives of men like David are written to motivate and inspire us: David stood against the nine-foot Philistine because he knew the battle was the Lord's (1 Samuel 17:47); and God would bring victory, as indeed He did. David won great victories that day: he defeated human fear, human faithlessness, and the urge to look to another to solve the communal problem. Great and hard fought victories all, even greater than the one over Goliath who, like any mere man, could fall at any moment to a chance sword-stroke or stone's mark. David defeated the same cowardly and selfish spirit that tempts the modern-day shepherd boy into ignoring those who plead for our assistance. Truly David was a god that day, and in his godliness, he allowed the One God to use him as His weapon, sweeping aside the giant with a single mark from the shepherd boy's sling.

Feeding the Spiritual Poor

Thus, we feed the poor. Yet currently we have considered only the materially poor, but there are poorer people than these we encounter every day. We speak of the spiritually impoverished. Those who are showered daily with God's blessings, some of which include: the ability to live, breathe, utilize all of their limbs, see, hear, talk, feel the warming rays of sunshine, enjoy a sufficiency of food and drink, laugh at good humor, experience the joy and strength of friendship, live in a country free from oppression or civil war, hold employment, and have free time enough to taste the myriad wonders of the natural world. Yet, despite all these blessings, some are still dissatisfied with their lot in life. Other people, they reason, do not respect them as much as they deserve. Their job certainly does not pay them what they feel they are worth. The overriding summary of their heart is that in all things they are not 'getting their fair share.' These are the spiritual poor, and they are the most in need of our charity, for truly they are the most destitute of all.

What then is our role for such people? Certainly it is not to despise or patronize them, or harbor any self-righteous thoughts. But there are a couple of necessary roles a god must play in such circumstances. One is to attempt to open their eyes to the pleasure that is available in simply being alive on this extraordinary planet and such enjoyment stems from a pervasive Hand of goodness behind the design through simple witness and encouragement. No easy task, because the temptation is to chastise the immense ingratitude and the nonsensicality of bitterness, which are doubtless unsuccessful and unhelpful routes.

Although children can be educated by rebuke; adults, in the main, cannot. Perhaps we can do little more than lend a sympathetic ear to perceived troubles and woes. But care must be taken over the manner in which this sympathizing is done and this is encapsulated in our second role.

The second role we have, which is more powerful to do immediate good, is to deliberately affect the tone of conversations we have. The spiritual poor will generally speak in negative tones: tones of bitter complaint. Agreeing with the complaint easily establishes friendship through camaraderie, but this acts to justify and augment the bitterness and is thus an error. Our task must be to create a positive spirit and sometimes that will require nothing short of a complete and discontinuous change of subject, so all included walk away enhanced in spirit and not in bitterness. Truly these poor we have with us always and we must love them as our own. And this work of love is not without benefit for ourselves: sometimes there is no clearer way to value of the wealth of our own blessings than by talking with someone blind to their own. Above all we must be guided by the notion that there is certainly enough pain and ill-feeling in the world already and thus take great care not to create any more, or fuel those spirits in others.

For the reader who grows suspicious that we have diverted from scripture we assure we have not wandered from the Biblical pathway. It has always been the scriptural directive to fill our minds and mouths with those good and positive things that build the spirit up, rather than the bitter and conspiratorial whisperings that sow dissatisfaction and discord. We note these passages from God's Word:

> Prohibition of spreading discord:
> There are six things the LORD hates, seven that are detestable to him: haughty eyes, a lying tongue, hands that shed innocent blood, a heart that devises wicked schemes, feet that are quick to rush into evil, a false witness who pours out lies and a man who stirs up dissension among brothers. (Proverbs 6:16-19)

Day 6 Exhortation: Gods

Stirring up dissension among brothers (or 'sowing discord,' KJV) is mentioned last in the list. This placement, as the culminating sin, the grand finale to the abominable catalogue, implies it is the worst offence of all. Given that the preceding list of crimes includes lies and murder; that is a sobering thought indeed.

Provocation to focus on good things:
Finally, brothers, whatever is true, whatever is noble, whatever is right, whatever is pure, whatever is lovely, whatever is admirable--if anything is excellent or praiseworthy--think about such things. (Philippians 4:8)

Achieving the High Calling: Awareness of Redemption

Paul's command to Philippi (above) is valuable indeed, but concentrating the mind on good things is complicated by the intrinsic reflex of human nature to be preponderantly drawn to evil thoughts, not good ones. This we know both from scripture (Jeremiah 17:9) and experience. The model of creation John has shown in his gospel assists with practical advice for overcoming the difficulty. One only achieves the status of the 'god' (Day 6) from traveling through Day 5, the waters of death – and death duly earned with our sins. In other words, we are in a similar position to the criminal on Death Row who, against all justice and by an inexplicable stroke of mercy, has been granted unqualified freedom. Surely this is a man flooded with intense relief, humility and gratitude! His appreciation of even the simple things of life, such as feeling sunshine and inhaling fresh air, must be sharply enhanced. This spirit of gratitude drives our focus to the godly things of life and is itself enabled by an accurate appreciation of the condemnation from which we have been released. We have escaped the sentence of death (Day 5) through the victory of Jesus Christ, in order to walk the Earth in Day 6 as the New Man with a higher calling: as a god. Truly we are the richest men and women on Earth: a truth that cannot, and must not, fail to shine through to everyone we meet.

Day 6 Exhortation: Gods

Call to Arms

So then, in summary, what have we seen? We have seen a closely averted catastrophe at the beginning of John 21, where Peter, James and John so nearly abandoned their calling as gods to return to the world of men. They were saved by Christ, as he saved them before, and as he saves each of us on many occasions. We encourage ourselves by reflecting that these faithful eleven who had walked with Jesus from the beginning did indeed remain faithful to their godly commission to the very end of their lives. Perhaps we obtain an imbalanced view of these wonderful and privileged few if we constrain our understanding purely to the gospel accounts, since the gospels record the opening three years of their walk on God's path: faltering at every turn, uncertain of their high calling and how it might ever be achieved. In the end they each heard their calling to be a god and they each heeded and performed it. Peter, for example, stumbling in rash outbursts and falling in his denial of Jesus, is transformed into a pillar of the early church (Galatians 2:9) and a principal light to the Gentiles:

> [Peter] said to them: "You are well aware that it is against our law for a Jew to associate with a Gentile or visit him. But God has shown me that I should not call any man impure or unclean… I now realize how true it is that God does not show favoritism but accepts men from every nation who fear him and do what is right… While Peter was still speaking these words, the Holy Spirit came on all who heard the message. The circumcised believers who had come with Peter were astonished that the gift of the Holy Spirit had been poured out even on the Gentiles…Then Peter said, "Can anyone keep these people from being baptized with water? They have received the Holy Spirit just as we have." So he ordered that they be baptized in the name of Jesus Christ. (Acts 10:28-48)

Day 6 Exhortation: Gods

We take both comfort and pleasure in their success. Indeed they were gods and will rise to be gods again: their success is our joy and our motivation.

To that end we must, whilst taking bread and wine, return from relishing their success to regard our path ahead. We have considered the necessary role of a god; and the many associated responsibilities: to care for every man on this planet as a loving father cares for an infant child. We also encouraged ourselves with the many privileges: the indescribable pleasure of being released from the death sentence, not just to walk the Earth again (which would be more than enough!) but to walk the Earth as a god! This is our blessing, insanely huge, absurdly undeserved and our response should be truly joyful: for by the grace of God we have every day of the rest of our lives to celebrate that victory and revel in its pleasure. Moreover even the pleasure we rightly feel in this life pales by comparison with the thought of the beauty God will establish in His coming kingdom, which kingdom forms the fullness of God's love towards us. Truly we who are unlovable are dearly loved; and blessed to the point of being indescribably rich: a richness none can steal, whose pleasure never fades, and which keeps on increasing every day. Ultimately the responsibilities and privileges are best expressed using the same phrase: All things are ours: the whole world and everything in it (entirely as one would expect, if we are indeed gods) and this too is a scriptural thought (1 Corinthians 3:21-23). We have limitless responsibilities to all men, a very few of which we have considered above and absolutely no excuses to transfer these responsibilities onto another. We are gods! (*gods!*)

And so now we must behave as such.

DAY 7 *No reference, does not appear in John*

EXPOSITION:
The Absent Day

> And there are also many other things that Jesus did, which if they were written one by one, I suppose that even the world itself could not contain the books that would be written. Amen. (21:25)

Amen. Yet our study is not yet completed. Even though we have reached the very last word of John's gospel, remarkable as though it may seem, the message of his testimony is not completed either. Even the silence at the end of his gospel speaks a message as powerful and as thought-provoking as any of the portions that preceded it.

7.1 Silent Witness

The seventh day, the day of rest, is absent from the record of John's gospel: this is emphasized in Table 7_1.

Day 7 Exposition: The Absent Day

Day	Natural Creation	John's (Spiritual) Creation: The Person and Ministry of Jesus Christ
1	Light	"the true light that gives light to every man" (1:1-3:21)
2	Water Drawn Above	"the water I give him will become in him a spring of water welling up to eternal life" (3:22-5:47)
3	Food	"I am the bread of life" (6:1-6:71)
4	Lights to Rule	"I am the light of the world" "And yet if I do judge, my judgment is true" (7:1-13:38)
5	Waters Beneath	" 'It is finished.' With that, he bowed his head and gave up his spirit" (14:1-19:42)
6	The New Man	"My Lord and my God!" (20:1-21:25)
7	God Rests; Creation is Very Good	*doesn't appear*

Table 7_1: Comparison of physical and spiritual creations, emphasizing both the relationship between the respective components, and the absence of Day 7 in the latter cycle presented in John.

Why is there no Day 7 in John? Does John consider that the seventh day is not really part of the creation sequence, maybe because nothing was actually created on that day, and therefore omits it from his model? This is extremely unlikely, because the seventh Day is of paramount importance in the natural creation, as we see from Genesis.

> By the seventh day God had finished the work he had been doing; so on the seventh day he rested from all his work. And God blessed the seventh day and made it holy, because on it he rested from all the work of creating that he had done. (Genesis 2:2-3)

Day 7 Exposition: The Absent Day

God attributes special importance to the seventh day precisely *because* no work was done. It was the day on which He rested in the completed beauty of His perfect world. The reason God created each of the components on Days 1-6 was so that He could enjoy them in His rest on the seventh day. All the six days existed for Day 7: Day 7 was their culmination, their justification, quite literally, their *raison d'être*.

Why then is this most important of days missing from John's record? Table 7_1 shows the spiritual seventh day equates to the time period in which all is perfect and God dwells harmoniously with His whole spiritual creation. This refers to the Kingdom era, obviously! This parallel explains *why* this era is absent from John's Creation: the kingdom is still in the future. Yet there is more to it than this. Table 7_1 highlights how John's gospel is arranged in a way that emphasizes loudly that the pattern is incomplete *without* the Kingdom. The table resembles a jigsaw puzzle with a piece missing! How better to state that the progression of God's plan with man is currently incomplete! The blatant omission of the seventh day is itself the irresistible proclamation of the surety of the Kingdom's arrival: as certainly as there are seven days in the week. Such is the beauty and intelligence of the gospel's design.

Day 7 Exhortation: The Beautiful Woman

EXHORTATION 7: *John 8*
The Beautiful Woman

Consider the account at the beginning of John 8, where the Pharisees bring the woman caught in the act of adultery to Jesus (8:1-11). [1] We are told from the outset the whole scenario is a deliberate attempt by the Pharisees to trap Jesus.

> The teachers of the law and the Pharisees brought in a woman caught in adultery. They made her stand before the group and said to Jesus, "Teacher, this woman was caught in the act of adultery. In the Law Moses commanded us to stone such women. Now what do you say?" They were using this question as a trap, in order to have a basis for accusing him. (8:3-6)

---

[1] We have no apportioned text from which to draw an Exhortation, since in Day 7 we are beyond the boundaries of the written gospel. We focus on this account because it has erstwhile received no attention.

Day 7 Exhortation: The Beautiful Woman

<u>The Trap: Condemning the Prostitute</u>

Why does this question form a trap? One immediate answer concerns a conflict between Jewish law and Roman law. Under the terms of the Roman occupancy the Jews were forbidden to conduct executions, yet the Mosaic Law called for any adulterer to be stoned (Leviticus 20:10). The Pharisees attempt to make Jesus side with either the Jews or the Romans, and thus against the other party (reminiscent of the trap they set Jesus of whether to pay the Roman taxes, Matthew 22:15-21).

But maybe there is more, for as always the spiritual depth of the material in John is difficult to overestimate. Recall John has already presented the meeting between Jesus and a Samaritan woman at Jacob's well (4:1-42). Note a few vital details of that exchange:

1 The conversation becomes broadly publicized. (4:28-30).
2 Jesus reveals himself to the woman as both the Messiah (4:25-26), and the fount of living waters (4:10-14).
3 The woman is a Samaritan; therefore the Pharisees would not have anything to do with her: the Samaritans being viewed as second-class citizens in Israel at that time (4:9).
4 The woman has a promiscuous history, with five or six sexual partners (4:16-18). This would have further repulsed the Pharisees from interacting with her in any way, or approving of anyone else doing so.

By assembling these four observations, we can postulate the Pharisees are well aware of, and angered about, Jesus conversing with the Samaritan woman. They know of the encounter by reason of its high publicity, (pt 1) and they are doubtless incensed by reason of both of Jesus' declaration as Messiah (pt 2) and of the low social status of the woman to whom he chooses to make this revelation (pts 3-4). Actually, the Pharisees' complaint against Jesus is broader than just this one relationship. They complain generically of Jesus' association with those they consider the morally lower classes (Luke 7:33-35): the spiritual physician is constantly rebuked for his attendance on the spiritually sick. We reasonably suppose this defines the nature of the Pharisees' trap here in John 8. What the Pharisees have done is to ensnare a woman of equal repute to those they complain about Jesus associating with and present this woman to Jesus. We focus on this stereotypical case of the Samaritan woman in John 4 because it has especial pertinence to the later development of our thoughts. [2] There is also an especially vicious dimension to the accusation, which centers around the notion of the virgin conception by which Jesus was born. Doubtless these hard-hearted Pharisees do not believe Mary's story and thus have concocted an accusation which matched their opinion of Jesus' own mother.

The adulteress is brought to Jesus and the Pharisees ask whether or not he will condemn her. This is the nature of the deeper trap. If Jesus says the woman should not be condemned then he contradicts the Mosaic Law, and Jesus himself stands condemned. Appreciate the craftiness of the Pharisees' evil, for if Jesus rules that the woman *should* be condemned, they will have ample grounds to call him to publicly renounce and apologize for his associations with such women (including the woman at Jacob's well who was guilty of the same infractions of the Mosaic Law). By this the Pharisees might hope to 'stop him in his tracks' in terms of the popularity he was so rapidly gaining. Thus Jesus stands to be condemned by whichever answer he gives and we feel it is this spiritual attack, more so than the divide between the Jewish and Roman authorities, which fuels the nature of the trap.

<u>Writing on the Ground</u>

Jesus' counter forms one of the most surprising verses in all of scripture.

---

[2] Note the suspicious nature of the capture itself: the woman was caught 'in the very act' of adultery (8:4). Adultery is not, of course, a solitary occupation; so it is mysterious the man was not also captured. Highly possibly, therefore, the man was employed by the Pharisees to act as *agent provocateur* in securing the woman's capture: indeed he may even have been one of their number.

Day 7 Exhortation: The Beautiful Woman

But Jesus bent down and started to write on the ground with his finger. (8:6)

An incomprehensible response! The words Jesus wrote on the ground are not themselves recorded, which makes it all the more intriguing. Normally we might suppose that something excluded from scripture is not particularly important. Lest we suspect that this is the case here, the importance of this insoluble puzzle is tantalizingly heightened by repetition.

Again he stooped down and wrote on the ground. (8:8)

The enigma of what Jesus actually wrote has puzzled Bible students for many years and we must approach with humility a problem which has stumped many fine students. Nevertheless speculation is ever available and we proffer a solution here for consideration. This proposed solution is again based on the context of the conversation Jesus had with the Samaritan woman at the well.

We start by considering a passage from Jeremiah:

> The heart is deceitful above all things and beyond cure. Who can understand it? …O LORD, the hope of Israel, all who forsake you will be put to shame. Those who turn away from you will be written in the dust because they have forsaken the LORD, the spring of living water. (Jeremiah 17:9-13)

Three things tie Jeremiah's prophecy to events in John. Firstly, the prophecy describes the nature and destiny of those with 'deceitful hearts' immediately marking it as a relevant text to the Pharisees plotting to ensnare Jesus. Secondly it says such men have "forsaken the LORD, the spring of living water." This is especially apposite for two reasons. Not only is this is exactly what the Pharisees did in rejecting Christ, but it also makes a direct link with the conversation in John 4: the only place in scripture where the reader is introduced to Jesus under the metaphor of living waters. This therefore acts as a counterpoint

Day 7 Exhortation: The Beautiful Woman

of some finesse to the Pharisees' strong disapproval of the promiscuous Samaritan woman in John 4. She herself did *not* forsake the living waters, but rather approached them in faith, believing. With this interpretation, how true is made Christ's prophecy against the Pharisees (Matthew 21:31): that tax collectors and prostitutes were entering the kingdom of God ahead of them! Finally, observe the destiny of these men from the quote in Jeremiah: *their names are to be written in the dust.* (or 'in the earth,' KJV). Although definitive interpretation of what this means is not available, it is clearly not a good fate to meet. Yet it forms an attractive contrast to the fate of the righteous, whose names are written in heaven (Hebrews 12:22-23, Luke 10:20), and we can conclude that to have one's name written in the earth denotes the fate of the faithless.

To summarize Jeremiah's prophecy: Those with deceitful hearts forsake the living waters and thus have their names written in the earth. John's gospel has already taken care to introduce the Pharisees as those with deceitful hearts (8:6) and Jesus as the fount of living waters (4:13-14). Jeremiah tells us such people will be "written in the dust." So, whilst we cannot know for certain what Jesus was writing in the dust of the temple floor (at least not in this age), the above passages provoke us to theorize he was writing the *names of the accusers* in the ground for them to see. This would remind them of Jeremiah's quote: "Those who turn away from you will be written in the dust." Perhaps this quote actually came to their minds, one by one, from the oldest, who had most familiarity with their Biblical scrolls, to the youngest, and convicted them to leave.

Weightier Matters of the Law

The Pharisees do not initially take Jesus' writing on the ground as sufficient answer to their challenge, however. Indeed they seem to consider it avoidance tactics and press harder for an answer to whether the woman should be stoned. Jesus replies:

> "If any one of you is without sin, let him be the first to throw a stone at her." (8:7)

Day 7 Exhortation: The Beautiful Woman

A compelling answer, which all of the Pharisees' sophistry is bereft to defeat, or even escape! Jesus does not deny the culpability of the woman, but calls into question the qualifications of those who have taken it upon themselves to condemn her.[3]

Central to Jesus' response is that the Pharisees are lacking the most important quality for human judgment – empathy – the ability to identify with the one who stands condemned and thus seek their escape from destruction. The purpose of empathy is not to condone either the sin or the sinner, but rather to enable that most precious and powerful judicial tool: mercy. The absence of mercy from the Pharisees' hearts – as it is absent from the natural world – formed the core of Jesus' appraisal of the Pharisaical judicial system.

> "Woe to you, teachers of the law and Pharisees, you hypocrites! You give a tenth of your spices--mint, dill and cumin. But you have neglected the more important matters of the law--justice, mercy and faithfulness. You should have practiced the latter, without neglecting the former." (Matthew 23:23)

The Pharisees are condemned, not by Christ, but ultimately by their own conscience. For all their plotting they have neglected

---

[3] Jesus does not mention the Roman law prohibiting the Jews from stoning, he (seemingly) invites the Pharisees to proceed. This is a small but fascinating detail, because it neatly balances the other occasion in which the Pharisees tried to trap Jesus with a 'Catch-22' situation: concerning the conflict over tax-paying (Matthew 22:15-21). In that instance (Matthew 22) Jesus appears to *support* the Roman position by saying: "Give to Caesar what is Caesar's…" – although certainly without stating that supporting the Roman law was the basis of his answer. In this instance (8:1-11) the reverse is true: Jesus seems to *disregard* the Roman law by inviting the Jews to cast stones, though again without suggesting that disregarding the Roman law is the basis of his answer. By comparing the two outcomes the truth is learned: in both cases, as in every case, Jesus is focusing wholly on enacting the Divine purpose, regardless of how such actions might be interpreted within the tortuous labyrinths of human jurisdiction. This is doubtless a powerful lesson to be drawn from the subtle comparison and one for us to implement in the decision-making processes we are faced with in our own lives.

Day 7 Exhortation: The Beautiful Woman

the weightier matters of the law: justice and mercy (c.f. Micah 6:6-8) and one by one they guiltily slink away. What they are thinking we do not know, but it is highly likely that they are encouraged to arrive at their conclusions by what Jesus is writing in the dust. And this writing, as we have hypothesized using Jeremiah's prophecy, may well have declared their own names.

Go, Sin No More

We might be tempted to think this is the end of the matter, but the narrative continues, as does the exhortation we gain from it.

> Jesus straightened up and asked her, "Woman, where are they? Has no one condemned you?" "No one, sir," she said. "Then neither do I condemn you," Jesus declared. "Go now and leave your life of sin." (8:9-11)

This exchange should not be considered an anticlimax to the 'real' message involving the dismissal of the accusing Pharisees: this portion of the account is as exhortational as any other. Jesus will not condemn the woman ("For God did not send his Son into the world to condemn the world, but to save the world through him" 3:17), but neither will he tolerate her sin: he commands her unambiguously to immediately desist from her adulteries. And there is more. Not only is her *sin* intolerable to Jesus but also whilst she has not (yet) separated herself from her lifestyle *her very presence* is unacceptable to Jesus: she is dismissed with the word 'Go' (see Section 2.4). This instruction is particularly telling, not only in the immediate context of the Pharisees' trap, but also in the broader context of Jesus' conversation with the Samaritan woman in John 4. Compare what Jesus says to the two women:

> To the Samaritan: "Go, call your husband and come back." (4:16)
> To the adulteress: "Go now and leave your life of sin." (8:11)

Day 7 Exhortation: The Beautiful Woman

How consistent is the Lord Jesus! The two women are conducting lifestyles with the same spiritual weakness, in this instance sexual promiscuity, and he directs them in exactly the same way! Favoritism is not shown to either woman. Most powerfully of all we see Jesus is not swayed by the presence of an audience, as most of us almost certainly would be, because his approach is identical in both cases. He says the same to the Samaritan woman in private as to the adulteress in the hostile presence of the Pharisees. Both women are treated with kindness, justice and mercy: highly probably a disciple was made in both cases. But, lest we attempt to misuse these scriptures and the powerful force of mercy for leniency in tolerating sinful lifestyles, we must notice that whilst they are unconverted from such lifestyles both women are, like Cain before them, dismissed from the divine presence. Neither woman is beautiful enough to share the presence of the Master. We do not refer to a physical beauty, but to a spiritual beauty, a heavenly beauty, one might say the beauty of the soul. And the souls of the women standing before Jesus at that time were disfigured with the choice of lifestyles they embraced.

The Bride of Christ: Scriptural Precedents

This exhortation will fail in its duty if it merely studies Biblical characters and contains no portion of self-examination. We have introduced the concept of the Beautiful Woman, one sufficiently beautiful to be a bride for the Lord Jesus Christ at the Marriage of the Lamb. The Beautiful Woman forms a pervading scriptural metaphor that impinges heavily on both our thoughts here and the lives we each lead.

To begin to understand the relationship between Christ and his Bride we consult the first mention of the word bride in scripture. This may seem a bizarre place to go, since this reference will not (seemingly) concern the time or person of Jesus. Yet as a rule of some generality the first mention in scripture of an important word often reflects its deepest spiritual meaning throughout the rest of the Bible. There is no obvious reason why this should be, although perhaps God knows 'first

Day 7 Exhortation: The Beautiful Woman

impressions last' in the human mind, and uses this method to teach us. Nevertheless, peculiar as it may seem, the rule seems to hold good in a surprising number of cases, (and indeed we have employed this thinking already in this work in the case of 'sun, moon and stars,' Section α.4). For further justification here are some examples of precedental usage of a key scriptural word; where its prime spiritual meaning comes to the fore.

> First appearance of 'Heart'
> The LORD saw how great man's wickedness on the earth had become, and that every inclination of the thoughts of his **heart** was only evil all the time. (Genesis 6:5)

> First appearance of 'Jerusalem' and 'Bread and Wine'
> Then Melchizedek king of **Salem** [Jerusalem] brought out **bread and wine**. He was priest of God Most High, and he blessed Abram, saying, "Blessed be Abram by God Most High, Creator of heaven and earth. And blessed be God Most High, who delivered your enemies into your hand." Then Abram gave him a tenth of everything. (Genesis 14:18-20)

> First appearance of 'Love'
> Then God said, "Take your son, your only son, Isaac, whom you **love**, and go to the region of Moriah. Sacrifice him there as a burnt offering on one of the mountains I will tell you about." (Genesis 22:2)

The first mention of the human heart denounces it a host of permanently evil thoughts in the strongest possible language. The first mention of Jerusalem occurs coincident with the first mention of bread and wine, itself a matter of interest, when Abram receives a blessing from Melchizedek and gives Melchizedek, the High Priest of God, a tithe of all he has. Thus the first communion bread and wine is shared between God's Friend (James 2:23) and the King of the City of Peace (Jerusalem). Additionally the subservience is emphasized to the High Priest of whom no origin is recorded from the premier of natural Israel. This becomes a very important principle in establishing the role of Jesus Christ as the Great High Priest. Likewise, the first mention of 'love' in scripture does not concern romance between man and woman; but rather the love of a father for his only son, a son whom he dearly loves, and whom he is asked to sacrifice that the will of God may be perfected. Instructive precedents all!

Demonstrably therefore each first mention does indeed tap the very deepest spiritual meaning each word will adopt as the pages of scripture unfold. These 'origins' are truly fascinating, but we will not explore them further because they do not directly concern our thoughts here. We leave the potential treasure houses of learning that lie on these several pathways for other explorers; as we press on towards our particular goal. We are concerned with the word 'bride' for ultimately there is only one Bride of importance in scripture: the one who is constituted by the church of the faithful believers baptized into Christ. The Bride who will marry God's Son.

The Bride: At Any Price

Having justified the notion that the first mention of an important word in scripture can define the deepest spiritual association of that term, we turn directly to scripture's first mention of the word bride:

> "Make the price for the **bride** and the gift I am to bring as great as you like, and I'll pay whatever you ask me. Only give me the girl as my wife." (Genesis 34:12)

This quote is completely removed from its context, the better to consider the abstract principle and not the narrative. The 'bride' is the one for whom any price will be paid by the bridegroom. What a perfect revelation of the relationship between Christ and his church! Is this not the ideal description of the life Christ displayed, and continues to display, for his chosen Bride for whom he willingly paid the ultimate price at Calvary?

Day 7 Exhortation: *The Beautiful Woman*

Because of the importance of the bride, particular spiritual significance is attributed to occasions when women are dismissed from, or found welcome in, the presence of Jesus. The two women we are concerned with in this exhortation, in John 4 and John 8, are necessarily dismissed from his presence. They are not condemned by Christ, who would save all, but they cannot remain in his presence whilst they conduct their lives the way they do.

The Beautiful Woman: New Jerusalem

We translate these thoughts onto the spiritual plane and direct them at ourselves for exhortation. First of all, where is this Bride of whom we speak? The scripture identifies her as the Church of the Faithful. In the Apocalypse revealed to John, she is described as (a) 'New Jerusalem' (b) populated exclusively with righteous people, and (c) clothed by the good works which these people perform.

> (a) One of the seven angels who had the seven bowls full of the seven last plagues came and said to me, "Come, I will show you the bride, the wife of the Lamb." And he carried me away in the Spirit to a mountain great and high, and showed me the Holy City, Jerusalem, coming down out of heaven from God. (Revelation 21:9-10)
>
> (b) The glory and honor of the nations will be brought into it [New Jerusalem]. Nothing impure will ever enter it, nor will anyone who does what is shameful or deceitful, but only those whose names are written in the Lamb's book of life. (Revelation 21:26-27)
>
> (c) Let us rejoice and be glad and give him glory! For the wedding of the Lamb has come, and his bride has made herself ready. Fine linen, bright and clean, was given her to wear. (Fine linen stands for the righteous acts of the saints.) Then the angel said to me, "Write: 'Blessed are those who are invited to the wedding supper of the Lamb!'" And he added, "These are the true words of God." (Revelation 19:7-9)

Day 7 Exhortation: The Beautiful Woman

The implications of these verses, though relatively obvious, utterly confound most modern Christian practice! For example common Christian opinion holds meeting together as a community, for example in sharing communion, as non-vital to one's relationship with God. The relationship between the baptized individual and God is often claimed a solely personal one and any interactions as a community are perceived optional extras which do not truly impinge on the relationship with God. "I don't need to go to church to find God": the common expression. Even without the consideration of scripture's Beautiful Woman, this attitude is perhaps a selfish over-focus on the individual because it disregards those other children of God who may need the company and caring attention that *we* may be able to provide, even if we do feel self-sufficient on our own.

This attitude is spreading as a virulent spiritual disease, but is confounded, indeed hopefully cured, by a true appreciation of the scriptural theory of the Beautiful Woman. The model of the Beautiful Woman provokes us to consider that in baptism we are called to *two* complementary roles. Firstly we are called to 'put on Christ,' in simple language to *be* Jesus Christ, irrespective of whether we are male or female. This is the 'male' aspect of our relationship with God: a highly personal one, in which we interact with God through prayer as an adopted son. Additionally we are called to a 'female' aspect: to construct this Beautiful Woman (the Church) and clothe her with actions provoked from love towards each other, so that she might form a Bride for our Lord.

If we don't meet together with our community, and take part in caring for our brothers and sisters within the family of God, we are simply not participating in making the Beautiful Woman for Christ to marry. And if we are not taking part in making the Bride then, logically, we will not be included in the marriage when the Bridegroom returns. Given that the marriage represents the Kingdom of God, we learn those who will not take part in the communal aspect of building the Beautiful Woman for Jesus to marry are acting to exclude themselves from the Kingdom of God! A sobering prospect…

Day 7 Exhortation: The Beautiful Woman

Bride and Bridegroom: Awaiting the Wedding

We attempt to appreciate this argument from God's perspective. Although we cannot understand the infinite mind of the Maker, God commonly teaches us using the analogy of a loving Father towards little children when explaining both His purpose and our role within it. In this scenario the Almighty is the Bridegroom's Father. His chief concern is that His beloved Son should marry, and marry well, (what father would think differently?). Thus as God looks down from heaven to regard the Earth, the principal thing He is looking for is a suitably Beautiful Woman to marry His Son. The Bible has shown us the Bride is not a singular person: she is an entity constructed from many disciples behaving in a loving fashion towards each other; desiring the presence of the Groom. This implies we *necessarily* have a responsibility to meet together as a Church to construct this Beautiful Woman through our caring acts towards one another. Indeed we have reasoned a suitable Bride is a principal feature God is looking for!

We also learn the Bride, composed of many people, can only be clothed by the mutual acts of love within the community they form (Revelation 19:7-8). This realizes another vital detail for our exhortation. It shows that meeting together of itself is useless unless it enables those acts of kindness. To merely turn up, listen, and slip away from a worship service, quietly congratulating oneself for attendance, does nothing whatsoever towards constructing the Beautiful Woman. It is a daunting task, and an equally breathtakingly exciting privilege, to realize that the task of creating a Beautiful Woman fit to marry God's own Son falls into our hands.

And there is more. Why does our Lord remain away? Why have we had to wait so many centuries for his return? This picture we have painted of the impending marriage gives a sobering response. We genuinely suppose one of the many reasons that our Lord's coming is yet before us, even in the 21st century, is that His Father does not yet see a sufficiently Beautiful Woman for him to marry, and thus His Son's return is not yet warranted. All too often when we ask: "How long till our Lord returns?" we imply, sometimes bitterly, the delay lies entirely with God's timelines *irrespective* of our actions. Seldom do we consider, as the model of the Beautiful Woman gives us prerogative to consider, that the date of our Lord's return is at least partially *under our own control*. Is it truly the Bride who awaits the Bridegroom? By no means! The Groom stands ready at the altar, fully robed and prepared for the marriage union. Rather it is the Bride who remains half-naked and unready, because she is clothed, as we have learned, by the righteous acts of the saints. There is therefore perhaps some level of covering which the Father awaits, and does not yet see, until which point the Wedding remains delayed. When the Bride is suitably adorned for the marriage, the Bridegroom will undoubtedly arrive to greet her. Who therefore awaits whom?

Invitation to the Beautiful Woman: 'Come' not 'Go'

One final thought. Those adulterous women, spiritually unattractive, were dismissed from the Bridegroom's presence with the command 'Go.' By contrast therefore, we might expect the Beautiful Woman whom the Bridegroom will marry to be bidden towards Christ with the command 'Come' (see Section 2.4). Pleasingly, we find exactly this.

> The Spirit and the bride say, "Come!" And let him who hears say, "Come!" Whoever is thirsty, let him come; and whoever wishes, let him take the free gift of the water of life. (Revelation 22:17)

The metaphor of the waters of life, which we first encountered at the start of this pattern in John 4, appears again in this verse. This confirms we are indeed following a connected scriptural thought. Now the woman at the fount of living water is acceptable to dwell in the presence of Christ. Indeed, because she is not one, but composed of many who are one, she invites all who will listen, and will 'come,' to join with her and live with Christ. Our acts of kindness towards each other beautify this woman, and as her beauty is augmented we draw the Bridegroom

Day 7 Exhortation: The Beautiful Woman

from heaven towards her. In this, then, let us bring to life this apocalyptic metaphor, and the quote that follows from it:

Even so, come, Lord Jesus. (Revelation 22:20)

Amen.

CONCLUSIONS

Here we appraise the bigger picture of all we have seen in our studies in John and draw our concluding thoughts. As we mentioned in the introduction, this objective crystallizes into two broad questions, the latter subdividing into two particular avenues:

1. Having considered the evidence, can we conclude that John's gospel presentation of the person and ministry of Jesus Christ is patterned according to a spiritual creation sequence?
2. Why would the creation pattern be employed in a gospel narrative?
    - What is gained for the glory of the Father and Son from a gospel structured as the creation sequence?
    - Are there other parts of scripture structured according to creation's six days and how are we edified from seeing them this way?
    - How does perception of John's spiritual creation help us become better disciples of Christ?

Conclusions

Ω.1 Perceiving the Creation Sequence in John's Gospel

Day	Arena	References (Genesis/John)	Theme (Genesis/John)
1	Heaven	Genesis 1:3-5	Light
		John 1:1-3:21	Light, Illumination, Understanding
2	Waters	Genesis 1:6-8	Water drawn above from beneath
		John 3:22-5:47	Water from above, life out of death, baptism, resurrection
3	Earth	Genesis 1:9-13	Revelation of Earth Plant life for food
		John 6:1-6:71	Bread, food, sustenance Word of God
4	Heaven	Genesis 1:14-19	Population of heavens Lights to rule
		John 7:1-13:38	Light to rule, authority and judgment
5	Waters	Genesis 1:20-23	Population below waters above: Tanniyn [no ruler]
		John 14:1-19:42	'Things below': Cross, Death [world's ruler taken]
6	Earth	Genesis 1:24-31	Population of Earth: New Man, to rule all creation
		John 20:1-21:25	The Resurrected Christ: New Man, to rule all creation

Table Ω_1: Natural and Spiritual creation sequences, detailed respectively in Genesis and John's gospel.

Conclusions

Here we consider the first question above: Is the material presented in John's gospel arranged to fit a spiritual equivalent of the creation sequence? This author suggests the concluding answer is "yes." The evidence on which this answer is based has been presented in detail in the preceding chapters and is summarized in tabulated format, to most readily appreciate the structure of the argument, in the three tables following (Tables Ω_1, Ω_2 and Ω_3).

Firstly, Table Ω_1. This table restates the major themes of the natural creation recorded in Genesis alongside the major themes of the successive portions of John's gospel. In both cases the respective Biblical references are given. This produces the proposed divisions of John's gospel by which the preceding chapters in this book are organized.

Table Ω_2 expands on Table Ω_1. It presents the breakdown of events and accounts in the gospel comprising each proposed creative 'day,' which are used to justify the thematic descriptions given in Table Ω_1.

Creative Day	Reference in John	Evidence for Creation Model
DAY 1	1:1	**1** Obvious mirror of natural creation's introduction
	1:1-9	**2** Presents Jesus as "the light of the world"
	1:10-18	**3** Focuses on Jesus being understood, recognized, known, seen (illuminated)
	1:19-28	**4** Focuses on understanding John the Baptist and his work
	1:29-50	**5** More focus on understanding. Jesus Christ says: "Come and see," Philip says: "Come and see"
	2:1-11	**6** Wedding at Cana. Central point is who understood Jesus' ministry, see 2:9
	3:1-21	**7** Concerns what Nicodemus should have seen (3:3), understood, and been

229

Conclusions

			illuminated by, but wasn't
		overall	**8** In this whole section light is the general vehicle of the text. Counting appearances of 'light' and 'water' and 'bread' in the gospel text we find a heavy preponderance of light: "light" : 11 occurrences [c.f. total "water" + "bread": 7]
DAY 2		3:22-36	**1** Concerns baptism, includes <u>re</u>appearance of John the Baptist
		3:31	**2** Jesus declared as being "from above" not "from beneath"
		4:1-26	**3** Jacob's well: presents water from Jesus (from above), water from the well (from below): explains superiority of the former
		4:10-14	**4** Explicit presentation of Jesus as the living water
		4:43-54	**5** Centurion's son is healed (drawn up) from the brink of death to life
		5:1-14	**6** Impotent man is "raised up" to walk, when healed at Pool of Bethesda
		5:16-30	**7** Subject is resurrection: the ultimate lifting up to life from that which is dead below
		overall	**8** In this section water is the general vehicle of the text. Again counting the appearances of 'light,' 'water' and 'bread' we find an almost exclusive presence of the keyword 'water' "water": 14 occurrences [c.f. total "light" + "bread": 1]
DAY 3		6:1-15	**1** Jesus feeds 5 000 with 5 loaves and 2 small fish
		6:25-33	**2** Jesus introduces spiritual bread and

Conclusions

		contrasts it with the manna (natural bread) of Moses' day
	6:35	**3** Jesus is explicitly presented as the "bread of life"
	6:35-59	**4** Jesus introduces the sacraments, the bread of his flesh, shows man cannot be sustained without it
	overall	**5** In this section bread is the general vehicle of the text. Again counting keywords 'light,' 'water' and 'bread' we find an exclusive presence of 'bread' "bread": 21 occurrences [c.f. total "light" + "water": 0]
DAY 4	7:14-24	**1** Jesus is presented as the authority from God, Pharisees are instructed to stop judging by appearances and make "right judgment"
	7:25-52	**2** Debate over Jesus' authority as the Christ, prophet
	8:1-11	**3** Jesus comments on having authority to judge
	8:12-30	**4** Jesus is presented as the "light of the world" (which echoes Day 1) who judges (judgment part is new to Day 4)
	8:31-59	**5** Jesus is senior in authority even to Abraham
	9:1-41	**6** This focal chapter concerns natural and spiritual blindness to the Light and resulting judgment therefrom
	10:1-21	**7** Concerns Jesus' authority as the Shepherd of the flock
	10:22-42	**8** Concerns Jesus' authority as the Son of God
	11:1-42	**9** Jesus raises Lazarus, explicitly for the purpose of demonstrating his position as coming from God (11:41-42)

Conclusions

	12:1-10	**10** Jesus is dined in honor and anointed for Kingship
	12:11-19	**11** Jesus enters Jerusalem as sign of his Kingship, fulfilling the prophecy of Zechariah (Zechariah 9:9)
	12:20-36	**12** Jesus declares judgment by his impending crucifixion: "Now is the time for judgment on this world" (12:31)
	13:1-17	**13** Jesus demonstrates spiritual rulership – in service
	13:31-38	**14** Jesus is glorified, and issues new commands
DAY 5	14:1-29	**1** Thomas, Philip and Judas all independently fail to understand what Jesus is saying
	14:30-31	**2** Jesus announces: "the prince of this world is coming"
	15:18-27	**3** Focuses on the world, that in its sinfulness it will persecute, hate and kill believers
	16:5-15	**4** Jesus (the ruler, see Day 4) announces his departure from the world
	16:17-33	**5** The disciples' failure to understand Jesus is again emphasized, Jesus announces their scattering and their desertion of him
	18:1-14	**6** Judas Iscariot betrays Jesus and has Jesus arrested: the 'prince of this world' stands in power
	18:6	**7** All "fall to the earth" as Jesus announces his presence (which echoes the reverse of Day 2, where people were raised up in the presence of Christ)
	18:15-27	**8** Peter denies any association with, or knowledge of, Christ

Conclusions

	18:28-40	**9** All choose Barabbas, Jesus Christ is rejected
	19:1-42	**10** Jesus is tortured, executed by crucifixion, & buried. Spiritual creation's ruler has been removed
DAY 6	20:1-9	**1** Jesus is resurrected as the firstfruits of the new creation (1 Corinthians 15:23), is presented as the New Man
	20:10-18	**2** Jesus' authority is elevated: he is called "Rabboni" by Mary, (previously he is only called "Rabbi" in John's gospel)
	20:19-31	**3** Jesus twice passes through locked doors that would prevent all other men
	20:21-22	**4** Jesus commissions his disciples to forgive or retain sins, and explains they too are now sent from God
	20:28	**5** Jesus' authority is elevated: he is called "God" by Thomas, (previously he is only called "Son of God" in John's gospel). God allows Jesus the name above every name after his resurrection (see Philippians 2:1-11, Appendix C)
	21:1-14	**6** Jesus miraculously supplies a meal of bread and fish (which echoes Day 3)
	21:15-24	**7** Jesus reinstates Peter, and calls his disciples to follow him
	21:25	**8** Jesus performs acts too wonderful and numerous for the world to record

Table Ω_2: Recapitulation of the reflections of the six days of creation, in sequence, throughout John's gospel record of the person and ministry of Jesus Christ.

Structure in the Spiritual Creation

We showed earlier the six days of the natural creation are structured in two cycles of three, in the arenas of Heaven, Waters

Conclusions

and Earth. This creates 'pairs' of Days: Day 1 with 4; Day 2 with 5; Day 3 with 6 (see Figure α_1). Table Ω_3 shows these same pairings also appear between the same days in the spiritual creation in John's gospel, through key declarations, scenes and details.

Days 1 & 4: Partners in Heaven	
Day 1 (1:1-3:21)	**Day 4** (7:1-13:38)
First of two mentions in John's gospel that Jesus is the light of the world. (1:9)	Second of two mentions in John's gospel that Jesus is the light of the world. (8:12)
Days 2 & 5: Partners in Waters	
Day 2 (3:22-5:47)	**Day 5** (14:1-19:42)
First of two mentions in John's gospel of "joy being complete" (3:29). John the Baptist makes this comment in the context of Jesus' disciples baptizing (3:26): i.e. bringing the gift of life out of death.	Second of two mentions in John's gospel of "joy being complete" (15:11-17:13). Jesus makes this comment in the context of bringing the gift of his life laid down in death. (15:13)
Days 3 & 6: Partners in Earth	
Day 3 (6:1-6:72)	**Day 6** (20:1-21:25)
First of two occasions in John's gospel where Jesus supplies a meal of bread & fish. (6:1-15)	Second of two occasions in John's gospel where Jesus supplies a meal of bread and fish. (21:1-14)

Table Ω_3: Paired days within John's Creation, mirroring the partnering in the six days of natural creation. The partnerships are established by John's subtle use of repeating scenes and phrases in the central teaching of the gospel at each respective point.

Additionally evidence of the creation sequence in John can be obtained independently by summarizing the gospel using some frequently employed key words. This method has the benefit of being slightly more objective than most, since it rests on the words the gospel author was inspired to choose, rather than a criteria operating within the mind of the reader. Whilst not essential to the main flow of the argument, this summary presents an interesting view of the substructure of John's gospel and therefore it, and the rationale which generates it, are appended to this work (Appendix B).

In conclusion, the material summarized in Tables Ω_1, Ω_2 and Ω_3 and their expansions in the preceding chapters, provides the basis on which the proposal of the creation model in John's gospel, 'John's Creation,' rests.

$\Omega.2$ Comparing 'John's Creation' with Other Expositions

The generic scholars' approach divides John's gospel into five portions: the Prologue (1:1-18); Early disciples (1:19-51); Book of Signs (2:1-12:50); Book of Glory (13:1-20:30); and Epilogue (21). The latter is sometimes taken to be apocryphal, although one of many suspicions against this notion is that its authenticity was never challenged prior to the 17th century. [1] Although many scholars acknowledge this general structure very few present any justification of it: its only common reference is seen in a trend of authors to describe the prologue as a summary of the gospel entire. This done, most commentators present their exposition of John wholly independent of the supposed structure and describe John in terms of central themes.

Carson suggests the central theme of John's gospel as the unity Jesus has with his Father, presented in the style of dualisms: contrasts between light and darkness, sight and blindness, truth and lie. [2] Weller differs by arguing John's gospel as constructed entirely around eight miraculous signs, with the intervening text acting as either introduction to or exposition of those signs. [3]

---

[1] Madame Cecilia, "Catholic Scripture Manuals: St John," 1923, Burns, Oates and Washbourne, London, U.K., p 366
[2] Carson D. A., "The Gospel According to John," 1991, Eerdmans, Grand Rapids, MI, p 22
[3] Weller P., "Signs in John's Gospel," Detroit Christadelphian Book Supply, Livonia, MI, p 5

Conclusions

Newbigin identifies John's principal themes as: life, light and darkness, truth and glory. [4] Additionally he generalizes John's gospel soundly by saying: as "One could, in fact, describe the whole book as an exposition of what it will mean to 'follow Jesus.'" [5] Whilst never departing from the Trinitarian stance this present author believes so damaging to the appreciation of the person and work of Jesus (see Appendix C), Newbigin offers thoughtfully crafted appreciation of John's gospel, largely through the essential tool of humility and an open ear in the presence of God's Word. He later adds the themes of perseverance and liberation to his list and expands the theme of truth (in a manner similar to Carson's proposed dualisms) by emphasizing how the gospel commonly presents truth through description of the apostles' misunderstandings of it. [6]

Ray, as Newbigin, faithfully quotes John's own purpose in writing his gospel: so that all might believe on the name of Jesus for their salvation (20:31). [7] Nevertheless Ray commits the grave error of ranking human reasoning equal to the Word of God, stating openly that "the tradition of the [Catholic] Church is an equally infallible authority" to the New Testament writings. This error is compounded by the insistence that "the authoritative interpretation of the Bible is the prerogative of the Catholic Church" in direct contravention of scripture's teaching that the Bible does not require a private interpreter before its meaning can be generally known (2 Peter 1:20-21). [8] His reasoning is heavily influenced by these premises and no overall theme or structure to the gospel is identified. Ray bases his study primarily on the "trusted Revised Standard Version, Catholic edition" (yet in the same paragraph advises against using versions of the Bible where "denominational biases are more likely to intrude into the

---

[4] Newbigin L., "The Light Has Come," 1982, Eerdmans, Grand Rapids, MI, p 1
[5] *Ibid*, p 19
[6] *Ibid*, pp 141, 152
[7] Ray S. K., *Op. cit.* p 34
[8] *Ibid*, p 20

translation."[9]) In general the work is presented in the form of a study guide where the reader is directed equally to the scriptures and the Catholic Catechism for answers, with resulting implied answers suffering from the fundamental divergence of the two sources.

Errico identifies the main theme of John's gospel as the eternal, living Word.[10] Whilst this theme is doubtless as accurate as those seen by other authors, he does little to expand on it and focuses on presenting the gospel as a series of Semitic idioms when read from Aramaic, rather than Greek, texts (for which Errico employs the work of Aramaic expert George Lamsa in co-authorship). This offers a valuable broadening of understanding of the cultural scenes of the gospel's time. Errico recognizes Jesus as the source of life from God, even confidently affirming his resurrection of Lazarus as prime example of that truth, yet utterly confounds the gospel message by denying the miraculous aspect of any of the other signs. This entails going to remarkable lengths to postulate, for example, why the water made wine actually remained water or how the feeding of the five thousand arose from thousands of loaves secreted on the persons of the multitude, despite the gospel's certain declarations to the contrary.[11]

Whittaker presents the gospel of John through the intriguing notion of narrating it as a continuing conversation between Jesus and Nicodemus.[12] He achieves this by postulating the presence of Nicodemus in the background of a good number of the gospel's scenes and considers Jesus' statements as an ongoing extension of the conversation in the third chapter. Whilst this analysis lacks firm proof of concept the exposition is engaging and frequently offers edifying insight, demonstrating the value of viewing the Word of God from a novel standpoint.

---

[9] *Ibid*, p 24
[10] Errico R. A., Lamsa G. M., *Op. cit.*, pp 7, 88
[11] *Ibid*, pp 35, 90
[12] Whittaker H., "Bible Studies: An Anthology," 1987, Biblia, Cannock, U.K. pp 22-25

Conclusions

Alongside this there are a few authors whose expositions are defined according to an explicit structure as well as general themes. Staley proposes a 'concentric' model, where John describes a symmetric process of God reaching out to man and enabling man to reach out to God, a pattern he sees loosely adhered to through the gospel's chapters. [13] This concentric model has also been hypothesized in the supposed Prologue (1:1-18). [14] Another author even suggests John's gospel is hinged entirely around Jesus' words in 10:22-29, after which the 'direction' of the whole gospel is changed and God's purpose, hithertofore obscured, is gradually revealed. [15] Whilst these structures present interesting concepts, this author is challenged to detect them any more than very loosely within John's gospel narrative.

Sadly, many authors reduce John's gospel to a purely reactive text, written to stem the flow of a particular heresy. Strachan argues that John was written to combat Gnosticism, [16] Meeks to combat Judaism, [17] Ray to combat both. [18] Whittaker, in another publication, agrees with Meeks, arguing the main theme of John's gospel to be a comparison between Jesus and Moses for countering the resurgence of heretical Judaism in the early years of the Church: indeed he argues the gospel written "with the express purpose of stemming that drift." [19] These analyses seem very unsatisfactory, since the result is invariably a weakened gospel, written only to rebut a particular doctrinal scheme. Whilst there is no doubt a revelation of truth necessarily combats error,

---

[13] Staley J. L., "The Print's First Kiss: A Rhetorical Investigation of the Implied Reader in the Fourth Gospel," 1985, Society of Biblical Literature Dissertation Series 82, Scholars Press, Missoula, MT

[14] Flanagan N. M., in "The Collegeville Bible Commentary: New Testament," 1992, Ed. R. J. Karris, Liturgical Press, Collegeville, MN, pp 981-982

[15] Wyller E. A., Studia Theologica 1988, 42, pp 151-167

[16] Strachan R. H., "The Fourth Gospel: Its Significance and Environment," 1941, Student Christian Movement, London, U.K., pp 44-45

[17] Meeks W. A., "The Prophet-King: Moses Traditions and the Johannine Christology," 1967, Novum Testamentun Supplements, Brill, Leiden, Netherlands

[18] Ray S. K., *op. cit.*, p 34

[19] Whittaker H. A., "Studies in the Gospels," Biblia, Cannock, U.K., p 54

this (or indeed any) resultant effect of a text should not be back-extrapolated to be necessarily defined as its purpose. (i.e. just because John's gospel may provide excellent comfort for the bereaved, for example, is not evidence John wrote it for this purpose.) The power of John's stunningly deep presentation of the person of Jesus Christ bespeaks much more than a mere rebuttal of heresy, but rather a more positive and direct revelation of the glory of the Father through His Son *per se*. As this author and others have detailed, John defines his own purpose as an evangelistic extension of exactly this tenet, which declaration is held to the fore in the thread of this work:

> But these [words] are written that you may believe that Jesus is the Christ, the Son of God, and that by believing you may have life in his name. (20:31)

The existing literature yields a broad spectrum of suggestions of the themes and structure of the gospel of John. To this we add the notion proposed and argued here, that John presents the life and person of the Lord Jesus Christ according to the structure of the creation pattern, for the reasons of revealing Jesus Christ as the express image and fullness of the Father as both Creator and firstfruit of the new, spiritual, creation.

Consequent benefits and justifications of this structure are detailed in the section immediately following. Here we simply conclude by noting that different themes and structures have been seen in John's gospel by different authors, many of which are complementary, rather than contradictory. The creation theme proposed in this work does not explicitly contradict any of those other themes mentioned here, variously identified themes above can flow uninhibited around and within the creation structure. Importantly 'John's Creation,' as a model, compares especially favorably to the themes and structures detailed above in terms of its close adherence to the scriptural text throughout the gospel, as detailed in Table Ω_2.

Conclusions

Ω.3 *The Value of the Creation Sequence in John's Gospel*
Here we address the first avenue of the second question:

Why would the creation pattern be employed in a gospel narrative?
- What is gained for the glory of the Father and Son from a gospel structured as the creation sequence?

We have seen how our understanding and appreciation of the central gospel tenets and even the details is enriched by the perception and application of this pattern. Secondly with our study of Day 7 we have seen how the cunning use of the prominent absence of the Kingdom from the model (Table 7_1) necessarily demands its presence: the silence at the end of the gospel speaking louder than words in testifying to the Kingdom's arrival to complete the pattern. This intelligently underscores that although John's gospel is concluded the outworking of God's plan is not; one final stage is yet to arrive. These are two reasons why the spiritual creation sequence is powerful and productive in John; and we shall find three more. These concern: the pre-eminence given to the kingdom era; the different insight lent into the prime reason for the sacrifice of Christ; and the ability to perceive Christ as creator within the model of the spiritual creation.

The Pre-eminence of God's Kingdom from John's Creation

A recurring theme of all six creative days in John's gospel was the superiority of the spiritual creation's component over its natural counterpart; and always for the same reason: where death is found in the natural form, life is seen in the spiritual. This is not a vague generalization, but explicitly justifiable in each instance, as Table Ω_4 clarifies.

Conclusions

Day	John's Creation	Relation To	Genesis Creation	Reason why
1	Spiritual Light	Excels	Natural Light	because it retains the Living Word of God – natural light is non-sentient
2	Spiritual Water	Excels	Natural Water	because it gives eternal life – those who drank earthly water died later
3	Spiritual Bread	Excels	Natural Bread	because it gives eternal life – those who ate manna (natural bread) died later
4	Spiritual Judgment	Excels	Natural Judgment	because in highest form it gives life – highest human judgment brings death
5	Spiritual Death	Excels	Natural Death	because spiritual death can produce eternal life – earthly death is just death
6	Spiritual Premier (Christ)	Excels	Natural Premier (Adam)	because Christ rules the new spiritual creation that lives to God – Adam rules the first creation that dies
7	Kingdom	?	Eden	?

Table Ω_4: A summary of the relationships between the spiritual components of John's Creation, and the natural components of the Genesis creation.

From the common pattern it is trivial to complete the last row of Table Ω_4: the Kingdom of God will stand in excellence above Eden, because it will be populated by those who will live for evermore, not those who are doomed to die. But despite this blatant apparence, the superiority of the Kingdom over Eden's state remains a truth seldom appreciated. Commonly the

Conclusions

Kingdom is spoken of using phrases such as 'Eden Restored' or 'Paradise Regained.' These phrases are erroneous, they vastly underestimate the quality of the Kingdom Age! God's plans never project backwards. We are not directing our lives *backwards* to the time of Eden, but *forwards* to a new and unprecedented future in our relationship with God. John's gospel, by use of the creation pattern, compellingly demonstrates the components of the spiritual creation always stand in excellence to their natural precursors. The Kingdom is not to be Eden restored: it is to be Eden *excelled*, and how exciting and pleasurable it is to learn that! This forms a third answer to why John arranges his gospel according to the creation sequence, because it gives this unparalleled emphasis to the pre-eminence of the Kingdom over and above even the 'goodness' of Eden.

The Pre-eminence of Christ's Sacrifice from John's Creation

All scripture promotes the sacrifice of Jesus Christ as the pre-eminent event in human history. The gospel of John amplifies this vital reality in adding another dimension to our perception, and does so through the pattern of the spiritual creation sequence.

Natural creation taught all six creative days existed *for* Day 7 (Section 7.1). The spiritual parallel to this underscores the Kingdom's pre-eminence: everything in the spiritual creation is justified only by the coming Kingdom. Day 1: Jesus shined as a light in the world, partly to illuminate us, but ultimately so the Kingdom would come, and there be some granted with the gift of life to populate it. Likewise Days 2, 3 and 4: Jesus drew some up towards the Living Water; Jesus provided – indeed formed – the Living Bread; and Jesus became the Light to Rule; all primarily for the Kingdom. But when we strike Day 5, that darkest of days, we gain an unusual gem of God's teaching. Jesus died: resigning his life of flawless obedience to the Father through ignominious and agonizingly painful flagellation and crucifixion. Some scriptures teach us he died as a consequence of our sins (1 Corinthians 15:3), others that it was part of his Father's greater design (Philippians 2:8). Yet John, as always,

Conclusions

leads our thoughts to the deeper understanding. His creation pattern shows us Day 5, as all Days, was *for* Day 7. The primary reason Jesus was crucified was for the coming Kingdom to exist! Only by his death could the Kingdom have a living population, cleansed of sin, which will share harmonious fellowship with the Father in a world filled with His Glory (Habakkuk 2:14). Without the crucifixion, the Kingdom cannot be achieved. What an important dimension of Christ's sacrifice this emphasizes! What a *better* sacrifice we are now blessed to see!

Thus our fourth answer why John sculpted his gospel with the creation framework is to proclaim the Kingdom age as *raison d'être* to all preceding ages. The additional emphasis seen in Jesus' life is how his ministerial acts were all thoughtfully and deliberately pointing towards that greater, final goal.

Understanding Christ as the Creator through John's Creation

John's Creation expounds fundamental truths about the preeminence of Jesus Christ. In so doing verses of scripture otherwise indecipherable are understood and embraced. Here are some examples of scriptural verses that imply Jesus is the creator of the world, or at least the channel by which God created everything.

> [Jesus] was in the world, and **the world was made by him**, and the world knew him not. (1:10, KJV)
> [Jesus] was in the world, and though **the world was made through him**, the world did not recognize him. (1:10, NIV)
> For even if there are so-called gods, whether in heaven or on earth (as indeed there are many "gods" and many "lords"), yet for us there is but one God, the Father, from whom all things came and for whom we live; and there is but one Lord, **Jesus Christ, through whom all things came** and through whom we live. (1 Corinthians 8:5-6)

How are we to understand these quotes? Some suggest Jesus is (part of) God Himself, that he dates back to the beginning of time, and was therefore cognizant of and instrumental in the

Conclusions

Genesis creation, as much as was his Almighty Father. Whilst this accounts well for the verses above, the broader scriptures teach this is an inaccurate understanding of the true nature of the Lord Jesus Christ. [20]

So how *are* we to understand these quotes? The Bible unambiguously states the creation came through Christ: a puzzling teaching. Yet John's remarkable gospel explains the matter. With the pattern we have presented we are now in a position to realize that Jesus was indeed the conduit for the creation, and in some senses even the creator. But this does not refer to the *natural* creation detailed in Genesis 1! Rather we have been shown a New Creation: the spiritual creation, whose presence we have seen in the New Testament (see Section $\alpha.4$), expounded to its fullest and most explicit (six-day) level here in the gospel of John.

Now we are perfectly placed to understand the quotations about God performing the whole *spiritual* creation through/by His Son the Lord Jesus Christ. Consider: what is the creation? If we are thinking down at the human level, we are likely to suppose: "The creation is land and sea and air. It is trees and animals: cats, dogs, pigs, cows, elephants and giraffes…" *ad infinitum*. But this is not, interestingly, the Biblical description even of the natural creation, let alone the spiritual. What is the Biblical picture of the creation? A light that shined in darkness (Christ!); life-giving water drawn up to a heavenly position (Christ!); bread sufficient to feed all men (Christ!); a light that shined to rule (Christ!); death, who dwelt in the waters beneath (Christ!); and a man in a new form, designed to care for it all (Christ!). Christ both created and epitomized all of these things in his ministry, yet we remain aware that this creation came, as all good things come, from the Father of lights Himself (James 1:17). Thus God did indeed create all these things, the whole

---

[20] The belief of Jesus being God is sufficiently commonplace as to warrant serious consideration: to that end we present a thesis of the nature of Jesus Christ, with particular reference to the descriptions in John's gospel, in Appendix C.

Conclusions

creation by and through His Son, the Lord Jesus Christ. The verses refer to this latter creation, the spiritual creation; and nowhere is this more explicitly propounded than the gospel of John, where the notion of Christ as the conduit of creation is introduced (1:1, 10).

We also recall a fascinating detail from Day 2:

> I tell you the truth, the Son can do nothing by himself; he can do only what he sees his Father doing, because whatever the Father does the Son also does. (5:19)

As we noted earlier (Section 2.5) the broader interpretation of this verse implies both Father and Son will create a dispensation of creation. In the light of the quotes above from John and Corinthians it seems reasonable to include this verse as a corroboration of the role of Creator Jesus plays in revealing the spiritual creation to us.

Additional corroboration comes from the letter to the Hebrews:

> **In the past** God spoke to our forefathers through the prophets at many times and in various ways, but **in these last days** he has spoken to us by his Son, whom he appointed heir of all things, and **through whom he made the universe**. (Hebrews 1:1-2)

In the former times 'the past' God spoke to the prophets in diverse ways, and in the latter days He created the universe through His son. The very structure of the sentence places the 'making of the universe' in the 'latter days' – confirming, as we deduced from John's gospel, to which creation this refers. Thus we find a further reason why John founds his gospel on the creation model. When the model is tied to the Lord Jesus Christ, we learn the unparalleled pre-eminence which Jesus holds in the eyes of the Father: that he has been the very one through whom, and by whom, the Father has worked to bring His second creation, the spiritual creation, into our lives. Once again, John

Conclusions

has extended our understanding of the scriptures with his breathtakingly simple, yet profound, description of the person and ministry of Jesus Christ.

Ω.4 *Letters to the Seven Churches*

Here we address the second avenue of our second question:

Why would the creation pattern be employed in a gospel narrative?
- Are there other parts of scripture structured according to creation's six days and if so how are we edified from seeing them this way?

There is evidence that the creation pattern does appear in other scriptures and, perhaps not surprisingly, it emerges in another of the apostle John's Biblical writings: the Revelation of Jesus Christ.[21]

In the early portion of the Revelation John receives a commission from the 'One like the Son of Man' to write to seven churches. These letters, dictated by revelation from the Lord, contain understated presence of the creation sequence. Since the pattern is subtle, we need to take care to handle all seven letters the same way, so we do not imprint the pattern purely by our desire, rather than its genuine appearance in the text. To ensure each letter is appraised commonly, we monitor three parameters: the description of the One like the Son of Man, (which changes from letter to letter); the core element(s) of the message; and the nature of the promise made to the faithful. The findings are shown in Figure Ω_1.

The creation pattern is seen in the match between the colors of the two right hand columns in Figure Ω_1: this is far higher than would be statistically predictable by chance. There is a small degree of subjectivity in the color assignment: the reader is

---

[21] The thoughts presented in this section draw heavily from the excellent, unpublished work of R. Walker and G. Walker entitled "The Revelation of Jesus Christ."

Conclusions

strongly encouraged to read Revelation 2-3 and self-determine what the appropriate color assignment should be at each point. But even allowing for small differences introduced by subjective interpretation it seems that the creation pattern is indeed present once again.

In the following explanation we present the reasoning by which the colored representation of the seven letters in Figure Ω_1 is established. (The color scheme is shown in the key to Figure Ω_1 and introduced in detail in Appendix B.)

Letter 1: Ephesus (Light)

The Speaker to Ephesus: He is seen walking amongst seven stars and seven lampstands (or candlesticks) (Revelation 2:1). This is a manifestation of light, for which the color yellow is chosen (as Appendix B).

The Message to Ephesus: One of encouragement and praise for those who have persevered and endured (Revelation 2:3). None of the colors of this study (Figure Ω_1) can be used for 'perseverance' or 'endurance' without overly straining the text, thus this box is left blank.

The Promise to Ephesus: Those who overcome in Ephesus will 'eat of the tree of life' (Revelation 2:7). This is best represented by the color we chose for food and sustenance: green.

Thus for the letter to Ephesus we have yellow/blank/green where we should have three yellows (Figure Ω_1). Not the greatest of matches, although there is some yellow present, at least.

Letter 2: Smyrna (Life out of Death)

For the second portion of creation in Genesis we saw fresh water drawn out of salt water, which John translated to the spiritual plane as the drawing of life out of death, most commonly seen in the act of baptism. This metaphor abounds in the letter to Smyrna.

Conclusions

Church	S: Speaker M: Message P: Promise	Seven Letters	John's Creation
1 EPHESUS	S: 7 stars & 7 lampstands M: Persevered & endured P: Eat of the tree of life	yellow / white / green	yellow / yellow / yellow
2 SMYRNA	S: First & Last; alive not dead M: Rich not poor; alive not dead P: Not be hurt by second death	blue / blue / blue	blue / blue / blue
3 PERGAMOS	S: 2 edged sword from mouth M: Faithful P: Manna + new name	green / green / green-blue	green / green / green
4 THYATIRA	S: Eyes of fire and brass feet M: Judgment of Jezebel P: Iron sceptre & morning star	yellow-red / red-yellow / red-yellow	red-yellow / red-yellow / red-yellow
5 SARDIS	S: 7 Spirits & 7 Stars M: Reputed alive, but dead P: White robes, not blotted out	white-yellow / black / white	black / black / black
6 PHILADELPHIA	S: Keyholder of David M: Open door, none can shut P: Temple pillar + new name	purple / purple / purple	purple / purple / purple
7 LAODICEA	S: Ruler of God's Creation M: Neither cold nor hot P: Share the Son's throne		

Key:
- Light, Understanding (yellow)
- Life out of Death (blue)
- Bread, Word of God (green)
- Light, Rulership (red)
- Death in Life (black)
- The Man to Rule (purple)

Figure Ω_1: Characterizing parameters of the letters to the seven churches in Revelation 2-3. The far right hand column shows the colors of the creation model from John's gospel (as Appendix B) and the near side right hand column shows the colors attributed to the details of the seven letters using the same color scheme. Where no match is found, a blank (white) box is shown.

Conclusions

The Speaker to Smyrna: He is seen as one who is alive and was dead (Revelation 2:8).

The Message to Smyrna: They will live and not die and though they appear poor they are rich (Revelation 2:9-10).

The Promise to Smyrna: Those who overcome will live and remain untouched by the second death (Revelation 2:11).

Three blue blocks for Smyrna: a perfect match with Day 2 of John's spiritual creation.

Letter 3: Pergamos, or Pergamum (Bread)

Metaphor for God's Word	Reference
Bread	"Jesus answered, It is written: Man does not live on bread alone, but on every word that comes from the mouth of God." (Matthew 4:4, quoting Deuteronomy 8:3)
Spirit	"The Spirit gives life; the flesh counts for nothing. The words I have spoken to you are spirit and they are life." (6:63)
Sword (& Spirit)	"Take the helmet of salvation and the sword of the Spirit, which is the word of God." (Ephesians 6:17)

Table Ω_5: The scriptural metaphors used for God's Word: Bread, Spirit and Sword.

The Speaker to Pergamos: He is seen as one with a sharp, two-edged sword (Revelation 2:12, 16). We expect Day 3 to be centered on bread, so at first consideration this may seem to be a mismatch. However, we have already established that the bread is itself a metaphor for the word of God (Sections $\alpha.4$, 3.2). There are two other scriptural metaphors for the Word of God: spirit and *sword* (see Table Ω_5). Therefore 'sword' has a link to 'bread' because scripture employs both as metaphors for the Word of God. This also teaches us Day 3 is centered on "sustenance from God," as it has been from the very beginning. The sword protruding from Jesus' mouth gives a further clue that the third

Conclusions

letter is centered on the words of God (as Revelation 1:16, 19:15), giving the picture that Jesus strikes by speaking, a concept ratified by the prophet Isaiah (Isaiah 11:4).

The Message to Pergamos: The Pergamos brethren had been faithful (Revelation 2:13). For interpretation we employ the Bible's single, unambiguous origin for faith: "So then faith comes by hearing, and hearing by the word of God" (Romans 10:17, NKJV). Thus 'faith' comes explicitly from the all-sustaining Word of God: another match with the spiritual component of creation's Day 3.

The Promise to Pergamos: Those who overcome will eat of hidden manna and be given a new name on a white stone (Revelation 2:17). The manna is obviously a good representation of bread, but the new name does not appear to be: seeming most reminiscent of Day 6, the new man. Thus Pergamos' promise is represented in Figure Ω_1 as half green (matching Day 3) and half purple (the Day 6 color).

Overall the letter to Pergamos forms another excellent match with the respective portion of John's spiritual creation.

Letter 4: Thyatira (Light and Judgment)

The Speaker to Thyatira: He has eyes of fire and feet of brass (Revelation 2:18). Once again we employ the Biblical precedents for both of these elements, and discover that they form excellent matches with the anticipated components of light and judgment. Here is the evidence:

> Fire = Light
> By day the LORD went ahead of them in a pillar of cloud to guide them on their way and by night in a pillar of **fire** to give them **light**, so that they could travel by day or night. (Exodus 13:21)
> The **lamp** of the wicked is snuffed out; the flame of his **fire** stops burning. (Job 18:5)
>
> Brass = Judgment

So Moses made a bronze snake and put it up on a pole. Then when anyone was bitten by a snake and looked at the bronze snake, he lived. (Numbers 21:9)
Solomon went up to the bronze altar before the LORD in the Tent of Meeting and offered a thousand burnt offerings on it. (2 Chronicles 1:6)

The eyes of fire and feet of bronze in the apocalyptic vision prompt us therefore to remember the respective parallels these form, by scriptural precedent, with light and judgment.

The Message to Thyatira The message to Thyatira focuses on the judgment meted on Jezebel, the false prophetess (Revelation 2:22-23).

The Promise to Thyatira: Those who overcome will be rewarded with two things: the morning star (Revelation 2:28) and an iron scepter (Revelation 2:27). These are good parallels with the elements of the fourth creative Day: Lights to Rule.

Letter 5: Sardis (Death)

The Speaker to Sardis: He is seen holding seven spirits and seven stars (Revelation 3:1). The "spirit" does not match any of our colors, the "stars" are represented with yellow, as we did with Ephesus and Thyatira.

The Message to Sardis: The Church at Sardis is dead (Revelation 3:1). This is a perfect match with Day 5! Additionally Sardis have a reputation for being alive even though they are dead, hence they are "death in life": the exact antithesis of Day 2's "life out of death" (Smyrna) and perfect match with John's gospel's Day 5 (the crucifixion of Christ).

The Promise to Sardis: The (few) faithful in Sardis will be dressed in white and not blotted out of the book of life (Revelation 4:4) – no obvious match to the creation theme.

Letter 6: Philadelphia (The New Man)

The Speaker to Philadelphia: He is the keyholder of David (Revelation 3:7). This corresponds exactly to the Keyholder we found in Day 6 of John's Creation (Section 6.2).

Conclusions

The Message to Philadelphia: As an extension of the keyholder theme, an open door has been placed before them that no man can shut (Revelation 3:8). This matches the theme of Jesus passing through the locked doors in Day 6 of John's gospel.

The Promise to Philadelphia: Those who overcome will be pillars in the temple of God, and they will be given a new name. The Bible shows that to be a pillar in the temple of God translates as being a prime member, a spiritual leader amongst the flock (e.g. Galatians 2:9). The reference to the new name is also reminiscent of Adam and Christ as new and premier creatures amongst the natural and spiritual creations.

Three purple blocks for Philadelphia: a perfect match with Day 6 of John's Creation from Letter 6.

Letter 7: Laodicea

It is not obvious how to approach the seventh letter. We could attempt to parallel it with the seventh Day, and assess it against the seventh Days of the natural and spiritual creations: Eden and the Kingdom. We would necessarily find that Laodicea fails woefully in realizing a Kingdom scenario. But to observe that a human assembly in the first century falls far short of the idyllic standards of the Kingdom era is hardly a surprise and thus the comparison itself seems unfair, particularly given John did not attempt to represent a Kingdom scene even in his own gospel. Thus we shall merely concentrate on the first six letters matched against the components of the six creative Days and not incorporate Laodicea. This seems unsatisfactory to not fully integrate the seventh letter within our studies, yet no obvious solution lends itself, so we cannot present one.

Structure in the apocalyptic letters

Just as we saw the repeated cycles of Heaven, Waters, and Earth in the natural and spiritual creations leading to three pairs of partnered days (Figure α_1, Table Ω_3) so we see the same structure evident in the letters to the seven churches (Table Ω_6).

Conclusions

Days 1 & 4: Partners in Heaven	
Letter 1: Ephesus (Revelation 2:1-7)	**Letter 4: Thyatira** (Revelation 2:18-29)
The speaker holds seven stars in his right hand, seven sources of light. (Revelation 2:1)	The 'star' reappears: given to those who overcome. (Revelation 2:28)
Days 2 & 5: Partners in Waters	
Letter 2: Smyrna (Revelation 2:8-11)	**Letter 5: Sardis** (Revelation 3:1-6)
The speaker is seen as the one who died and came to life again (Revelation 2:8), Smyrnans are told to be faithful to death, to receive the crown of life (Revelation 2:10).	In the perfect antithesis of Letter 2, those in Sardis have a reputation of being alive, but they are dead (Revelation 3:1).
Days 3 & 6: Partners in Earth	
Letter 3: Pergamos (Revelation 2:12-17)	**Letter 6: Philadelphia** (Revelation 3:7-13)
The faithful are given a new name, written on a white stone (Revelation 2:17).	The faithful will be adorned with the new name of Jesus (Revelation 3:12).

Table Ω_6: The six letters to the churches in Revelation 2-3; evidencing the same partnered-pair structure as the days of the natural creation (Figure α_1) and the spiritual creation (Table Ω_3, see also Table 6_2).

What John Saw

As with our current study of John's gospel we might be provoked to ask what function the creation pattern serves in the seven letters. This is not immediately apparent, and doubtless requires much careful study of Revelation to determine, which is not our direct business in this work.

However one interesting clue is the comparison between John's encounter with the 'One like the Son of Man' in the opening chapter and the view of the speaker in the letters (Table Ω_7).

Conclusions

verse in Rev 1	Facet of "One like the Son of Man"	Seen in Letter
12	Seven golden lampstands	1: Ephesus
13	One like the Son of Man	
13	Robe reaching down to his feet	
13	Golden sash around his chest	
14	His head and hair white like wool	
14	His eyes like blazing fire	4: Thyatira
15	His feet like bronze glowing in a furnace	4: Thyatira
15	His voice like the sound of rushing waters	
16	Seven stars in his right hand	1: Ephesus & 5: Sardis
16	Sharp two-edged sword protrudes from his mouth	3: Pergamos
16	His face like the sun shining in full brilliance	
17	The First and the Last	2: Smyrna
18	The Living One	
18	He was Dead but now Alive for ever	2: Smyrna
18	Keyholder of Death and Hades	6: Philadelphia

Table Ω_7: What John Saw. Fifteen facets of the One like the Son of Man observed by John at the beginning of his apocalyptic vision. On the right are indicated where the churches in the seven letters see the same features.

John sees every aspect of the 'One like the Son of Man' the six churches see, as well as other facets above and beyond those revealed to the first century churches. Perhaps the answer to the mystery of why the creation pattern can be seen embedded in the apocalyptic letters starts with this observation. Nevertheless we proceed no further along this path; the reader is invited to pursue this further investigation at his leisure. For our study of the gospel of John we merely note that there are indeed other passages of scripture whose complexity can be better discerned by the application of the creation model, and cite the apocalyptic letters to the seven churches as an example.

Ω.5 Guides to Discipleship from John's Creation

Finally we address the third avenue of our second concluding question:

Why would the creation pattern be employed in a gospel narrative?
- How does perception of John's spiritual creation help us become better disciples of Christ?

Creative Day	Natural Component	Spiritual Component	Component of Discipleship
1	Light	Illumination, understanding	Understanding God
2	Water drawn above	Life out of death	Baptism
3	Food on Earth	Bread from Heaven, Words of God	Feeding from Bible reading and communion
4	Lights to rule	Understanding bringing responsibility	Responsibility in service to others
5	Populace below waters above	Death in Life	Maturing Humility
6	The Ruling Man	The Ruling Man	Rulership within church body
7	Completion in Eden	Completion in Kingdom	Completion in Kingdom

Table Ω_8: The natural components of the creation sequence listed alongside the spiritual equivalents we have established from the study of John's Creation and their role in the life of a disciple of Jesus Christ.

Conclusions

Can the model of John's Creation be applied usefully in the life of the disciple? At surface consideration this seems an unlikely source of exhortation. Yet, with the components of the spiritual creation we have elucidated, comes an intriguing developmental guide for the individual believer (Table Ω_8). Consider how the believer must incorporate all these facets into a sincere discipleship and is best advised to follow the steps in sequence.

Disciple's Day 1: Understanding

This is the necessary precursor of all. As an immediate caveat clearly none of us *fully* fathom any aspect of God's plan: either the depth of the sacrifice God has made in giving His Son, the depth of the love Jesus felt for those he came to save, or the plan God has for our future. Thus we cannot legalistically prescribe what depth of understanding must come first. Nor would we desire to do so given the experiential knowledge of the disasters that transpire every time humans set about translating the Spirit of God into a set of legalistic requirements! Nevertheless John's creation pattern assures us the beginning of our walk with Christ does not begin at birth, or as an infant, but only with a degree of enlightenment from the Word of God to the situation of the sinner and the Savior and the necessary relationship they must go on to develop. The Lord himself underscores the vital importance of 'knowing God,' so vital that he uses it as a definition of eternal life!

> "Father, the time has come. Glorify your Son, that your Son may glorify you. For you granted him authority over all people that he might give eternal life to all those you have given him. Now this is eternal life: that they may know you, the only true God, and Jesus Christ, whom you have sent." (17:2-3)

We have also seen the partnerships of Days: Day 1 partners Day 4, as the light is refined into a role of responsibility. This has consequences for our study of discipleship in John.

Conclusions

Understanding brings the consequence of responsibility, for anyone who understands what he is doing is necessarily answerable for his actions, thus we deduce understanding the role the believer is called to play also instigates responsibility before God to respond to that call.

> Evil men do not understand justice, But those who seek the LORD understand all. (Proverbs 28:5, NKJV)

Disciple's Day 2: Baptism

The illumination of understanding will draw the true disciple of Christ towards Day 2: the waters of baptism. To embrace the New Creation, those things above, one must enact the 'drawing above' of Day 2 in the baptismal resurrection. The association must be made of one's initial state with the waters beneath and the death they hold and the drawing out to the life above achieved through the sacrifice of Jesus Christ.

> "But I, when I am lifted up from the earth, will draw all men to myself." [Jesus] said this to show the kind of death he was going to die. (12:32-33, see also Romans 6:3-5)

Day 2 necessarily follows Day 1: it does not precede Day 1, nor is it contemporary therewith. Hence baptism cannot precede understanding, nor does it occur simultaneously with understanding (albeit the disciple's understanding is never 'completed' in this dispensation, of course). John's spiritual creation sequence provides this excellent guidance for the disciple's footsteps. Illumination comes first: discrete understanding of the gospel message must be reached before any useful baptism can be achieved.

Nevertheless baptism comes very early in the sequence: stage two in a creative series of six. This prompts us to view baptism appropriately as a beginning and not an end. The creation pattern gently contradicts the notion of baptism as a state of 'achievement,' as it can often be viewed. The majority of the disciple's work (four days of six) lies *beyond* this point! Thus the

Conclusions

disciple is advised not to overly delay baptism. We should remember our Creator, and what He has done for us, in the days of our youth (Ecclesiastes 12:1) and remember Him in the positive response of a timely baptism, since there is so very much to be done in His service beyond this point.

Disciple's Day 3: Communion

Day 3: Bread to feed the world, and again the order of days is instructive. First understanding, then baptism, then communion: two lessons emerge. Firstly, sharing memorial bread and consideration of God's Word are essential parts of the disciple's universe, not a voluntary practice. Creation shows us why: the works of day 3 sustained all life on Earth (Genesis 1:29). Those who do not eat frequently grow malnourished and weak. Thus reflection in the scriptures and sharing communion bread in a spirit of penitence and thankfulness towards the Father and encouragement and love towards one's siblings are essentially restorative functions. They help grows the character God would have us exhibit and thus our constant feeding is both required and greatly beneficial.

> As the rain and the snow come down from heaven, and do not return to it without watering the earth and making it bud and flourish, so that it yields seed for the sower and bread for the eater, so is my word that goes out from my mouth: It will not return to me empty, but will accomplish what I desire and achieve the purpose for which I sent it. (Isaiah 55:10-11)

Secondly, communion's appearance on Day 3 demonstrates fellowship only exists between those who have who have seen the light and passed through the baptismal waters. We do not determine with whom we have communion! On the one hand we might like to expand our community to include any we consider a 'nice' or 'Christian' person. Conversely we might like to reduce our community amongst the baptized believers to just those of whom we personally approve. Yet this is not a matter determined at our discretion! Communion (Day 3) can only exist – and

Conclusions

conversely must always exist – between all those and only those who have walked the path through illumination and baptism.

With the completion of Day 3 we arrive at the end of the first cycle of Heaven, Waters and Earth (Figure α_1). With Understanding; Baptism and Communion the disciple's universe is similarly completely defined. But at the end of Day 3 the natural universe was unpopulated: likewise the disciple's universe remains empty if he does not grow beyond Day 3 of his discipleship. Through illumination, baptism and communion the structure of the disciple's world has indeed, through God's grace, been established, and this calls for Days 4-6 to populate his spiritual world.

Disciple's Day 4: Responsibility

Responsibility is the necessary and inevitable consequence of illumination, as we noted at the end of Day 1. Paul is very clear about this in his letter to the church at Thessalonica:

> He will punish those who do not know God and do not obey the gospel of our Lord Jesus. They will be punished with everlasting destruction and shut out from the presence of the Lord and from the majesty of his power on the day he comes to be glorified in his holy people and to be marveled at among all those who have believed. This includes you, because you believed our testimony to you. (2 Thessalonians 1:8-10)

Defining the responsibilities of adopting the life of Christ is a book in itself, nevertheless we can repair to the two directives crystallized by the Lord Jesus concerning the fulfillment of the Law: 'Love God, Love your neighbor.' (Matthew 22:37-40)

The disciple is no longer to be the center of his own universe, but to center himself around the service of his God and his fellow servants. This statement is easy to acknowledge, but to perform it in the reality of everyday life is the hardest task we face, and a level from which all of us frequently fall. Once again, as always, the Lord leads us where he wants us to follow:

Conclusions

> Having loved his own who were in the world, [Jesus] now showed them the full extent of his love... so he got up from the meal, took off his outer clothing, and wrapped a towel around his waist. After that, he poured water into a basin and began to wash his disciples' feet, drying them with the towel that was wrapped around him. (13:1-5)

The disciple is called to forego self-service and serve the needs of others for the glory of God from such actions as bring glory to the Father. We commonly fail partly because the calling is contrary to the philosophies of this present world that influence us daily. We are daily invited to focus upon ourselves, meditate within ourselves, study ourselves, challenge ourselves, better ourselves and endlessly absorb ourselves within ourselves. From the puerile '20-question' test of the popular magazine, to the (barely) more considered analysis of the Myers-Briggs test, to the furthest depths of modern philosophy, the common object is inevitably the same: to revel in further descriptions and classifications of oneself. It is the secret of popular appeal, for man has always been, and remains to this day, self-fascinated. But the message of the true God, the One God, invites and commands the disciple to set self-focus aside and focus upon, deduce, and respond in loving service towards, *the needs of others*.

Failures in the disciple's responsibility can exist on the scale of a church body, as well as the individual. For example: the church generally recognizes the importance of preaching, and this is good, subsequently non-members feel highly valued with attention. Upon joining the church in baptism those same individuals can sadly be wholly passed over, no longer holding the high status of a 'targeted acquisition.' Conversely new members may be immediately pressured into working towards the various efforts of the church itself before they are fully comfortable to do so. New members of the body of Christ do indeed need to recognize they have undertaken a life in service to others, not themselves. But equally the existing 'older' members of that church have every responsibility in allowing and enabling

Conclusions

new members to effect that transition for themselves, whilst providing the caring support of a loving family throughout. For all of us, serving the needs of our brethren will populate the heaven we established with our understanding of the gospel. These will be, indeed must be, the sun, moon and stars that govern our night and day.

Disciple's Day 5: Death

Day 5 is intriguing: the disciple must die. We do not refer to the mortal collapse of the human frame, for here we traverse the spiritual creation. We refer to a spiritual death. We might suppose that this 'death' has already been covered in the baptism of Day 2, and indeed we have seen Days 2 and 5 partnered in the creative cycles (Figure α_1, Tables 6_2, Ω_3, Ω_6). What we see here is that the creation structure suggests even the aspects of death experienced in the baptism of Day 2 must be developed at a later point in discipleship. Since sin itself continues beyond the point of baptism, alas, this is not a surprise. We know from the character of Day 5 this will involve some element of 'casting down' in discipleship: we interpret this as humility, for humility is the ultimate 'casting down' of the human spirit (James 4:10).

The day of baptism (Day 2) carries a joyful spirit, as well it should, and a spirit of elevation, for the new life embarked upon is from above. But for exactly these reasons baptism cannot always carry the full spirit of humility – understandably, being such a joyful day! But this abject spirit must come, to complement the uplifting spirit of Day 2's baptism. Furthermore the gravity of true humility is hardly possible from the new convert, for a true understanding of the weight of sin is required, and this comes with years and not moments.

This 'death' itself is an absolute rejection of one's nature: a realization that, contrary to humanist philosophy, we are not 'good' after all and those who would see 'good' prevail must ultimately suffer, and applaud, destruction of the human spirit. Paul's impassioned cry: "O wretched man that I am! Who will deliver me from this body of death?" (Romans 7:24) shows true discernment of this thought and is a far deeper cry from the heart than can be appreciated by cursory reading. Again, this cry was not made from a new convert; the letter to the Romans is one of Paul's later writings,[22] this underscores our thought that only the mature disciple can realize the humility this section represents.

For those in Western civilization this can present a particularly hard development, because it requires an emotional response to the call of Christ. Western civilization is currently steeped in worship of the brain, being happily drawn towards, even worshipping, anything with the scent of intellectualism. Intellectualism can pose a dangerous spirit in the disciple's life, and over-focus on the intellect will stunt growth of the necessary humility and devotion of the disciple's heart towards his Maker. Discipleship requires the abandonment of the reliance upon the tools of man to solve his own manifold problems: for spiritual locks will not be turned with natural keys. One cannot be reborn with the Spirit in one's heart until it is cleared of self-reliance, so that the 'regenerate' may truly 'Abba,' 'Father' cry (Romans 8:15).

Disciple's Day 6: Rulership

The disciple is called to a life of submission: to the authorities (Romans 13:1-2), to his friends (13:14-15) and even to his enemies (Matthew 5:39-41). Yet without all contradiction the disciple is also called to rule: both in present and future roles. There will come a time when the call "Come and dine" (21:12, KJV) will be made again. The Lamb will beckon his faithful to the Wedding Supper as he comes to claim his Bride and we know Jesus' disciples will have a rulership role at that time (Revelation 5:10). But there is also a present role of rulership for the disciple and one that fully emulates the submission we have mentioned. The Bible portrays the relationship between God and ourselves using the metaphor of a father and his children. The father provides constant, attentive care towards our every need; whilst fully cognizant of our inability to reflect, or even comprehend,

---

[22] The exact date of Paul's letter to the Romans is uncertain; predictions range from AD 56-59. But all agree the letter was one of his later works, being written during his last missionary journey.

the true degree of gratitude we owe. Here indeed is the spiritual ruler, the Servant Ruler, and such is the disciple called to be. Each baptized believer is called to surrender his needs and predilections in favor of the needs of those to whom he witnesses: whether within or without the family fold. He is called, as part of service to the Father, to spend his energies seeking out his neighbor's spiritual needs and attempting, to his best ability, to provide the service of the Lord Jesus himself towards them. Neither recognition nor gratitude should he seek for this service. In this way the spiritual ruler begins to emulate his Heavenly Father, who behaves this way towards us all every day.

Once again the order of days is essential: Day 6 can only follow Day 5. The disciple can only rule in the spiritual community if he has truly "died" to Christ, not just in baptism but much more importantly in later mature humility: a condition easier to recognize than to describe in words. But it is evident from logic that one who is not humbled cannot take the role of the Servant Ruler, for one who is not humbled will not primarily seek the needs of others. The disciple who has undergone the elevation of baptism, but not the later counterpart of death in the humbling waters beneath, is not well equipped to rule in God's house.

> Nor are you to be called 'teacher,' for you have one Teacher, the Christ. The greatest among you will be your servant. For whoever exalts himself will be humbled, and whoever humbles himself will be exalted. (Matthew 23:10-12)

Disciple's Day 7: Perfection

For this day the disciple must certainly wait, for perfection comes with God's gracious provision and not with the disciple's efforts. One can certainly appreciate the beauty of this Earth, and bask resplendent in the joys that both the natural and spiritual creation have to offer now – and perhaps in so doing grasp a cameo facsimile of the Kingdom's glory. Indeed this is to be encouraged since the process educates us in the appreciation of the provision of the Loving Father! But for the full experience of

Conclusions

the bounty God's Hand has prepared the disciple must happily and excitedly wait.

Nor is this to suggest we can extrapolate our highest joys of this present age to gain an accurate measure of the Kingdom's Joy. This is evident from a parallel argument. Paul rebukes those who postulated the physical form of the resurrected from regarding only the mortal frame:

> How foolish! What you sow does not come to life unless it dies. When you sow, you do not plant the body that will be, but just a seed, perhaps of wheat or of something else... (1 Corinthians 15:36-37)

To attempt to predict the form of a plant from regarding the physical characteristics of the seed is a futile, even misleading, exercise. One could never look at an acorn, for example, and deduce the form (or the size!) of the oak tree that will subsequently appear! The acorn does not bear the slightest resemblance to the tree in its size, constituents or complexity! Similarly when we regard our mortal selves, with our finite, human minds, we see only acorns. God has promised from the acorns who faithfully die in the soil of His love and goodness some new thing will grow. But we can no more hope to deduce or extrapolate what form that final joy will take than we could deduce the size and shape of an oak tree from seeing only the acorn.

> Then the end will come, when he hands over the kingdom to God the Father... When he has done this, then the Son himself will be made subject to him who put everything under him, so that God may be all in all. (1 Corinthians 15:24-29)

Finally, the ultimate completion: God is all, and in all. We shall not pretend to explicitly understand this prophecy but we shall certainly anticipate it in all hope and joyful expectation!

What more need we say?

Conclusions

Ω.6 And Last

A 20th century philosopher once wrote:

> "When I am working on a problem, I never think about beauty. I think only how to solve the problem. But when I have finished, if the solution is not beautiful, I know it is wrong." [23]

These are not divinely inspired words, yet experience with handling God's Word corroborates their accuracy. God's patterns are always of the most delicate beauty. This is no surprise of course, given the infinite beauty we see in creation all around us. From the most awesome interactions, such as a mighty ocean storm pounding against a granite coastline, to the most delicate interplay, such as the diffraction of morning sunlight through dewdrops on the fragile silk of a spider's web, we everywhere regard the beautiful signature of the Almighty's handiwork.

Any intense beauty pervading the structure of a Bible study is evidence of its veracity. Thus if the reader is able to witness beauty in the creation structure proposed to underpin John's gospel, it acts as ratification of that model, and evidence of God's Hand at work. We also repair to the concept: 'by their fruits you shall know them' (Matthew 7:15-20): a directive of the Lord's specifically designed to test those broadcasting new ideas. If this study has been considered to yield any fruits which the reader can find valuable, in terms of the understanding and appreciation of the scriptural message, then this suggests veracity to the concept itself. The fruits of this study have, at least for the author, brought a wealth of new appreciation of the intricacy and power of both the gospel of John, and the broader scripture as a whole.

The creation model we perceive applies across a whole breadth of scales! It exists on the very largest scale: declaring the pre-eminence of the Lord Jesus Christ in the plans of the

---

[23] Fuller B. in *"Peter's Quotations,"* L. J. Peter, 1977, Bantam Books, New York, p 37

Conclusions

Almighty as the conduit (and creator) of the new creation (Section $\Omega.3$). Similarly we observe it on the smallest scale, reflected in the detail of the gospel. We find out why Jesus sits at the top of the well when speaking to the Samaritan woman (Section 2.3); why he instructs his disciples to collect together the fragments of bread that had fallen to the ground after the multitude have eaten (Section 3.4); and why Thomas is right to cry "My Lord and my God!" when regarding Jesus after his resurrection (Section 6.1). Perceiving the presence of a divine pattern in scripture is a wonderful thing: it allows the reader to correctly perceive the spiritual weight of each interaction as the narrative of the gospel unfolds. The content and ordering of the accounts in John's gospel take on an overall form and an associated powerful message when interpreted through comparison with the creation sequence, without which the gospel structure remains thoroughly mysterious.

Our primary response when uncovering gems mined from the scriptural store must be excited gratitude – to realize we have been blessed to glimpse a system by which the Hand of God has been working from the foundation of the world! Doubtless we have done no more than peek a hair's breadth beneath scripture's surface at the beautiful patterns swirling within. Yet still what gratitude must be ours towards our Heavenly Father for this blessing of scripture, to realize the depth of the provision of love made for us, who are unlovely, by the One who loved us first. What pause it gives us to reflect upon the myriad ways God is working in our lives: although the slightest dullness in our senses renders so many of them unobserved. How well we are exhorted to honor the name of our God.

> "Be still, and know that I am God; I will be exalted among the nations, I will be exalted in the earth." (Psalm 46:10)

God's revelation of scripture before our eyes is also a provocation to draw our thoughts kingdom-wards and we deliberately direct our concluding thoughts in this direction. We always struggle to imagine what the kingdom will be like: perhaps that is why it doesn't appear in literature as often as it might, because we always like to be so sure of what we are writing. But although it is genuinely difficult to imagine God's kingdom, as we stand on the shores of the present gazing myopically towards it, it is nonetheless a thrilling prospect to consider! How awesome it will be to regard our Lord with eyes finally open! What remarkable set of feelings will be unleashed as we are able to turn the pages of the Bible we may have read hundreds of times, and see for the very first time the deeper meanings and messages that were in front of our faces the whole time! How will we feel when we do this? Will we feel foolish: that we never saw such things before? Will we feel exhilarated, by the staggering increase in knowledge of the interplay God had structured with His children through the ages? Or will we feel utterly humiliated by sensing the extent of love shown towards us that we never took the trouble to properly discern or respond to? Maybe all of the above. Or perhaps the written expression of God's Word will play no further role as we enjoy full communion with the Living Word himself. Either way we will doubtless obtain a greater understanding of the One who made us, and, in so doing, be drawn to love that Maker more deeply and properly.

But for now, we must conclude. We have presented the gospel of John according to the spiritual creation model with which it is so carefully crafted: 'John's Creation,' as we have termed it. And regardless of whether we are able to find agreement on every facet of the structure, we surely have gained from sharpening our mind's perceptions on those things above, rather than allowing them to be further blunted by the clamor of things below. We know the feeble intellects we have at our disposal will often derail our thoughts from the road of truth into the ditch, but by studying God's Word the Bible we better perceive the real world God has made, which lies behind the mask of those things that evidently appear. Every time we make the effort to walk that path pointing upwards, towards knowing our God better, we learn to plant slightly surer footsteps than the time before – it is, as all things, a learning experience after all. And with every step we pull further away from the land where we

Conclusions

began: the human world in which we were conceived and born – not in order to patronize or despise its inhabitants, for they are but ourselves, and our own sons for whom we must now take care. But little by little we learn to become aliens and strangers there, in pursuit of the land beyond, just as the faithful preceding disciples who walked before us did many years before.

> All these people were still living by faith when they died. They did not receive the things promised; they only saw them and welcomed them from a distance. And they admitted that they were aliens and strangers on earth. People who say such things show that they are looking for a country of their own. If they had been thinking of the country they had left, they would have had opportunity to return. Instead, they were longing for a better country--a heavenly one. Therefore God is not ashamed to be called their God, for he has prepared a city for them. (Hebrews 11:13-16)

This, then, is His promise. And in it we trust, knowing that as long as we walk therein we will always both bear and be borne those good fruits; the like of which we have been served so delicately handled so intimately in the gospel of John.

For it is, after all, a most extraordinary book.

APPENDIX A:
The Uniqueness of John's Gospel

Perhaps the most compelling observations of the uniqueness of John's gospel are given in the brief preface. Nevertheless those arguments, though powerful, are still largely subjective, based on general observation rather than statistical data. This appendix provides one factual measurement of the degree John's gospel departs from the records of Matthew, Mark and Luke. This necessarily requires we also demonstrate a similarity between Matthew, Mark and Luke (i.e. a justification of their description as 'synoptic') as well as a demonstrated difference in John. Should we fail in the former criterion and succeed only in the latter we will merely demonstrate that all four gospels are different from each other.

We test the similarities and differences of the four gospels by observing the parables and healing miracles of Jesus. We select these two material types because they are relatively common and relatively unambiguous to distinguish.

A.1 Comparing Parables in the Four Gospels

Firstly we need to define what we shall recognize as a parable. Simply to rely on the word 'parable' appearing the text is clearly inadequate and leads to inconsistencies: e.g. the parable of the talents (Matthew 25:14-30, Luke 19:12-27) is labeled as a parable in Luke's record (Luke 19:11) but not in Matthew. We employ the following definition:

A parable shall be recognized as a moral teaching from Jesus contained either within a hypothetical story or communicated by an abstraction of principles from the physical to the spiritual plane.

The definition of the term 'parable' is not itself critical: what *is* critical is that once a definition has been formulated, that *same* definition should be applied commonly to all of the four gospel records for genuinely comparative information to be yielded.

Appendix A: The Uniqueness of John's Gospel

Table A_1 gives a comparative listing of the gospel parables according to the above definition.

Parable	Matthew	Mark	Luke	John
Salt of the Earth	5:13	9:49-50	14:34-35	
Lamps & Candlesticks	5:14-16	4:21-23	8:16-18, 11:33	
Dismemberment	5:29-30			
Rich Man Taking Ease			12:16-21	
Treasure in Heaven	6:19-21		12:33-34	
Light of the Eye	6:22-23		11:34-36	
Serving Two Masters	6:24			
Lilies, Birds, Grass	6:25-30		12:27-28	
Mote & Beam	7:3-5		5:41-42	
Pearls before Swine	7:6			
Son's Request for Food	7:9-12		11:11-13	
Two Paths	7:13-14		13:24-30	
Trees & their Fruits	7:16-20		6:43-45 & 13:6-9	
Wise & Foolish Builder	7:24-27		6:46-49	
Direction of Wind				3:8
Children of the Bridegroom	9:15	2:19-20	5:34-35	
New Garment & New Wine	9:16-17	2:21-22	5:36-39	
Market Children	11:16-19		7:31-35	
A House Divided	12:25-30	3:23-27	11:17-23	
Good Samaritan			10:30-37	
Importunate Host			11:5-8	
Unclean Spirit	12:43-45		11:24-27	

Appendix A: The Uniqueness of John's Gospel

Sowing the Seed	13:3-23	4:2-20	8:4-15	
Wheat & Tares	13:24-30, 36-43	4:26-29		
Mustard Seed	13:31-32	4:30-32	13:18-19 & 17:6	
Leaven	13:33		13:20-21	
Treasure in a Field	13:44			
Pearl of Great Price	13:45-46			
Fisherman's Net	13:47-50			
Digestion		7:14-23		
Blind leading the Blind	15:14		6:39-40	
Sheepfold				10:1-18
Lost Sheep	18:12-14		15:3-7	
Lost Coin			15:8-10	
Prodigal Son			15:11-32	
Unjust Steward			16:1-12	
Rich Man & Lazarus			16:19-31	
Servant & Master			17:7-10	
Importunate Widow			18:1-8	
Pharisee & Publican			18:9-14	
Two Debtors	18:23-35		7:40-50	
Vineyard Laborers	20:1-16			
Walking in the Daylight				11:9-10
Corn of Wheat				12:24-25
Two Sons	21:28-32			
Wicked Husbandmen	21:33-46	12:1-12	20:9-18	
Fig Tree		13:28-31	21:29-33	
Marriage Supper	22:1-14		14:16-24	
Wise Builder & King			14:28-33	

Appendix A: The Uniqueness of John's Gospel

Ten Virgins	25:1-13			
Talents	25:14-30		19:12-27	
Vine & Branches				15:1-8
Total parables (52)	**34**	**11**	**38**	**5**
Total verses in parables	**188**	**66**	**224**	**31**
% of gospel	**18%**	**9.7%**	**20%**	**3.5%**

Table A_1: An exhaustive parallel listing of parables in the four gospel records.

Summary information is given in the last 3 rows of the table. The last line of the table, the percentage of the gospel devoted to the parables, is calculated as the sum total of the number of verses dedicated to parables divided by the total number of verses in the gospel.

Table A_1 gives good support to the idea that John's gospel differs from the other three. Parables are rare features of the gospel of John: only 5 exist compared to 11 in Mark, and more than 30 in Matthew and Luke. (The smaller number of parables in Mark is partially attributable to Mark being the shortest gospel. This is partially corrected by considering the percentage content.) Our hypothesis is well evidenced here: there are between three and six times more parables of Jesus in the synoptic records than in John's gospel.

Parables common between two gospels	Matthew	Mark	Luke
Mark	9		
Luke	24	9	
John	0	0	0

Table A_2: Number of parables that are shared between two gospels. John stands alone, sharing no parable with any other gospel.

Appendix A: The Uniqueness of John's Gospel

The commonality of parables between gospels is also revealing, as Table A_2 highlights.

Here the matter is conclusive. The synoptic records share between nine and twenty-four parables (Matthew and Luke's correlation is heightened by the sermon on the mount, which contains ten parables and appears in both of those gospels.) By contrast there is not even *one* parable in John appearing in any other gospel!

Indeed such is the similarity amongst the synoptic records we find eight parables appearing in all three records, including some of the most well known parables Jesus told. They include short parables such as "A house divided against itself shall not stand" (Matthew 12:25-27, Mark 3:23-27, Luke 11:17-19); and also longer records such as the parable of sowing the seed. The sower casts his seed into different types of soil and the seed lives or dies depending on the nature of the soil into which the seed is thrown (Matthew 13:3-9; Mark 4:2-9; Luke 8:4-8). This parable's explanation: how the different soils represent different human behaviors towards the seed as God's Word, is also included in all three synoptics (Matthew 13:18-23; Mark 4:13-23; Luke 4:9-15). These parables, long and short, are so familiar as to be household tales: we might suppose they would appear in every gospel. Yet John mentions none of them.

For the case of the parables of Jesus Christ, therefore, we have conclusively shown that John differs significantly from the gospels of Matthew, Mark and Luke (Tables A_1 and A_2).

A.2 Comparing Healing Miracles in the Four Gospels

In analyzing the healing miracles we use the same procedure: considering both the number of recorded miracles, and the commonality each miracle has between gospels. The list of healing miracles in the gospels is given in Table A_3.

Healing Miracle	Matthew	Mark	Luke	John
Many in Syria	4:23-25			
Demoniac in		1:23-28	4:33-37	

Appendix A: The Uniqueness of John's Gospel

Synagogue				
Faithful Leper	8:2-4	1:40-45	5:12-15	
Centurion's Servant	8:5-13		7:1-10	
Nobleman's Son				4:46-54
Peter's Mother-in-Law	8:14-15	1:30-31	4:38-39	
"Many that same evening"	8:16-17	1:32-34	4:40-41	
Legion	8:28-34	5:1-19	8:26-40	
Widow of Nain's Son			7:11-18	
Impotent Man at Bethesda				5:1-15
Sick of the Palsy	9:1-8	2:1-13	5:18-26	
Jairus' Daughter	9:18-19, 23-26	5:22-24, 35-43	8:41-42, 49-56	
Women with Issue of Blood	9:20-22	5:25-34	8:43-48	
Blind Men	9:27-31			
Dumb Man	9:32-34			
Blind Man at Bethsaida		8:22-26		
Blind Man Washing in Sent				9:1-7
Man with Withered Hand	12:10-13	3:1-5	14:2-4	
Dumb Man	12:22-30		11:14-26	
Syrophenician Girl	15:21-28	7:25-30		
Many in Tyre and Sidon	15:29-31	7:31-37	6:17-19	
Epileptic Son	17:14-21	9:17-29	9:37-45	
Arthritic Woman			13:11-18	
Ten Lepers			17:11-19	
Blind Bartimaeus	20:30-34	10:46-52	18:35-43	
Lazarus				11:1-46

Appendix A: The Uniqueness of John's Gospel

Malchus			22:50-53	
Total healing miracles (27)	17	14	18	4
Total verses	88	114	128	77
% of gospel	8.2%	17%	11%	8.8%

Table A_3: A parallel listing of all healing miracles in the four gospel records.

Prior to the main analysis we note a couple of attractive, if sideline, observations. There is an evident complement between the gospels of Matthew and Mark with respect to parables and healing miracles (compare Tables A_1 and A_3). Matthew leans towards the parables (18% of gospel), but away from the healing miracles (8.2%), whilst conversely Mark does the precise reverse (9.7% parables, 17% healing miracles) in almost exactly mirrored proportions! It seems Matthew favors the record of hypothetical teachings of the Lord Jesus for our education, whilst Mark concerns himself more with communicating the physical healing the Lord performed. It may even be possible to understand these preferences given the very little that we know about the two apostles. Matthew was a tax collector, and John Mark, it is commonly believed, was a young man.[1] Perhaps the tax collector, with a penchant for the more legalistic approach, was naturally drawn to the moral codes contained within the parables, whilst the younger man (if indeed he was such) was more readily impressed by the healing touch with which Jesus blessed people's lives. This is tenuous speculation at best, but the bias of the two gospels is genuine enough even if our suppositions are wide of the mark.

---

[1] This belief arises from the KJV translation of Colossians 4:10, which states that Mark was Barnabas' sister's son. Nevertheless this translation overstrains the Greek word 'anepsios,' meaning cousin (Strong J. H., *Op. cit.*, 'Greek Dictionary of the New Testament,' p 12.) Thus it is possible Mark was no younger than the other writers.

Appendix A: The Uniqueness of John's Gospel

An equally fascinating consequence of the pre-eminence of Mark in recording healing miracles may well expel a relatively common myth. It is commonly supposed Luke has a special association with Jesus' miracles of healing, presumably from the simplistic observation of Luke's trade as a medical doctor; that he would somehow take special interest in them. The evidence is minimal to the point of non-existent: at best one can find Peter's mother-in-law described as having a "fever," in Matthew and Mark (Matthew 8:14, Mark 1:30) and having a "high fever" in Luke (Luke 4:38): hardly an impressive distinction in total! The counter-evidence of Table A_3 is drawn from the broad base across all gospels and is compelling: it demonstrates no foundation to a special relation between Luke and the healing miracles. Rather it bears out the discovery that it is Mark, more than the other gospel writers, who is concerned with the healing miracles of Jesus.

Healing miracles common between two gospels	Matthew	Mark	Luke
Mark	12		
Luke	13	12	
John	0	0	0

Table A_4: Number of healing miracles shared between two gospels. John stands alone, sharing no healing miracle with any other gospel.

Returning to our principal duty, demonstrating the singularity of John's gospel, we find once again the evidence from Table A_3 is strongly favorable. Whilst healing miracles are common in the synoptic gospels, each containing between fourteen and seventeen, there are only four miracles of healing recorded in the gospel of John. (The total number of verses and percentage of the gospel attributed to healing miracles in John does not demonstrate John's gospel's uniqueness so well. This is because the single account of Lazarus' resurrection in John is recorded in great detail and totals more than half of the verses on healing in

Appendix A: The Uniqueness of John's Gospel

John, thus obscuring their true rarity.) To underscore the uniqueness of John's gospel we demonstrate the similarity between Matthew, Mark and Luke in showing how many healing miracles are shared between gospels (Table A_4).

The evidence in Table A_4 is conclusive. The similarity between synoptic records is very high: twelve or thirteen miracles found in any one synoptic gospel will be found in at least one of the others. Contrariwise John's gospel has no shared accounts. Indeed there are eleven healing miracles recorded in all three accounts of Matthew, Mark and Luke without a single one of them mentioned in John! These include the raising from death of Jairus' daughter and the healing of the woman with the issue of blood along the way (Matthew 9; Mark 5; Luke 8). "Who touched me?" asked Jesus, to the astonishment of the apostles who saw the crowds thronging him on every side (Mark 5:30-31, Luke 8:45). We read also of Legion the schizophrenic, who needed to see his affliction transferred elsewhere to know that he was healed; and two thousand head of (illegally kept) pigs charged to their death so one man might live and walk as a healed soul (Matthew 8:32, Mark 5:11-13, Luke 8:32-33). These are singular moments in the ministry of the Lord, present in all three synoptic records, yet, remarkably, all absent from John's witness. Conversely, not one of the four healing miracles listed in John's gospel: the raising of the nobleman's son; the healing of the impotent man at Bethesda; the restoration of sight to the man washing in Sent; or the resurrection of Lazarus; can be found in the other gospels!

Finally we combine the above results of Tables A_1 and A_3 and show the proportion of each gospel dedicated to parables and healing miracles (Table A_5).

Once again strong factual support is found for the uniqueness of John's account. In particular this is witnessed as a dearth of parables and healing miracles in John. One logically concludes John is focusing on different attributes of Jesus' ministry (and in any event his uniqueness has been incontrovertibly demonstrated). Our inquiry thus evolves into exploring *why* John's gospel differs so much from the synoptic records, and

Appendix A: The Uniqueness of John's Gospel

what those differences might teach us. For this we return to the main body of the text, at Section α.1, and proceed.

Parables + Healing Miracles	Matthew	Mark	Luke	John
Total gospel %	26	27	31	12

Table A_5: Percentage of each gospel, calculated in verses, which records parables and healing miracles.

APPENDIX B:
Creation in John's Gospel Summary

B.1 *The Science of Pattern Perception*

We have attributed the peculiar order and selection of material presented in John's gospel to the intensely spiritual view of Jesus' ministry that John forms (Section α.1). We know patterns in scripture often exist on a breathtaking range of scales, sometimes so small as to be encrypted thrice over in a single verse, sometimes so large as to span many books of the Bible and several centuries of the history of God's people. The sheer range of scale over which God has embedded teaching in the Bible, by the use of patterns, and patterns within patterns, is awesome indeed. Our task becomes to identify what patterns, if any, lie in John, and how we are to perceive them.

We must take care not to 'force' the perception of a pattern: thinking of an attractive idea and trawling through the gospel record selectively harvesting the material supporting the idea to corroborate it. We must take great care to examine patterns we purport to find and to explore the entirety of the text in which the pattern is perceived. Worse yet, it is a scientifically demonstrable fact that the human mind is a habitual fabricator of patterns where none truly exists. A known reflex function of the human brain is to create an ordered pattern, or a recognizable geometry, within a system where the pattern does not occur, and sometimes where there is simply no pattern at all.

For example: the psychological evaluation process known as the 'Rorschach test' utilizes this feature of the brain: the test is famed for the employment of inkblot patterns for personality analysis (Figure B_1).

Appendix B: Creation in John's Gospel Summary

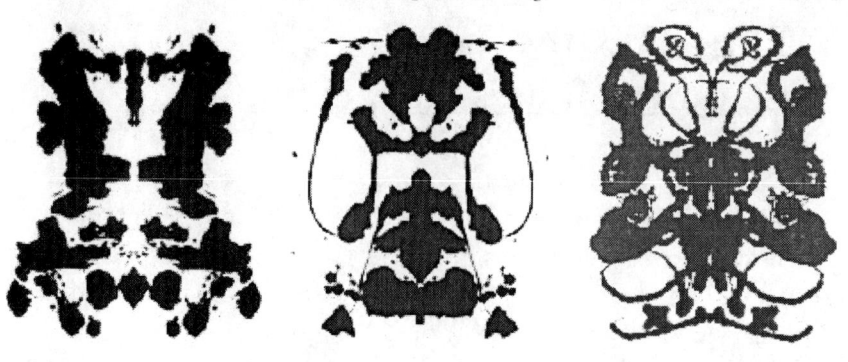

Figure B_1: Examples of Rorschach inkblot patterns.

Those who attest to the efficacy of the Rorschach test assert the patterns the subject sees provide an access to the deepest recesses of his subconscious mind. Nevertheless the inkblots are intentionally structureless entities: indeed the value of the test rests wholly on this very design! (For those more pragmatic, or less profligate, who are not in the habit of parting with considerable sums of money to be shown random designs, there is always the time-honored tradition of gazing heavenwards into cloud formations. Here meteorology plays the poor man's Rorschach, and many generations of humanity have mused on the various cloud-scenes they have conceived within the fickle human mind.)

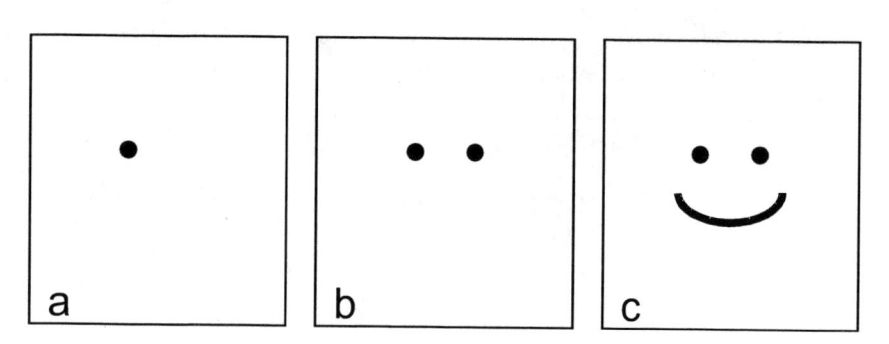

Figure B_2: A small number of geometric shapes: a) a dot, b) two dots, c) two dots and a curve. By part c) almost all observers are spontaneously picturing a smiling human face.

Appendix B: Creation in John's Gospel Summary

The pattern most commonly 'seen' by the human brain within an image known to be random is a human face. Whether it be in a rocky cliff face, in features on the surface of the Moon or Mars, or in swirling smoke clouds, people invariably impute human facial features amidst the morphology. This proclivity is demonstrated at its base level in Figure B_2.

In part a) there is a single dot; part b) adds a second dot; and part c) a curve. With just these three simple geometric shapes the vast majority of observers see a smiling human face. Considering the complexity of the human features the nonsensicality of such a perception is evident, (i.e. nobody's face looks like two dots and a curve!), yet, despite this realization, the image firmly remains. Even with the assurance that Figure B_2c) is merely two dots and a curve, are you able to eliminate the erroneous superposition from the mind, or does the image of a smiling face persist?

The brain is a desperately overzealous perceiver of patterns where none exists, and thus pattern perception *solely* using the human brain is an unreliable function. So pattern perception in John's gospel should not be solely based on the interpretation of the human mind; rather we must ensure that we are always regarding, and drawing from, the literal text of the gospel.

However there are also positive points to note with respect to finding patterns in scripture. We know we have been constructed by God, our brains molded after His design. We also know God has laid patterns within His word, because some are obvious to see. God knows the human proclivity to seek structure as we look for Him in His word, and He also desires us to seek Him, and desires us to explore His word to discover more about His character and His plan for us. Thus it is reasonable to suppose there are patterns laid in scripture that require us to dig to find them, which are not obvious at first appreciation. More encouragingly, we know God *wants* us to discover Him, He desires us to search this way. He is not hiding from us, indeed He is not far from us (Acts 17:27), and promises that those who seek Him (in truth) will find Him (Matthew 7:7).

Appendix B: Creation in John's Gospel Summary

B.2 Constructing a Summary of John's Gospel

Thus we look to summarize the gospel to facilitate appraisal of evident patterns. Attempting to summarize this gospel, indeed any book of the Bible, is an immensely difficult task, and one fraught with potential error, particularly since scripture is not padded with superfluous text to be minimized at will. Nevertheless we find that summary is possible by scriptural precedent, and therefore justifiable. Jesus says:

> "Love the Lord your God with all your heart and with all your soul and with all your mind. This is the first and greatest commandment. And the second is like it: Love your neighbor as yourself. All the Law and the Prophets hang on these two commandments." (Matthew 22:37-40)

Jesus is not dispensing with the bulk of the law when he says this, although he is providing accurate summary of the Old Testament in just two statements.

One manner in which we shall *not* be attempting to find a pattern in John is by simply reading through the gospel and jotting down everything we deem to be significant. This has such a high level of subjectivity it will yield a pattern revealing much more of the reader's mind than the word of God before it. Instead we will create a summary of John's gospel by reading it through and noting down the words John has used most frequently. These results will have a higher, though still imperfect, level of objectivity, because it is the gospel writer, gently compelled (there is no contradiction) by the Divine Hand, who has chosen the words which appear in the text. This allows the gospel summary to be constructed through a list of 'keywords': the words appearing most frequently. We thus avoid the disastrous consequences of high subjectivity 'pattern-spotting' by minimizing the influence of the reader's mind.

As a prerequisite task, we first excise words that are 'unimportant:' also a delicate task. We dismiss conjunctions, articles and pronouns from our study, for these will not bear the gospel message even though they are the words most commonly

Appendix B: Creation in John's Gospel Summary

appearing. Additionally we disregard the characters themselves: the Lord God, the Lord Jesus Christ, the apostles, the Pharisees, the priests and non-specific references to characters such as 'man' and 'woman.' It is evident upon *whom* the gospels are focusing and why. We know the focus of the gospel is on the Lord Jesus Christ, for the glory of God, revealed for the salvation of those men who will receive him and the condemnation of those men who will reject him. We are left with simple nouns and verbs: these words form the vehicles by which the gospel message is carried. This appended study focuses on the distribution of nouns that can be related to concrete objects in John, (though that is not to say that the verbs and repeating phrases could not themselves form fascinating studies also).

Only four concrete nouns appear more than twenty times in the Greek text [1] of John's gospel: Water (24 occurrences), Bread (24), Light (23) and Judge (21). Hereafter we refer to these words as 'keywords' of John's gospel. In addition we include a fifth keyword: the Greek word 'stauros,' which is translated as the English words 'cross' and 'crucify.' [2] We include it because the crucifixion event is of central importance to the gospel message. It would seem to engender an error to compile any summary of a gospel in which the sacrifice of Christ's crucifixion is not included. So we have five keywords: Water, Bread, Light, Judge and Cross, with which to construct our summary.

The summary is constructed simply as the list of the keywords (Table B_1) as they appear in order in John. The table includes the references to assess how comprehensively the gospel has been covered.

---

[1] Wilson B., *Op. cit.*, pp 312-399. This should not be assumed the definitive text of John's gospel. Linguistic scholars argue compellingly for an original written text in Aramaic, possibly contemporary with Jesus' ministry, and copied into Greek later: Errico R. A., Lamsa G. M., *Op. cit.* pp xxxviii-xxxi
[2] *Ibid.*

Appendix B: Creation in John's Gospel Summary

Light 1:4	Water 3:23	Bread 6:23	Light 8:12	Judge 18:31
Light 1:5	Water 4:7	Bread 6:26	Judge 8:15	Cross 19:6
Light 1:7	Water 4:10	Bread 6:31	Judge 8:15	Cross 19:6
Light 1:8	Water 4:11	Bread 6:32	Judge 8:16	Cross 19:6
Light 1:8	Water 4:13	Bread 6:32	Judge 8:26	Cross 19:10
Light 1:9	Water 4:14	Bread 6:33	Judge 8:50	Cross 19:15
Water 1:26	Water 4:14	Bread 6:34	Light 9:5	Cross 19:15
Water 1:31	Water 4:14	Bread 6:35	Light 11:9	Cross 19:16
Water 1:33	Water 4:15	Bread 6:41	Light 11:10	Cross 19:17
Water 2:7	Water 4:46	Bread 6:48	Light 12:35	Cross 19:18
Water 2:9	Water 5:3	Bread 6:50	Light 12:35	Cross 19:19
Water 2:9	Water 5:4	Bread 6:51	Light 12:36	Cross 19:20
Water 3:5	Water 5:4	Bread 6:51	Light 12:36	Cross 19:23
Judge 3:17	Water 5:7	Bread 6:51	Light 12:36	Cross 19:25
Judge 3:18	Judge 5:22	Bread 6:58	Light 12:46	Cross 19:31
Judge 3:18	Judge 5:30	Bread 6:58	Judge 12:47	Water 19:34
Judge 3:18	Light 5:35	Judge 7:24	Judge 12:47	Cross 19:41
Light 3:19	Bread 6:5	Judge 7:24	Judge 12:48	Bread 21:9
Light 3:19	Bread 6:7	Water 7:38	Judge 12:48	Bread 21:13
Light 3:20	Bread 6:9	Judge 7:51	Water 13:5	
Light 3:20	Bread 6:11	Judge 7:51	Bread 13:18	
Light 3:21	Bread 6:13	Light 8:12	Judge 16:11	

Table B_1: The gospel of John in order using just five keywords: Light, Water, Bread, Judge and Cross. The listing of the words is taken from a Greek text. [3]

The summary may seem featureless and illegible, but we take encouragement in its relatively high level of objectivity. Objectivity is not total, nor can it ever be, since all of our choices about words to exclude and include are to some degree subjective. Nevertheless because this summary has been

---

[3] *Ibid.*

formulated with primary basis upon the gospel text; rather than primary basis on the proclivities or impressions of the reader we can be confident the level of objectivity is higher in this summary than would result from other methodologies. It is this most raw of forms of the gospel we shall work with, hoping the gospel message to crystallize most accurately before our eyes having minimized the distorting influence of our attendant mind.

B.3 The Creation Sequence in John's Summary

At first glance Table B_1 shows grouping amongst the keywords. We do not automatically assume the grouping significant, because normal conversation has identifiably segregated subject areas in which certain keywords aggregate. Nevertheless we propose the degree of grouping is more than occurs by this natural effect, because even the *separate accounts* containing a certain keyword are also grouped together in John's gospel. For example the keyword 'water' is the central article in four accounts in John, and these accounts are listed consecutively in the gospel:

1. The miracle of water into wine at Cana (2:1-11)
2. Jesus' conversation with Nicodemus about being born of water and of the spirit (3:1-21)
3. Jesus' conversation with the Samaritan woman about the origin of the water of life (4:1-42)
4. The healing at the poolside of Bethesda (5:1-15)

We therefore conclude these keywords are deliberately sequenced in John's gospel. We compare the keywords in John, and their ordering, with the six days of creation, drawing from the previous work expounding the elements of the spiritual creation (Section $\alpha.4$). We find, astonishingly, the elements of the spiritual creation match with all of John's keywords!

To illustrate this graphically, we compose a figure (Figure B_3) which displays both the keyword summary of John (Table B_1) and the creation sequence. We replace each word in Table B_1 with a block of a chosen color, using a single color for each

Appendix B: Creation in John's Gospel Summary

keyword, to give us a bar of colors reflecting the keyword sequence. The result is shown in the left hand bar of Figure B_3. For a single word a standard length of the appropriate color is used, and the list of words is 'painted,' in sequence, from top to bottom, according to the list of words in Table B_1 and the color scheme shown in the key. From Table B_1 we see one period of the gospel is poorly represented. The period after the crucifixion with the resurrected Christ is represented with just two mentions of the word 'bread,' themselves non-central to the contextual argument. Thus we add the comment (in the purple box in Figure B_3) that Jesus is raised. Without this we would have represented the gospel of John finishing with Jesus dead: a terrible misrepresentation of any gospel (remember 'gospel' means 'good news'). Arguably *the* central message of the gospel is that Jesus finishes alive and remains alive at the right Hand of His Father to this day: indeed it is a belief around which all our hopes congregate (1 Corinthians 15:12-19).

When we compare this summary with the creation sequence the backbone of John's presentation is seen. The keywords of John's gospel directly relate to the principal elements of each of the creative Days! Light, Water and Bread perfectly summarize Days 1-3. Even this should be considered astonishing because there is no reason for the principal elements of creation to be the same as the commonest concrete nouns in John's gospel! Day 4 contains two of John's keywords, Light and Judge(ment), and their representation in Figure B_3 is scaled accordingly. The principal component of Day 5 is the great sea-beast who is related, by complex connection presented earlier (Section α.4), to the cross of Christ. Day 6 alone bears no relation to these keywords, and thus we mark the creation of Adam at the bottom of the right hand bar. Figure B_3 gives graphic demonstration of the central thesis of this work: the presence of the creation sequence in John – and in the correct order. This is an independent demonstration from the one given in the main body of this work, but an important corroboration nonetheless.

Appendix B: Creation in John's Gospel Summary

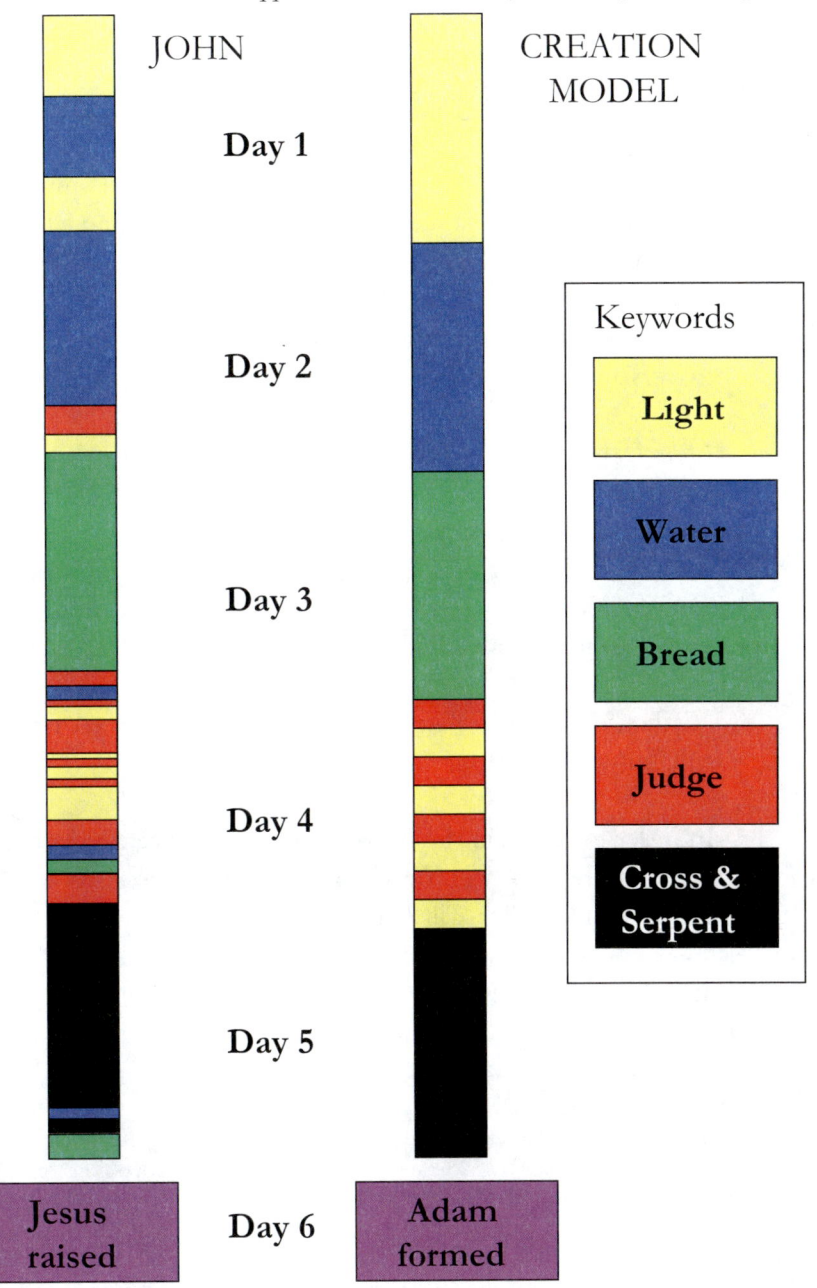

Figure B_3: Comparison between the keyword summary of John's gospel (left, from Table B_1) and the creation sequence in Genesis (right).

287

APPENDIX C:
The Nature of Jesus Christ

The singularity of the nature of Jesus Christ must be established in order to gain the full appreciation of the victory of his life and sacrifice. Likewise the presence of Jesus within the creation model in John's gospel, the central focus of this work, also requires an appreciation of Jesus' nature (a subject as controversial as it is important).

C.1 The Essence of Obedience and Submission

We learn Jesus' nature from Biblical scenes, of which few are more informative than the discourse between Jesus and his Father in the Garden of Gethsemane. The Bible describes the central sacrifice of Jesus, in resigning his own desires in preference to those of his Father.

> "Father, if you are willing, take this cup from me; yet not my will, but yours be done." (Luke 22:42)

In order to maintain the fullness of this sacrifice it is essential that one nature, one will, occupying the first person, is wholly submitted to the other will occupying the second person. This disallows commonly held notions such as Jesus and God being one in all facets of their being, [1] or Jesus being 'wholly God' and 'wholly man.' [2] It constitutes a serious degradation of this heart-

---

[1] This is the "Deity of Christ" doctrine in its Trinitarian form. Initially proposed by the scholar Tertullian, the Trinity was coded by a convention of bishops at Nicea in AD 325, and ratified in formal expressions by the Chalcedon Council in AD 451.

[2] This is the most common version of the Deity of Christ doctrine. The difficulty inherent in this doctrine is apparent from the logical contradiction it forms. Mathematical logic dictates it is impossible for any system to be 'wholly x' and 'wholly y' for any unenclosed x and y. The presence of one unenclosed variable necessarily detracts from the exclusive pervasiveness of the other. Acceptance of the doctrine therefore places one outside of the sphere of rational argument. This author finds the logical disproof of the Deity of Christ doctrine conclusive. Whilst it is true the revelation of God through His Son

Appendix C: The Nature of Jesus Christ

rending discourse to preach the presence of the Eternal Almighty in both proponents of the conversation, for the true submission of one party to the other is lost. Rather under either of these other doctrines, God, who is wholly present in both characters, is merely making a choice between two available options. Even with Jesus Christ expressed as "wholly God and wholly man" the submission that is made, of man to God, still occurs only within Christ: he is still, essentially, submitting to himself, which negates the idea of actual submission *per se*.

Rather, the total submission of a genuinely human Son to his Heavenly Father, though horrifically tragic in those things it touched upon, is the most wonderful encouragement for the true disciple of Christ! It demonstrates that, as a man brought death into the world, so another man, through the Spirit of God, was able to enable resurrection from the dead (1 Corinthians 15:21). Since we are only men ourselves, how vital it is to understand that with sufficient help from the Spirit of God a *man* (not an immortal, nor an illogically mortal/immortal hybrid) can be brought to redemption.

Likewise the Bible declares that Jesus was obedient to God, always doing what pleased Him.

> Although he was a son, he learned obedience from what he suffered and, once made perfect, he became the source of eternal salvation for all who obey him. (Hebrews 5:8-9)

> "When you have lifted up the Son of Man, then you will know that I am [the one I claim to be] and that I do nothing on my own but speak just what the Father has taught me. The one who sent me is with me; he has not left me alone, for I always do what pleases him." (8:28-29)

Jesus Christ is so challenging that it invariably presents the disciple with crisis, it does not present him with chaos. (see also 1 Corinthians 14:33).

Appendix C: The Nature of Jesus Christ

As with submission, the concept of obedience is entirely nullified unless the two involved have different wills. If Jesus is 'wholly God' (whether he is 'wholly man' as well or not) it does not constitute obedience to submit to a will that actually comes from inside him as much as from anywhere else. In fact, one cannot then distinguish between obedience and selfishness – for both include the practice of performing one's own desires.

By holding to the accurate scriptural description we are enabled to preach a truly powerful Christ. Jesus truly was one with his Father (10:30). He explains that those who follow him can likewise become one with each other in the same way as he and his Father are one. This is the true description of the power of unity from many parts.

> "My prayer is not for them alone. I pray also for those who will believe in me through their message, that all of them may be one, Father, just as you are in me and I am in you. May they also be in us so that the world may believe that you have sent me. I have given them the glory that you gave me, that they may be one as we are one: I in them and you in me. May they be brought to complete unity to let the world know that you sent me and have loved them even as you have loved me." (17:20-23)

These verses teach the oneness enjoyed by the Lord Jesus and Almighty God can be achieved between two human beings. This necessarily precludes one person being actually contained inside another, or one human being 'wholly himself' and 'wholly another' since this is impossible for two humans. We conclude the 'oneness' refers to an absolute commonality of understanding and intention, as detailed in the quote above: "for I always do what pleases him." (8:29) Even within this oneness Jesus teaches the absolute superiority of the Father over all, including himself:

> "If you loved me, you would be glad that I am going to the Father, for the Father is greater than I." (14:28, see also 1 Corinthians 11:3; 1 Corinthians 15:27-28)

Appendix C: The Nature of Jesus Christ

<u>Wearing the Name of God</u>

This total unity between Son and Father, combined with the obedience of the former to the latter allows Jesus the honor of wearing the Name of God Himself.

This too is part of a larger scriptural pattern: those who respond to the loving extension of God's Hand are rewarded with names that label them appropriately closer to the Father. Abraham and Moses, for example, were each given the name 'Friend of God' (James 2:23, Exodus 33:11) for their extraordinarily high level of faithfulness. Comparably David was blessed with the title 'Man after God's own Heart' (1 Samuel 13:14) – and for precisely the same reason. Additionally angels, who are always in the presence of God (Matthew 18:10), occasionally wear the name of God when dispensing His will:

> See, I am sending an angel ahead of you to guard you along the way and to bring you to the place I have prepared. Pay attention to him and listen to what he says. Do not rebel against him; he will not forgive your rebellion, since **my Name is in him**. If you listen carefully to **what he says** and do all **that I say**, I will be an enemy to your enemies and will oppose those who oppose you. (Exodus 23:20-22)

Clearly Jesus was far superior to Abraham, Moses and David: indeed in a wholly separate class. He never sinned, but rather cultivated the desire to perform a will that was not his own. Jesus is also superior to the angels, whose obedience is flawless, because he had the capacity to sin, being tempted in all ways just like any other human man (Hebrews 4:15), yet did not. Jesus' faith was total and absolute, and thus the corresponding title God chooses to bestow upon him is also total and absolute – the name of God Himself!

> But about the Son [God] says, "Your throne, O God, will last for ever and ever, and righteousness will be the scepter of your kingdom. You have loved righteousness and hated wickedness; therefore God, your God, has set you above your

Appendix C: The Nature of Jesus Christ

companions by anointing you with the oil of joy." (Hebrews 1:8-9)

To take the contrary view, that Jesus contained the nature of God, unfortunately, if unintentionally, belittles the Lord Jesus' life. For if Jesus *was* God all along (indeed "wholly God") he therefore deserved the name 'God' anyway, without his sacrifice. Rather the Bible preaches without equivocation that Jesus wears the name of God because he abandoned his own desires and submitted himself with uncompromised humility and obedience to his Father's will. This submission was seen at the ultimate level in Gethsemane and brought to fruition at Calvary.

> Your attitude should be the same as that of Christ Jesus: Who, being in very nature God, did not consider equality with God something to be grasped, but made himself nothing, taking the very nature of a servant, being made in human likeness. And being found in appearance as a man, he humbled himself and became obedient to death-- even death on a cross! Therefore God exalted him to the highest place and gave him the name that is above every name, that at the name of Jesus every knee should bow, in heaven and on earth and under the earth, and every tongue confess that Jesus Christ is Lord, to the glory of God the Father. (Philippians 2:9-11).

C.2 The Nature of Jesus Christ as Creator and Creation

All agree the opening chapter of John's gospel gives one of the deepest insights into the true nature of Jesus Christ. John opens his gospel by saying: "In the beginning..." mirroring the opening of the book of Genesis. This, as we have postulated, is not coincidental, nor does the parallel end there. We suggest John is deliberately presenting the spiritual creation of Jesus Christ as parallel to, and superseding over, the natural creation of Genesis. In that context we expect much symmetry between John 1 and the opening verses of Genesis 1 – which symmetry is clearly seen.

Appendix C: The Nature of Jesus Christ

1 In the beginning was the Word, and the Word was with God, and the Word was God.

What is the Word? We shall employ minimal interpretation to avoid distorting scripture: the Word of God is that which God speaks. Since God does not produce words at random His words may also be taken as explicit embodiment of the divine purpose (i.e. the Word was God). The parallel to Genesis 1 is compelling: all creation is effected by God speaking, by the imposition of **His Word**.

2 He was with God in the beginning.

The Word was from the beginning: again in harmony with Genesis 1.

3 Through him all things were made; without him nothing was made that has been made.

Again perfect harmony with Genesis 1: God, speaking the Word, made all things. The Genesis record does more than corroborate that the mechanism of creation was the verbal pronouncement of the Almighty. It also testifies to the absence of the Son of God at this point in history. The characters in Genesis 1 are: God, and the words that He speaks. In this way all creation came to be; John's opening chapter recapitulates this faithfully.

4 In him was life, and that life was the light of men.

This says that the Word of God brings life, and light. The 'Him' is still the Word of God – not Jesus – yet (although we will qualify this statement in the following). Support for the notion that the Word of God brings life occurs in many texts, e.g. 6:63. The Word of God also brings light, and that is very important, since we have already demonstrated "light" as a scriptural metaphor for "understanding" (Section $\alpha.4$).

Appendix C: The Nature of Jesus Christ

5 The light shines in the darkness, but the darkness has not understood it.

As light translates to 'understanding,' and conversely darkness translates to 'not understanding' (Section α.4), this verse is no longer merely an observation. It is now an attractive spiritual definition!

6 There came a man who was sent from God; his name was John.

This introduces John the Baptist. This too is evidence the preceding verses are not talking about Jesus, at least directly, because the chronology is linear. John the gospel writer starts with creation, and then introduces John the Baptist. Jesus has not yet entered the text.

7 He came as a witness to testify concerning that light, so that through him all men might believe.

John the Baptist proclaims the message of the light: the Word of God. This verse points both forward and back. John testifies to the light of the Word of God, which has been from the very beginning, and also proclaims the coming of Jesus Christ in the future, who will embody the illuminated (and illuminating) Word.

8 He himself was not the light; he came only as a witness to the light.

John the Baptist was not the fully embodied will and purpose (Word) of God.

9 The true light that gives light to every man was coming into the world.

This is a key verse, because it heralds the entry of Jesus Christ into John's gospel. Since Jesus comes as the light of the world the

Appendix C: The Nature of Jesus Christ

things spoken about the light of the world (e.g. verses 4-5), also become true about Jesus. So even though verse 4 describes the Word of God, which dates back to the beginning of time, it is possible to see the eternal Word in Jesus, because Jesus perfectly embodies that light. Similarly one can also retrospectively see Jesus in the Word of old, long before Jesus himself existed. [3]

> 10 He was in the world, and though the world was made through him, the world did not recognize him.

This verse has beautiful and powerful symmetry. Who is 'He'? From the context of everything we have seen so it could be either the Word, or Jesus. Wonderfully this dual truth exists on parallel, but separate, levels. The Word of God was unrecognized and ignored by all God's children, yet through that Word the whole natural creation was made (Genesis 1). By direct parallel Jesus Christ, the embodied light, the embodied Word, was equally unrecognized and rejected by God's people, and yet is the one through whom the whole spiritual creation is made (this latter observation being the central thesis of this work).

> 11 He came to that which was his own, but his own did not receive him.

This again is true of both God's Word and Jesus. Both are coming to the Jews; and both call them to be His people. Yet the Jews will not receive either the Word, or the Son. Stephen's damning tirade is especially germane in this regard. [4]

---

[3] For a parallel argument, see John 8:58.

[4] "You stiff-necked people, with uncircumcised hearts and ears! You are just like your fathers: You always resist the Holy Spirit! Was there ever a prophet your fathers did not persecute? They even killed those who predicted the coming of the Righteous One. And now you have betrayed and murdered him-- you who have received the law that was put into effect through angels but have not obeyed it." (Acts 7:51-53).

12 Yet to all who received him, to those who believed in his name, he gave the right to become children of God—

Again division is unnecessary between Jesus and the Word. The symmetry is beautiful, for the Bible speaks of the path to salvation – one path – as both accepting Christ and accepting the Word. On the one hand we are told salvation comes from receiving the Word (combine Romans 10:17 with Hebrews 11:6) and on the other hand that salvation comes from receiving Christ (14:20-23).

13 children born not of natural descent, nor of human decision or a husband's will, but born of God.

This introduces the notion of a new, second birth and therefore hints at the broader concept of the spiritual creation following the natural creation; on which subject Jesus expands within this gospel. John draws all thoughts towards the creation pattern.

14 The Word became flesh and made his dwelling among us. We have seen his glory, the glory of the One and Only, who came from the Father, full of grace and truth.

This caps the matter perfectly and completely; explicitly confirming what has been constructed in the opening verses. The Word, the purpose of God dating from the beginning of time (in fact before, if that has meaning, since God does not feel the constraints of time) has now been perfectly embodied in Jesus Christ, who dwelt amongst us. Because the embodiment is perfect, we can look at Jesus Christ and see those eternal things present from the very beginning of time, an idea we find corroborated elsewhere (e.g. 14:9).

Overall we learn the nature of Jesus Christ. The Bible declares Jesus' life began at birth by his mother Mary (Luke 2:6-7, Galatians 4:4), after the Holy Spirit of God had impregnated her (Luke 1:35). We therefore understand this as the beginning of

Appendix C: The Nature of Jesus Christ

Jesus' existence. Had Jesus existed beforehand one would anticipate a description of transformation, of his 'transition into the flesh,' but the language used at his birth (Luke 2, Matthew 2) is indicative of the origin of Jesus' life.

This interpretation is corroborated by both the second and third days of John's Creation. In Day 2, the geometrical arrangement of the living water and the earthly water at Jacob's well mirrored the structure of creation's second day – the pertinent lesson being that the "waters above" were themselves physically set apart from the "waters beneath" (Section 2.3). And in Day 3 Jesus refers to himself as the 'bread from heaven' in parallel to, and extension of, the manna given to the Israelites in Moses' day. Again the Old Testament testifies well to the coming Messiah, since the original manna was also called 'bread from heaven' and yet was also formed physically on the ground (c.f. 6:32-51, Exodus 16:4-16).

Jesus was a human man who, through the support of the Spirit of God to whom he submitted himself, lived a perfect life of obedience in humility before his Father. Is Jesus the Creator? Indeed he is, John's gospel eloquently demonstrates this, as we have argued. But he is not the Creator of the *natural* creation at the beginning of time (Genesis 1); he is the Creator of the *spiritual* creation (1:1-14) in these "last days" (Hebrews 1:1-2); as well as the perfect emulation of each component.

ISBN 141207430-4